I0821576

NEW GEOGRAPHIES

11 Extraterrestrial

Edited by
Jeffrey S. Nesbit &
Guy Trangoš

New Geographies 11
Extraterrestrial

Editors
Jeffrey S. Nesbit & Guy Trangoš

Editorial Board
Michael Chieffalo, Mariano Gomez-Luque,
and Julia Smachylo

Former Editors
Daniel Daou, Gareth Doherty, Ali Fard, Rania Ghosn, Ghazal Jafari, El Hadi Jazairy, Daniel Ibañez, Nikos Katsikis, Taraneh Meshkani, Pablo Pérez Ramos, Antonio Petrov, Stephen Ramos, Neyran Turan

Advisory Board
Eve Blau, Neil Brenner, Sonja Dümpelmann,
Mohsen Mostafavi, Antoine Picon, Charles Waldheim

Academic Advisor
Neil Brenner

Production Advisor
Meghan Ryan Sandberg

Copyeditor
Elizabeth Kugler

Proofreader
Tamar Kupiec

Graphic Designer
Sean Yendrys

Printed in Estonia by Printon.

Logo design with Johannes Breyer (Dinamo) and Elias Hanzer

ISBN: 9781948765503
LCCN: 2019954925

www.gsd.harvard.edu/publications

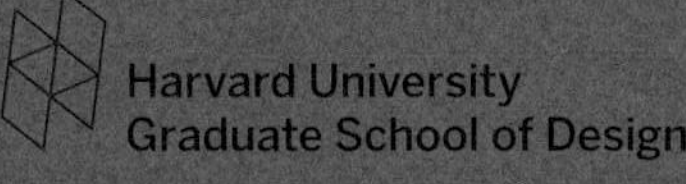

New Geographies is a journal of design, agency, and territory founded, edited, and produced by doctor of design candidates at the Harvard University Graduate School of Design. *New Geographies* presents the geographic as a design paradigm that links physical, representational, and political attributes of space and articulates a synthetic scalar practice. Through critical essays and projects, the journal seeks to position design's agency amid concerns about infrastructure, technology, ecology, and globalization.

New Geographies 11: Extraterrestrial has been made possible with support from the Graham Foundation for Advanced Studies in the Fine Arts.

All attempts have been made to trace and acknowledge the sources of images. Regarding any omissions or errors, please contact:

New Geographies Lab
Harvard University Graduate School of Design
48 Quincy Street
Cambridge, MA 02138

Distribution
Actar D
440 Park Avenue South, 17th Floor
New York, NY 10016
Actar.com

New Geographies 11: Extraterrestrial would not have been possible without the generous support of various individuals, departments, and institutions. We must first acknowledge Neil Brenner, the publication's academic advisor, for his continued intellectual guidance and moral support. We thank the Harvard GSD Publications Department for their assistance in the publication processes. In addition, we would like to acknowledge the excellent work by copyeditor Elizabeth Kugler and graphic designer Sean Yendrys. As *New Geographies* continues into its second decade, we thank our colleagues on the editorial board who continue to inspire the mission of the journal. We acknowledge and thank our faculty who serve on the advisory board for their keen and productive feedback. Finally, this project would not be possible without the support of the Graham Foundation, for which we are immensely grateful.

Cover Image
Earthrise Seen for the First Time By Human Eyes; Photographed by William Anders, Apollo 8, December 24, 1968
Credit:
From the book and exhibition *FULL MOON* by Michael Light, 1999. Negative NASA; digital image ©1999 Michael Light

Extraterrestrial
JEFFREY S. NESBIT & GUY TRANGOŠ

> Cosmographers mapped spaces well beyond the surface of the earth, recognizing the inseparability of terrestrial and celestial forms and patterns.
> —Denis Cosgrove, 2012

Extraterrestrial, often interpreted as the unknowable beyond, is distinct from our lives and landscapes on Earth. First used in 19th-century literature, extraterrestrial describes "anything or any being beyond the earth, or from some place other than the earth." However, when considered critically, a curious epistemological device emerges. This volume borrows extraterrestrial from pop culture to gather new knowledge on the impact of cosmic geographies extended into, and from, outer space. The term reveals those spatial interactions between Earth's surface and the layered or "extra" conditions added to, and projected from, it. *Extraterrestrial* positions the cosmos as a geographic space culturally projected through constructed imaginaries, technologies, and reflectivities. This issue centered on the extraterrestrial is not exclusively a history of science fiction, nor is it metaphorical—it explores the spatial, the imaginative, and the politically projective force to construct such space.

> The landscape of the earth is like a skin or veil, wrapping the globe in its different guises. Cities are like skins of this skin—second skins.
> —Chora et al., 1998

Outer space is an infinite void. Its darkness, vacuity, and lifelessness are a sharp contrast to the protected biosphere of our earthly existence. The atmosphere forms a protective veil between explicable Earth and unfathomable space. This thin boundary is physical as it defends Earth from radiation and supports all living systems. It is also sociocultural as it separates Earth from the construct of space, creating a cocoon in which the changing tide, the setting sun, or the shifting constellations are not reminders of our one universal system but banal daily features of life on Earth. Despite this, as musician Moby states, "We are all made of stars." However, these divides enable as much as they impede. They drive exploration and imagination outward and foster a deep desire to know and to occupy the world beyond. As a result, not only is space understood and interpreted from Earth, but through the changing social, political, and economic lenses of Earth. Planetary landscapes are imagined as rugged, mountainous forms or sweeping deserts. Asteroids are examined for their extractive potential under US law, and Mars is projected as real estate opportunity. These extraterrestrial ambitions also see the terrestrial surface become a territory in which imaginations of technical advancement and experimentation beyond human purview occur, such as projects involving the massive displacement of ground by the use of nuclear explosives. A desert becomes a lunar landscape, the Pacific seabed a graveyard for defunct asteroids, and the planet itself a staging zone for human survival elsewhere.

The year of this publication is significant in aerospace history, as 2019 marks the 50th anniversary of the Apollo 11 mission and humankind's first steps on extraterrestrial soil. This pivotal moment in the eternal timeline of human fascination with the cosmos changed both our interpretation of space and our understanding of our place within it. While this moment inspired some to protect our valuable "blue marble," the Space Race also fueled a continued technological quest grounded in an entwined nationalist and capitalist agenda, what we might refer to as the space-industrial complex. The first act following the giant leap for humankind was the planting of the US flag in the gray lunar dust—a symbol of a national achievement but also a marker of future territorial ambition. The subsequent half-century has seen numerous important scientific interests expand in space, and these have both stretched our knowledge of the universe and dramatically improved many lives on Earth. We have reached a moment, however, when the predominant public discourse on space is owned by the expansionist ambitions of private capital, historically derived from the Cold War era public agencies that once trumpeted and supported space exploration and research. As the 20th century proceeded, the imaginary realm of celestial, unknowable, and phantasmagorical space was surpassed by a sterile modernist technological rationality. Today, outer space is imagined increasingly as a privatized zone of tourism, material extraction, colonization, and warfare.

New Geographies 11: Extraterrestrial explores the historical and contemporary consequence of our planetary relationship with space. We interpret this duality through the conceptual lens of "extraterrestrial," which engages an entangled zone of expanding practices in geography, landscape, and architecture, stretching Earth to space, and conversely, space to Earth. This issue questions the means through which space is forged as a condition *extra* to our own *terra*. Complicit within this imagination resides a deep political and economic logic that serves to territorialize outer space as an exception to, and extension of, Earth. These critical processes are revealed as not *extra* at all, but rather distinctly of *terra*. Through a series of written, photographic, and representational investigations, this edition of *New Geographies* builds on earlier studies of outer space from science, technology, and society, as well as from the design disciplines, history, and critical geography. It reinforces the need for humanity's changing relationship with outer space to be recorded, critiqued, and theorized from a breadth of academic traditions and projected within design discourse.

This issue brings together experts contributing to the social, political, and cultural imaginary implicit in extraterrestrial. Three primary thematic territorial devices structure these explorations: a technologically constructed space between, a material culture constructed and discharged, and a space politically and economically reflective, all revealed through historical and contemporary society.

The first third of this volume considers our political and economic ambition within extraterrestrial environments. These texts primarily engage notions of the frontier, which outer space so patently presents to governments and private interests seeking new territories for control and expansion. Elizabeth Kessler opens the critical essays with an analysis of the Golden Record. The "message" attached to the Voyager 1 and 2 spacecraft was a means to represent humankind and Earth to "extraterrestrials." While its intended audience will most likely never view its content, many on Earth have, and the very act of projecting Earth into outer space serves to alter our human relationship to space through technology. Felicity Scott introduces a different form of projection into space as she considers the nationalist rhetoric and other "strategic fictions" territorializing space through political and corporate interests. Gretchen Heefner turns her focus to Earth, the Arctic during the Cold War in particular, where she considers the extraterrestrial through the construction of US military bases in extreme environments. Following the discourse of environmental dominance, Julie Klinger examines outer space as a site for new patterns of resource extraction within the context of destruction, enclosure, and abandonment. Rajji Sanjay Desai investigates the processes by which human satellites are decommissioned and disposed. She charts a sectional sweep from High Earth Orbit to the bottom of the South Pacific Ocean as these technologies are operated and destroyed in the extraterrestrial, beyond human experience. David Salomon uses the *axis mundi* to stress the direct relationship between Earth and space—the *geo* and the *astro*. He formally constructs and politically aligns the notion of the extraterrestrial artifact by discussing numerous ways in which space interprets and reflects Earth. Salomon's analysis reminds us that Kessler's Golden Record and Scott's territorial imaginaries are both the product of, and a factor in, the changing human-space relationship, and Heefner's focus on the militarization of extreme environments is common to both Earth and space. In setting the conceptual tone and a political urgency, these contributions demonstrate how frontier conditions imagine and construct contested territorial boundaries.

The second third examines the extraterrestrial as a series of techno-cultural responses to space and landscape. Technological advancement through history has changed human relations to space, shifted our own sense of the universe, and inspired new ways of creating, making, and reading space on Earth. These investigations consider material expressions of our extraterrestrial relationships. Alessandra Ponte takes us to an early 20th-century infatuation with creating a massive model of Earth, a grand social observatory that represent our global complexity as a vast spectacle of light and mechanics. The unrealized effort came to reveal much about a growing desire for a planetary perspective. Lisa Messeri continues a planetary focus but interrogates the Moon to discuss graphic representations of lunar surfaces as devices that fostered a sense of extraterrestrial belonging between a planet and its moon. Our human desire to inhabit space between, explored by Fred Scharmen, uses two 19th- and early 20th-century visions of spacecraft designed for orbit around Earth. These reveal a technological imaginary animated by the prospect of human needs in space. Katarzyna Balug continues to explore a technological imaginary but one of Earth inspired by humans in space. She looks at inflatable architecture as an expression of such technologies and spatial complexities in the race for space. Building on the terrestrial-to-lunar effects of space exploration, Edward Eigen investigates the Lunar Receiving Laboratory, a sterile facility in which all astronauts, rock samples, and other lunar matter have been held in quarantine for fear of potential contamination of Earth by unknown hazards. Scott Kirsch continues this investigation into the impact and effect of outer space, focusing on cratered landscapes on Earth and on other planets. These zones question the presence of humans due to their creation of defense and nuclear testing, yet they are tied to features of a neighboring planet. This section concludes with Neyran Turan's call for a new environmental imagination in the face of climate change, drawing on the potential of design to imagine new planetary futures.

The final third engages the extraterrestrial as a critical tool for rethinking Earth itself through fictional sites of experimentation, reflection, and political projection. Nicholas de Monchaux looks to the creation of science-fiction representations and the cinematic simulation of space in film achieved by advanced technologies and how the "absence" of space and landscape provoke innovative and thoughtful projections. De Monchaux begins his essay with early flight simulators and those figures instrumental in history of technology to offer new relationships tied to cinematic production of fictional extraterrestrial space. Neil Leach focuses on science fiction and film to foreground his arguments of artificial intelligence, which he interprets as a "radically other form" of alien intelligence produced on Earth today. He calls for an approach to AI that is beyond anthropomorphism, one where the human is no longer the sole guardian of intelligent life. Turning to the question of extraterrestrial life explicitly, Rachel Armstrong breaks down the anthropocentric and earth-bound lenses through which life elsewhere is commonly imagined. She provides an alternative means to imagine life in our complex and infinitely diverse universe. Daniel Daou describes a political ecology based on a historical depiction of the cosmos—cosmology, cosmism, and cosmopolitics—to raise discourse centered on new forms of terrestrial definitions, moving from the global to the cosmic. This section concludes with a provocative essay by Rania Ghosn and El Hadi Jazairy, who speculate on the scale and extreme nature of the cosmos as a stage for three graphic stories. These design-based descriptions foreground the political impetus of our ecological crisis and offer new perspectives to project future environments in, and between, the extraterrestrial unknown.

These 18 text-based contributions are interspersed with photo-essays by Michael Light and Roland Miller. Both are established photographers who consider the critical premise of extraterrestrial in their work and capture both the sublime landscapes of space and the equally elusive landscapes of Earth in their photographs. While Miller foregrounds the technological apparatus of humans in space through his images, coproduced by astronaut Paolo Nespoli, Light explores the forms and textures of otherworldly terrains. As we have already mentioned, but requiring further articulation, two critical and representational reflections on the themes of this volume support the essays and other photographic contributions. The work of Design Earth (Rania Ghosn and El Hadi Jazairy) and NEMESTUDIO (Neyran Turan) both draw on design as an analytical, projective, and political tool through which to frame important questions and speculate through provocative visions. The volume ends with an interview with leading science-fiction author Kim Stanley Robinson. Here, Robinson considers the science-fiction worlds that he has created within the rubric of planetary urbanization. His strongly developed thoughts on our very human relationship with, and the imaginary potential of, space embed the space-Earth dialectic that is so central to extraterrestrial.

The *New Geographies* journal has a decade-long history of challenging and redefining our earthly spaces under capitalist urbanization. The journal has successfully explored issues of urbanization through the agency of design in diverse scales, geographies, and other related themes. This issue extends the inquiry into the vast extra-orbital cosmos. Such extra-orbital space, and its associated infrastructure and geography, appears minimally discussed in design fields. However, with a commercial space industry on the rise, recent discussions of military activity, and increased discourse around interplanetary colonization, space continues to press new challenges related to design and questions of territory. Extraterrestrial demands a deeper and interdisciplinary critique of our changing and increasingly complex Earth-space relationship.

1
Denis Cosgrove, *Geography and Vision: Seeing, Imagining and Representing the World* (New York: I. B. Tauris, 2012), 34.

2
Oxford English Dictionary (Oxford: Oxford University Press, 2019), s.v. "extraterrestrial." Striking for this issue, the epistemology of extraterrestrial continues to define "outside" through various forms, such as "outside the uterus," "outside a vehicle," and "out of sight."

3
Helene Binet, Raoul Bunschoten, and Takuro Hoshino, *Urban Flotsam: Stirring the City* (Rotterdam: 010 Uitgeverij, 2001), 10.

4
Moby, "We Are All Made of Stars," *18* (London: Mute Records, 2002).

5
Scott Kirsch, *Proving Grounds: Project Plowshare and the Unrealized Dream of Nuclear Earthmoving* (New Brunswick, NJ: Rutgers University Press, 2005). For more on labor and the deep sociopolitical impact of earthmoving practices with respect to nuclear efforts, see Gabrielle Hecht, *Being Nuclear: Africans and the Global Uranium Trade* (Cambridge, MA: MIT Press, 2014).

6
See Gonzalo Munévar, "Space Exploration and Human Survival," *Space Policy* 30, no. 4 (2014): 197–201. See also Moon Valley in Chile's Antofagasta Region located in the Atacama Desert, named by Jesuit priest Gustavo Le Paige.

7
Stewart Brand, *The Next Whole Earth Catalog* (Sausalito, CA: Point, 1980). See also Fred Turner, *From Counterculture to Cyberculture: Stewart Brand, the Whole Earth Network, and the Rise of Digital Utopianism* (Chicago: University of Chicago Press, 2010). Seen through a new resistance to the increase of technology, counterculture as described as "a culture antithetical to the technologies and social structures powering the cold war state and its defense industries." And yet, for Marshall McLuhan and Buckminster Fuller, technology was depicted as "tools" for social transformation.

8
See Nicholas de Monchaux, "Cities and Cybernetics," in *New Geographies 4: Scales of the Earth*, ed. El Hadi Jazairy (Cambridge, MA: Harvard University Graduate School of Design, 2011): 17–25. See also Rosalind Williams, "Redesigning Design," in *New Geographies 9: Posthuman*, ed. Mariano Gomez-Luque and Ghazal Jafari (Cambridge, MA: Harvard University Graduate School of Design, 2017): 12–17.

9
Earth became more understood and recognized in the design field as a singular, vulnerable body floating in space. See Buckminster Fuller, *Operating Manual for Spaceship Earth* (New York: Simon and Schuster, 1969), and the spacesuit was seen as a representation of our own bounded environment contingent on technology and politics. See Nicholas de Monchaux, *Spacesuit: Fashioning Apollo* (Cambridge, MA: MIT Press, 2011).

10
These three themes are greatly influenced by a body of work from diverse fields and scholars. See Lisa Messeri, *Placing Outer Space: An Earthly Ethnography of Other Worlds* (Durham, NC: Duke University Press, 2016); Peter Redfield, *Space in the Tropics: From Convicts to Rockets in French Guiana* (Berkeley: University of California Press, 2000); Felicity D. Scott, *Outlaw Territories: Environments of Insecurity/Architectures of Counterinsurgency* (New York: Zone Books, 2016).

11
A recent rise in interest from the design field includes the architectural enclosures in extraterrestrial space, such as the imaginative paintings from the 1970s described in Fred Scharmen, *Space Settlements* (New York: Columbia University Press, 2019).

Full Moon
MICHAEL LIGHT

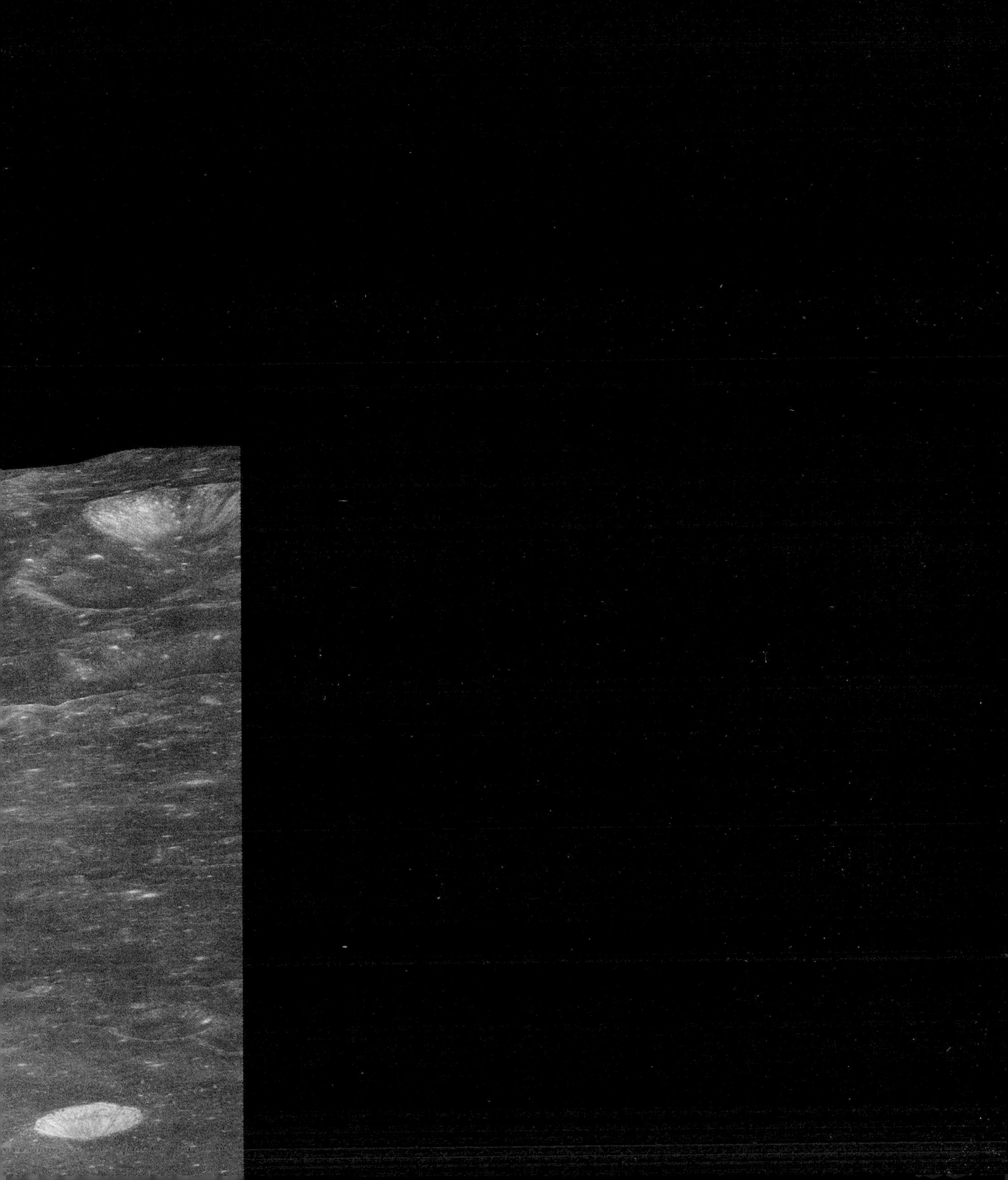

FULL MOON
Images from Michael Light book and exhibition, 1999

Edward White Spacewalking Above the Texas Coastline;
Photographed by James McDivitt, Gemini 4, June 3, 1965

Earthrise Seen for the First Time By Human Eyes;
Photographed by William Anders, Apollo 8, December 24, 1968

Rover Tracks and Mount Hadley Rising 15,000 Feet Over the Marsh of Decay;
Photographed by James Irwin, Apollo 15, July 26–August 7, 1971

Becoming Extraterrestrial through the Voyager Golden Record
ELIZABETH A. KESSLER

In 1977, NASA launched a pair of spacecraft—Voyager 1 and 2—on a tour of the solar system. Sent on a trajectory past Jupiter and Saturn, with the potential to observe Uranus and Neptune before continuing on to interstellar space, the Voyager probes marked the culmination of an ambitious program of planetary exploration that began in the 1960s and included flybys of Venus and Mercury, landers and orbiters to Mars, and the reconnaissance of Jupiter and Saturn. The cameras carried on these various planetary missions introduced a new genre of photography: the extraterrestrial landscape.

Science fiction had imagined such scenes, and astronomers had observed and photographed them through ground-based telescopes, but space travel provided a close-up, nearly eyewitness view of the surfaces and atmospheres of neighboring planets. Instead of strange, unexplored worlds, they became places visited and photographed by humanity's mechanical emissaries, and the pictures, although taken for scientific purposes, served as postcards addressed to eager, earthbound recipients.

In the case of Voyager 1 and 2, the spacecraft also carried an outbound message, a collection of images and sounds encoded on a golden disc and purportedly destined for extraterrestrials who might one day intercept and interpret it. Astronomers and alien-life enthusiasts Carl Sagan and Frank Drake oversaw the Golden Record's composition and production. They shared a long-standing commitment to the scientific viability of extraterrestrial communication, having previously collaborated on the Pioneer plaque, a single-panel dispatch for aliens carried aboard Pioneer 10 and 11.[1] In 2017 the 40th anniversary of the Voyager's launch—an event sandwiched between NASA's announcements in 2012 and 2018 that first Voyager 1 and then Voyager 2 had reached interstellar space, making them the first human-made artifacts to do so—brought renewed attention to the Golden Record.[2] Many accounts of the project celebrate the audacity and idealism of composing a message "for future times and beings," to borrow Sagan's phrase.[3]

What, however, did the Golden Record convey to its own time and to humans about the extraterrestrial? The odds of its discovery are slim, and earthlings are its more certain audience, as Sagan acknowledged. At the project's start, he wrote to scientists Philip Morrison, Stephen Jay Gould, A. G. W. Cameron; science-fiction writers Robert Heinlein, Isaac Asimov, and Arthur C. Clarke; and a few others to solicit their advice and suggestions. He

1
On the Pioneer plaque, see Carl Sagan, Linda Salzman Sagan, and Frank Drake, "A Message from Earth," *Science* 175, no. 4024 (February 1972): 881–884, and William R. Macauley, "Inscribing Scientific Knowledge: Interstellar Communication, NASA's Pioneer Plaque, and Contact with Cultures of the Imagination, 1971–1972," in *Imagining Outer Space: European Astroculture in the Twentieth Century*, ed. Alexander C. T. Geppert (New York: Palgrave Macmillian, 2012), 285–303.

2
Media coverage of Voyager's 40th anniversary and the crossing into interstellar space has been extensive. In addition, a collector's edition with all the music has been issued: *The Voyager Golden Record* (Mill Valley, CA: Ozma Records, 2017).

3
Carl Sagan, "For Future Times and Beings," *Murmurs of Earth: The Voyager Interstellar Record* (New York: Random House, 1978), 3.

4
Carl Sagan, correspondence, box 1253, folder 5, Seth MacFarlane Collection of the Carl Sagan and Ann Druyan Archive, Manuscript Division, Library of Congress, Washington, DC, 1976.

5
Carl Sagan et al., *Murmurs of Earth: The Voyager Interstellar Record* (New York: Random House, 1978). Efforts to issue an album of the musical selections were frustrated by copyright disputes between the various record labels.

ended the letter with a reminder that "the message ought to be justified on internal grounds for its principal objective which is the remote contingency of contact with another civilization; but at the same time, we should remember that . . . it may play a role in expanding the perceptions of the general public about our cosmic context. The latter will surely be the most immediate consequence of the design."[4] To ensure the message would reach humans, Sagan and Drake, along with several coauthors, published *Murmurs of Earth* (1978)—a collection of essays about the Golden Record, as well as reproductions of the images it carried—a year after Voyager's launch.[5] Both the project itself and the accompanying book encourage its earthbound audience to reorient itself to the temporal and spatial scale afforded by space exploration and to redefine what constitutes the extraterrestrial, or alien, landscape. In addition, and especially alongside the startlingly alien views of Jupiter and Saturn returned by the Voyager mission, the Golden Record imagines the possibility of humanity becoming extraterrestrial.

Cosmos, the PBS series that aired in fall 1980, cemented Sagan's celebrity, but by the time of Voyager's launch he was already a well-known figure courtesy of his popular science books, frequent magazine and newspaper interviews and profiles, and regular appearances on television, most famously *The Tonight Show*.[6] The Golden Record fits within Sagan's larger project to share scientific developments, especially those around space exploration, with the public and to inspire an appreciation for the significance of these advances. He firmly believed that the late 20th century was a pivotal moment in human history because science and technology had reached a level of sophistication that would deliver answers to profound questions about the origins of the cosmos and about humanity's very existence. "By far the most exciting, satisfying and exhilarating time to be alive is the time in which we pass from ignorance to knowledge on these fundamental issues; the age where we begin in wonder and end in understanding," he wrote a few years after Voyager's launch. "In all of the four-billion-year history of life on our planet, in all of the four-million-year history of the human family, there is only one generation privileged to live through that unique transitional moment: that generation is ours."[7]

A rare alignment of the planets enabled Voyager's tour of the solar system, allowing the spacecraft to use gravity from one planet to propel it on to the next. For the cycles of the cosmos to coincide closely with humanity's development of rocket technology was exhilaratingly fortuitous for scientists. It radically reduced the time required to reach the four outer planets and made it feasible to send spacecraft carrying cameras and other instruments to them. Studies in the mid-1960s estimated that a mission to Neptune using existing rocket technology would take 30 years; Voyager 2 reached the planet in 11 years, having already observed Jupiter, Saturn, and Uranus along the way.[8] In 35 years, Voyager 1 reached interstellar space. Forty thousand years in the future, the spacecraft will make its closest approach to another star after traveling 1.7 light-years. The confluence of nature and technology made manifest in the Voyager mission collapsed the distance previously separating Earth from other planets in the solar system and from the stars beyond our Sun. The spacecrafts' travels annihilated space and time on a cosmic scale.

The notion of annihilating space and time is, of course, most often associated with the effect of railroads on humanity's temporal and spatial experiences in the 19th century. As cultural historian Wolfgang Schivelbusch has described, railway travel dramatically altered experiences of distance, introducing "a geography based on the new conditions of speed, a condensed geography" even as the actual distances remained unchanged.[9] The space that separated an urban hub from the surrounding towns and villages appeared reduced because it could be covered in notably less time. Simultaneously, space seemed to expand as the railways connected previously remote regions to transportation centers. Although initially disorienting to train passengers, the technological shift induced a kind of sensory adaptation. Schivelbusch writes, "It did not take long for the industrialization

6
On Sagan's life and career, see Keay Davidson, *Carl Sagan: A Life* (New York: Wiley, 1999) and William Poundstone, *Carl Sagan: A Life in the Cosmos* (New York: Henry Holt, 1999).

7
Carl Sagan, *Broca's Brain: Reflections of the Romance of Science* (New York: Random House, 1979), xiv.

8
Several accounts of Voyager cite this 30-year figure to illustrate the improvement afforded by the planetary alignment. See Henry C. Dethloff and Ronald A. Schorn, *Voyager's Grand Tour: To the Outer Planets and Beyond* (Washington, DC: Smithsonian Books, 2003), 27, and Stephen J. Pyne, *Voyager: Seeking New Worlds in the Third Great Age of Discovery* (New York: Viking, 2010), 18.

9
Wolfgang Schivelbusch, *The Railway Journey: The Industrialization of Time and Space in the 19th Century* (Berkeley: University of California Press, 1986), 34.

of the means of transport to alter the consciousness of the passengers; they developed a new set of perceptions."[10] Passengers came not only to appreciate the moving, changing landscape as seen through the windows of the train, but also to adopt the mobility of vision as the new standard for perception, a way of seeing that Schivelbusch calls panoramic perception.

No one physically rides the Voyagers. No body feels the contraction and expansion of space and time introduced by planetary exploration. The technological shift might be less disorienting but also provides less opportunity for humanity to reorient itself to the cosmos. The Golden Record, the very concept of sending a message to extraterrestrials, attempts to compensate for this lack by calling attention to the astonishing and even inhuman scale of travel made possible through our surrogates. The message serves as a vehicle for our imaginations, and it invites us to mentally travel to the anticipated moment of its discovery. We leap ahead 40,000 years to that far-off point in time and space, contracting the distance that separates us from it, them from us. The Golden Record simulates an experience of space travel and encourages an awareness of how the technology of space exploration extends humanity's reach.

The Golden Record holds more than 100 images that, as Sagan writes, are intended to "send to any possible extraterrestrial auditors information about the Earth and its inhabitants that they are unlikely otherwise to find themselves in possession of."[11] Their sequence reflects the desire to instruct aliens as it moves from the simple to the complex. The first images establish terms and notations needed to read the later ones; the next series of photographs document the solar system, human biology and reproduction, the geography of Earth, and some features of the biosphere; and the final set—nearly half of the collection—is a study of human culture. Frank Drake oversaw the visual portion of the message, and space artist Jon Lomberg had the task of paging through old editions of *National Geographic* and stacks of coffee table books, as well as consulting the files of the United Nations photographic archive to find photographs to represent life on Earth and human civilization.

Although carefully chosen to depict peoples of various ages, genders, and races, the Golden Record's photos focus narrowly on one aspect of culture: humanity's use of tools. Fishing nets, cotton harvesters, grills, drills, microscopes, and X-rays are among the technologies on display. Several photos celebrate transportation; cars, highways, bridges, trains, planes, airports, and even a Sno-Cat are all represented. In series, they function as a preamble to views of radio telescopes, an astronaut, and a rocket launch—the technologies allowing humans to engage with extraterrestrial worlds and even beings. To underscore the teleology, an illustration from Sir Isaac Newton's *The System of the World* (1728) that proposes the possibility of launching an object into orbit precedes the shot of an astronaut. Modern human history, it would seem, has led to the moment when a person can float far above Earth with the blackness of the space beyond. The figure of the astronaut nearly fills the frame, a portrait mislabeled in *Murmurs of Earth* as James McDivitt.[12] The photo, however, shows his Gemini 4 crewmate, Ed White, on the first space walk by an American. It's an understandable mistake; the opaque sun visor on the space suit's helmet conceals any identifying features. Instead, through the cooperation of man and machine, he has become less of an individual and more of an extraterrestrial.

In an early section about the solar system, the Golden Record features three extraterrestrial landscapes, specially chosen by Sagan. They highlight the planets that American spacecraft had visited and photographed from close proximity at the time of the message's composition, reminding viewers of the new ways of seeing afforded by space exploration. Craters pockmark Mercury's surface, clouds swirl over Mars, and the distinctive bands in Jupiter's atmosphere wrap around the planet. According to the caption in *Murmurs of Earth*, these pictures, along with a photo of Earth taken from Apollo 11, would communicate the origins of the message to an extraterrestrial audience. "From an interstellar point of view, the solar system is a little family huddled around a little star, and if we wish to tell extraterrestrials that 'this is home,' Jupiter and Mars are as much a part of home as New York or New Delhi," it reads.[13] But to describe Earth's neighboring planets as home goes beyond locating the source; it speaks to how space exploration expands our experience of space and redefines what

10 Ibid., 14.

11 Sagan, *Murmurs of Earth*, 33.

12 Ibid., 120.

13 Ibid., 87.

constitutes the extraterrestrial, or at least what we consider alien.

Nearly 18 months after its launch, Voyager 1 returned its first extraterrestrial photographs. It made its closest encounter with Jupiter in March 1979; Voyager 2 arrived in July. In November 1980 and August 1981, they reached Saturn. For scientists, "Voyager images rewrote the textbooks on the outer solar system and clinched the argument on the utility of images for planetary science. The Voyager images emphasized the solar system's diversity and dynamism and thus helped to correct the geocentric perspective of planetary scientists," writes historian Peter J. Westwick.[14] The stunning postcards from other worlds also reached a much wider audience. Major newspapers and weekly news magazines—the *New York Times*, *Los Angeles Times*, *Washington Post*, *Newsweek*, and others—prominently covered the Voyager mission and published many brilliantly colored views of the planets and their moons. Articles in *National Geographic* and other popular magazines featured double-page spreads of Jupiter's Great Red Spot in lurid red with turbulent turquoise waves surrounding it and close-ups of Saturn's rings in a rainbow of saturated shades.

The vivid, even psychedelic hues, that characterized the Voyager's photos of Jupiter and Saturn contrast with the black-and-white extraterrestrial landscapes carried on the Golden Record. The exaggerated and enhanced colors make the planets' physical features more immediately visible, and they also call attention to the mediated qualities of all extraterrestrial landscapes. Even as they suggest an eyewitness view of distant worlds, photos of distant planets depend on a complex collaboration between humans and machines; a multistage series of translations from electronic data to the printed photograph; and a negotiation between the demands of scientific visualization and public relations.[15] Voyager's brilliantly colored views of Jupiter and Saturn represent the most flamboyant expression of this endeavor, and they remain startlingly alien even as subsequent missions have flooded us with images of these same extraterrestrial landmarks.

In April 1980, after Voyager 1 and 2 had left Jupiter behind and before their encounters with Saturn, Sagan speculated about the characteristics of extraterrestrial perception. "A possible sensory capability of an extraterrestrial organism: spectral sensitivity through the infrared and other frequency ranges which implies the ability to detect chemistry directly," he dictated into a tape recorder for his secretary to transcribe and file for his future reference.[16] He imagines an otherworldly way of seeing, one that transcends the limits of human vision. Although the Voyager images' brilliant colors do not represent the chemistry of the planets, they introduce a new way of seeing, one that magnifies distinctions that might otherwise be invisible to human eyes. The views of Jupiter and Saturn might then be imagined as doubly extraterrestrial: in subject matter and in mode of representation. They show the atmospheres of these alien planets with the expanded perception of an imagined extraterrestrial. In this regard, they extend the experience initiated by the Golden Record. They allow us to become extraterrestrials through other means.

14
Peter J. Westwick, "Visual Imagery in Solar System Exploration," *Exploring the Solar System: The History and Science of Planetary Exploration* (New York: Palgrave, 2013), 156.

15
On image processing and the Voyager mission, see Peter J. Westwick, *Into the Black: JPL and the American Space Program, 1976–2004* (New Haven: Yale University Press, 2007).

16
box 1253, folder 5, Seth MacFarlane Collection of the Carl Sagan and Ann Druyan Archive, Manuscript Division, Library of Congress, Washington, DC, 1980.

Strategic Fictions
FELICITY D. SCOTT

The US National Aeronautics and Space Administration (NASA) closed the heroic Apollo program in 1972 and its manned expeditions to Skylab in 1974. By 1976, the agency redirected attention from outer space exploration to focus on earth science research and environmental monitoring—one of many responses to perceived threats to US security born of resource scarcity, pollution, and population growth in the so-called developing world. Today, NASA plans to boost the role of private companies, such as SpaceX and Blue Origin, in future space missions. In April 2016, Representative Jim Bridenstine, Republican from Oklahoma, sponsored the American Space Renaissance Act (ASRA), announcing, "The purpose of this bill is to permanently secure the United States of America as the preeminent spacefaring nation." The bill breaks down into national security, civil, and commercial goals, each requiring architecture, infrastructure, and geography-based research. If Britain was the preeminent seafaring empire at the height of colonial rule on Earth, the US continues to seek to update this paradigm for a neocolonial world order. In September 2017, with no scientific or technical training, Bridenstine was nominated by President Trump to head NASA. Alluding to the shock of the Soviet Union's 1957 launch of Sputnik, Bridenstine declared, "This is our Sputnik Moment."[1] On November 8, after a contentious hearing, the United States Senate Commerce Committee voted (13 to 14 along party lines) to send the nomination to the full US Senate for confirmation. His appointment was confirmed on April 19, 2018, and he assumed office four days later, becoming the first elected official to head NASA.[2]

In a flashback to a proposal launched in the mid-1970s by Princeton University physics professor Gerard K. O'Neill, Bridenstine proclaimed that Earth's Moon should be mined for fuel and even serve as a "proving ground" for travel to Mars, a key aspect of Trump's "Make America Great Again" space agenda.[3] But if O'Neill claimed strip mining on the Moon would be in the interest of saving Earth's environment, Bridenstine makes no such claim. Bridenstine's interests are aligned with Trump's earliest post-election-victory announcements, his plan to cut NASA's budget for earth science research and redirect the agency's attention to outer space. Climate change studies are now rejected as "politicized science."[4] In retrospect, the military, psychological, and economic agendas at work in this new "renaissance" seem to appeal to NASA's earlier heroic Space Race narrative, but also to the complex of nationalism and privatization fostered by Professor O'Neill under the seductive but misleading fiction that colonizing space would

1
Kenneth Chang, "Jim Bridenstine to Be Nominated by Trump to Head NASA," *New York Times*, September 2, 2017, https://www.nytimes.com/2017/09/02/science/jim-bridenstine-nasa-trump.html.

2
Kenneth Chang, "Trump's NASA Nominee, Jim Bridenstine, Confirmed by Senate on Party-Line Vote," *New York Times*, April 19, 2018, https://www.nytimes.com/2018/04/19/science/jim-bridenstine-nasa.html.

3
See Jacqueline Klimas, "Trump's NASA Pick Faces Blistering Criticism on Capitol Hill," *Politico*, November 1, 2017, https://www.politico.com/story/2017/11/01/jim-bridenstine-nasa-confirmation-hearing-244416.

involve techno-scientific aid for global humanity. It is not surprising that O'Neill's visions of space colonization are repeatedly likened to European discovery of the New World and the ideology of Manifest Destiny associated with the 19th-century American frontier. At a moment when US expansion and economic growth seemed threatened by resource scarcity, environmental degradation, nuclear fallout, or political pressures at home and from developing countries, space colonization promised continuity in US economic supremacy and pioneering know-how. This constellation of politics have returned with force. As reported in *Scientific American* with some alarm in July 2017, "Echoing Trump's 'America first' theme, [Vice President Mike] Pence said Trump intended to carry nationalism into space with renewed emphasis on human space exploration and discovery 'for the benefit of the American people and all of the world.'" Reversing NASA's decades-long participation in international partnerships, the Trump administration now calls for "American boots on the face of Mars."[5]

O'Neill's vision for space colonization first made headlines in May 1974, when he convened the first Conference on Space Colonization at Princeton University. The colonies, according to O'Neill, were initially to take the form of a pair of giant cylinders rotating to simulate gravity, with alternating strips of land areas (valleys) and windows (solars), the shell fabricated from metal cables "bunched to form a coarse mesh in the window areas" and subdivided into smaller glass or plastic infill panels.[6] The interiors of these man-made habitats would replicate, or so O'Neill insisted, the most beautiful parts of Earth. For him, this beauty was exemplified by Carmel Bay, California; Grand Teton in Wyoming; the island of Bermuda; and "attractive villages in Italy and Southern France." With an abundance of material goods, endless sunshine, "virtually unlimited" resources harvested from the Moon and outer space, freedom to circulate, and, as he repeatedly underscored, "independence from large-scale governments," pioneering colonists were promised attractive, self-sufficient, profitable, Earthlike environments.[7] Yet, unlike on Earth, there would be no unproductive workers, no pollution, no limits to energy consumption, no garden-destroying pests. Fresh strawberries would be available throughout the year.[8]

When O'Neill testified before the US House of Representatives in July 1975, his proposal wavered between the language of plentiful economic development and threats of scarcity, insurrection, and war. With rhetorical flair, it was pitched at the nexus of "American know-how" and appeals to freedom and economic opportunity, cast in distinctly nationalist terms and encouraging a shift from government funding of science to private industry. O'Neill even proposed the 1969 Moon landing should be understood not as a scientific venture but as a "prospecting survey" for space colonization.[9] Moreover, his claims to the "promise" of a productive, profitable, isolated, normative, and distinctly American form of life, as illustrated in NASA's renderings, repeatedly refracted through American populations. In this sense the lush, protected suburban lifestyle in outer space was racially marked, as De Witt Douglas Kilgore cogently argues in *Astrofuturism: Science, Race, and Visions of Utopia in Space* (2003). Kilgore notes, "O'Neill's argument for future diversity therefore contains a catastrophic tension between an unmarked whiteness representing technological modernity and a marked blackness (racial/cultural others) representing the atavistic survival of preindustrial culture as tourist trophy or exotic spectacle."[10] Like a flashback to the US in the 1950s, space colonies sought a society wherein political questions seeking to challenge extant social and economic hierarchies and injustices—from civil

4
Oliver Milman, "Trump to Scrap NASA Climate Research in Crackdown on 'Politicized Science,'" *Guardian*, November 23, 2016, https://www.theguardian.com/environment/2016/nov/22/nasa-earth-donald-trump-eliminate-climate-change-research.

5
Irene Klotz, "Pence Calls for 'New Era of Space Exploration' at NASA," July 7, 2017, *Scientific American*, https://www.scientificamerican.com/article/pence-calls-for-ldquo-new-era-of-space-exploration-rdquo-at-nasa/. Originally published on Space.com as "Pence Calls for Return to Moon, Boots on Mars," July 6, 2017, https://www.space.com/37411-nasa-moon-mars-vice-president-pence.html.

6
Gerard K. O'Neill, "The Colonization of Space," *Physics Today*, 27, no. 9 (September 1974): 33. For a diagram of the rotating cylinders, see Gerard K. O'Neill, "A-III. The Colonization of Space," "Appendix A: Proceedings of the Princeton Conference on the Colonization of Space, May 10, 1974," in *Space Manufacturing Facilities* (Space Colonies), Proceedings of the Princeton/AIAA/NASA Conference, May 7–9, 1975, ed. Jerry Grey (New York: American Institute of Aeronautics and Astronautics, 1977), Figure A-2.

7
O'Neill, "A-III. The Colonization of Space," A7.

8
Ibid., A10.

9
Future Space Programs 1975: Hearings before the Subcommittee on Space Science and Applications of the Committee on Science and Technology, 94th Congress (July 23, 1975), (testimony of Gerard K. O'Neill), 168.

10
De Witt Douglas Kilgore, *Astrofuturism: Science, Race, and Visions of Utopia in Space* (Philadelphia: University of Pennsylvania Press, 2003), 176–177.

rights struggles and antiwar protests against the unjust war in Southeast Asia to calls to regulate the unchecked environmental pollution from industry—would be eliminated. In their place was found a culture privileging corporate profit.

During his testimony, O'Neill alluded to the country's role in a shifting geopolitical landscape and the violent reshufflings of power in the wake of decolonization. Testifying that space colonies were key to economic and resource security, he claimed, "Both the oil-consuming nations and the underdeveloped third world [*sic*] are vulnerable to the threat of supply cutoff from the Middle East."[11] Promising to transmit solar satellite energy back to Earth via giant microwave beams, O'Neill stated that US energy independence would be assured without the political backlash caused domestically by strip mining and nuclear proliferation, and in volumes far beyond the Alaska pipeline. Given the scale of the market for energy, payoff for investors would also be enormous. "We can put the Middle East out of business!" he exclaimed.[12] Moreover, taking lessons from the cynical rhetoric of the development sector, he asserted that what was good for the US was good for the world. The US would be able to supply cheap energy to developing countries or even provide humanitarian aid, thereby overcoming growing hostility toward the US as "exploiters of scarce resources." Furthermore, appealing to a rising Malthusianism, it was even suggested that this energy supply would reduce population growth in the global south.[13] In such claims to offering panaceas and even aid we find American nationalism taking its most brutally coercive, biopolitical forms and doing so under the language of the good.

O'Neill in fact never imagined an equitable scenario. "The human race," he proclaimed in his 1977 book, *The High Frontier*, "stands now on the threshold of a new frontier, whose richness surpasses a thousand fold that of the new western world of five hundred years ago."[14] "It would be naïve to assume that its benefits will be initially shared equally among all of humankind," he acknowledged, reassuring potential investors of his intent. "The world has never worked that way."[15] By 1977 O'Neill was willing to acknowledge the most effective governance structure for a space colony would be far from democratic: "a dictatorship is what works," he noted in an interview with Stewart Brand and Jane McClure, since "there's nothing that produces conflict more than an ill-defined situation of authority."[16]

O'Neill repeatedly appealed to US sovereignty and national good and to bettering international relations when pitching space colonization. When so doing, to underscore again, he marshaled a symptomatic transition toward the dominance of the private sector as a driving force, shifting the rhetoric from colonies to manufacturing facilities and from scientific missions to prospecting surveys. We thus need to ask again, For whom was a future in outer space being imagined? His images of Earthlike environments suggested an extension of suburban life, the normative American subject, and his form of life persisting as key tropes to conceive social, economic, and political relations to come. Yet we still need to return to the question of who would profit from such an expansion and against whom such an apparatus might work, overtly or covertly. Positioning himself strategically within this battlefield during his 1975 testimony to US Congress, O'Neill spoke directly to the language of private interest.

> We have a product for which there is a big market, and which satisfies a need. Where there is a big market there is reason and justification for big investment. We're talking about something which is more like the kind of decision a large manufacturing company has to make when it decides whether to invest in a new plant, than like the traditional idea of our space program: a research-oriented effort from which you never expected to have a direct-dollar return.[17]

As evident in Bridenstine's conception of the Moon as yet another site for resource exploitation to serve US interests, aspects of the 1970s cultural imaginary, with its neo-imperialist disposition, persist today.[18] The Moon still serves as a potential station for missions of territorial expansion to other parts of

11
Future Space Programs 1975 (testimony of O'Neill), 129.

12
Ibid., 134.

13
Ibid., 135.

14
Gerard K. O'Neill, *The High Frontier: Human Colonies in Space* (New York: Morrow, 1977), 8.

15
Ibid., 11.

16
Gerard K. O'Neill, "Instead of Frictionless Elephants: Talking with Gerard O'Neill," interview by Jane McClure and Stewart Brand, in *Space Colonies*, ed. Stewart Brand (New York: Penguin Books, 1977), 151.

17
Future Space Programs 1975 (testimony by O'Neill), 187.

the solar system. However, in contrast to O'Neill's dream of constructing giant lunar, post-planetary colonial territories, artificial landscapes to erect new worlds, today other planets, particularly Mars, are the primary object of extraterrestrial colonizing missions. Soon after the 2016 presidential election, the *New York Times* reported that "we've been having a kind of Mars moment lately," going on to position the Moon as key. "Among the attractions of a lunar base," science writer Dennis Overbye reported,

> would be the ability to mine ice at the Moon's poles to produce rocket fuel. According to recent studies, refueling at the Moon, or nearby, would be the cheapest way to get to Mars. It could be the mother of all infrastructure projects, perhaps a notion attractive to Mr. Trump's developer instincts, in effect paving a highway to Mars and beyond.[19]

Mock missions simulating extended stays on Mars have also proliferated in recent years, including NASA's ill-fated Hawaii Space Exploration Analog and Simulation, or HI-SEAS, missions, wherein mock astronauts retreat into a geodesic dome known as a "habitat" on Mauna Loa, a Hawaiian volcano.[20] Moreover, the detection of a "large, watery lake beneath an ice cap on Mars" made headlines on July 28, 2018. Now, proclaimed one scientist, "there are all the ingredients for thinking that life can be there, or can be maintained there if life once existed on Mars."[21]

The dream of an unregulated outer space continues. As Kenneth Chang details in "Opportunity in Orbit," from the perspective of entrepreneurial American companies—such as Moon Express, SpaceX, Blue Origin, and Planetary Resources, and initiatives such as Google Lunar XPrize—regulating entities, including NASA's 1967 Outer Space Treaty and the Federal Aviation Administration, merely pose obstacles to commercial exploitation. NASA's treaty, Chang posits, "may now be getting in the way of entrepreneurs with plans to push farther and faster into space than national agencies like NASA."[22] Jeff Bezos, Chang reports, returning us even closer to O'Neill's strategic fiction, "talks about Blue Origin less as a business than as part of a glorious future for humanity, with millions of people living and working off the planet," a path that "humanity must pursue if it is to continue to prosper." With energy and raw materials derived from and heavy manufacturing moved to "elsewhere in the solar system," Earth, Bezos "joked, would be zoned for residential and light industrial use, allowing much of Earth to return to a more natural state."[23] Beyond the rhetoric of humanity, prosperity, and environmental care, the persistent mobilization of fear and claims to threat of war attending such colonizing dreams remain, repeatedly threatening imminent disaster if such corporate bodies aren't given a free rein. As reported by Olivia Solon in the *Guardian*, "Humans must prioritize the colonization of Mars so the species can be conserved in the event of a third world war," stated SpaceX founder Elon Musk, foreseeing the advent of a new "dark age."[24]

That we find ourselves again at a dangerous nexus of territory, private capital, and war was rendered all too explicit in President Trump's declaration on June 18, 2018, to "direct the Pentagon to establish a sixth branch of the armed services dedicated to protecting American interests in outer space," thereby replacing any potential for new forms of self-government by something closer to martial law. This, Trump announced, would be "great not only in terms of jobs and everything else, it's great for the psyche of our county."[25] A *New York Times* editorial responded on July 28, reminding readers that this new military branch, called the

18
See Tiqqun, *Introduction to Civil War*, trans. Alexander R. Galloway and Jason E. Smith (Los Angeles: Semiotext(e), 2010).

19
Dennis Overbye, "Where Will NASA Go in the Age of Trump?" *New York Times*, December 13, 2016, D6.

20
See Kenneth Chang, "In a Dome in Hawaii, a Mission to Mars," *New York Times*, October 21, 2014, D1, and Marina Koren, "When a Mars Simulation Goes Wrong," *Atlantic*, June 22, 2018, https://www.theatlantic.com/science/archive/2018/06/mars-simulation-hi-seas-nasa-hawaii/553532/.

21
Kenneth Chang and Dennis Overbye, "Lake on Mars: Finding Stirs Hope for Life," *New York Times*, July 26, 2018, A1.

22
Kenneth Chang, "Opportunity in Orbit: Entrepreneurs Seeking to Make Money on the Moon May Find a 50-Year-Old Treaty in Their Way," *New York Times*, November 28, 2017, D1.

23
Kenneth Chang, "Bezos Lifts Veil on His Secretive Rocket Company," *New York Times*, March 9, 2016, B8.

24
Olivia Solon, "Elon Musk: We Must Colonise Mars to Preserve Our Species in a Third World War," *Guardian*, March 11, 2018, https://www.theguardian.com/technology/2018/mar/11/elon-musk-colonise-mars-third-world-war.

25
Katie Rogers, "Trump Orders Establishment of Space Force as Sixth Military Branch," *New York Times*, June 18, 2018, https://www.nytimes.com/2018/06/18/us/politics/trump-space-force-sixth-military-branch.html.

Space Force, comes with a dream of "dominance in space." Space is seen as a "'war-fighting domain' like the land, sea and air," a reconception of outer space that is itself likely to "spur an arms race in space and make war-fighting more likely."[26] Once again, conceptions of the future in outer space are deployed as weapons in a battle to inflect or control the path capitalism might take and to shift the global socioeconomic, political, and environmental apparatus in a manner facilitating certain dispositions or tendencies. But these tendencies remain unstable, subject to revalencing, reversals, and even to reconceiving in terms of new ethical and political frameworks of justice—a task for history and theory, a task now seemingly ever more urgent as "Trump in Space" gains momentum.

26
Editorial Board, "Trump in Space," *New York Times*, July 28, 2018, A3.

A Vast Frontier
GRETCHEN HEEFNER

In early 1951, Lt. Gen. Lewis A. Pick was given orders to build an air base. As chief engineer for the US Army Corps of Engineers, it was Pick's job to oversee all military construction at home and abroad. The outlines of the proposal were not particularly unusual, although the location and timing of the request were unexpected: the US Air Force wanted a base in northwestern Greenland built within the year. Pick was handed a "small photograph of a bleak, wind-swept, rocky plateau partially covered by snow." That is where he was to build. While Pick knew how to build an air base, he also knew enough to recognize the difficulties—what Pick called the "imponderables"—of constructing something in such a "hostile" and "extreme" environment.[1] Pick was not sure it could be done.

Complicating matters, Greenland was not the only extreme environment Pick had to consider. As he sent a scouting crew up north that February 1951, a different team of engineers moved into the sand seas of the Sahara; still more set up labs to test the effect of altitude and rapid temperature shifts on basic equipment. The Cold War forced American military engineers and planners to consider the world's extreme environments, not simply as exotic places to explore and visit, but as sites of mobilization and construction. In military writings "extreme" came to signify two things. First, it was shorthand for environments considered outside the bounds of modern human habitation, "hostile" places where modern man could not —or perhaps should not—live. Yet "extreme" was more than mere description; it was also an opportunity: these were places where the US military could demonstrate technical and spatial mastery.

The story of military engineers rearranging the extremes raises important questions about the infrastructure of modern exploratory knowledge. What does it mean that the US military took such an active, and arguably lead, role in understanding the Earth's extremes? Does it matter that our contemporary understanding of how to deal with the extreme—wherever that may be—has military origins? More important, how does this story of extreme terrestrial environments reframe how we imagine and understand exploration for the extraterrestrial? While in the early 1950s Pick and other military planners were not yet thinking about space exploration, the terrestrial extremes they encountered shaped the institutions and ways that people would later think about how humankind could survive in extraterrestrial space.

Such questions and concerns were far from Pick's mind in the 1950s. He and his team of military engineers had a job to do. It was their task to take abstract ideas and sketchy plans and fabricate a *constructed* environment; to take landscapes apart and put them back together as they saw fit. Military

1
Lewis A. Pick, "The Story of BLUE JAY," *Military Engineer* 45, no. 306 (1953): 278–286.

2
Walter G. Vincenti, *What Engineers Know and How They Know It: Analytical Studies from Aeronautical History* (Baltimore: Johns Hopkins University Press, 1993), 6; Najmedin Meshkati, "Engineering Diplomacy: An Underutilized Tool in Foreign Policy," June 5, 2018, http://www.sciencediplomacy.org/perspective/2012/engineering-diplomacy, June 2014.

engineers were primed to do what the National Academy of Engineering defines as "design under constraint."[2] Or what the aeronautics pioneer Walter Vincenti described as the "the practice of organizing the design and construction of any artifice which transforms the physical world around us to meet some recognized need." For engineers such as Pick, the descriptions were accurate enough. In Greenland average winter temperatures hovered around −30°F. Snow and ice were everywhere. The icy tundra lacked the natural resources usually used for construction. Yet the engineers still had to build an air base. Under these conditions, seemingly simple tasks became arduous undertakings. The men learned to keep their gloves on when manipulating tiny tools lest the skin on their fingers stick to the cold metal, leading to "metal burn." According to the famous polar explorer Paul Siple, work in the "hostile wasteland" had long been reserved for the "bold adventurers" intent on uncovering the world's unknown.[3]

The environment these military engineers confronted in 1951 was clearly of this earth, yet it was decidedly outside of and beyond their realm of normal knowledge and experience. For all the engineers knew—or perhaps did not know—Greenland could have been the moon. The first survey teams returned from the Great North with grim stories of snow, ice, permafrost, and winds so fierce that the engineers were left gasping for air. Lack of daylight made finding specific locations for runways and barracks difficult. Soil samples were inconclusive. The corps's libraries, normally a wealth of information, lacked appropriate manuals for building and working in such conditions. The corps had recently started a cold-climate research center, the Snow, Ice and Permafrost Research Establishment (SIPRE), complete with labs and test sites in Alaska. But work on permafrost had yet to bear conclusive or particularly actionable recommendations. There was so much they had to learn before heading north: Would the sea lanes be open? Would 200,000 tons of supplies reach Greenland? Would the ships make it past Baffin Bay or the Melville Pack? And what of daily life? Would they be able to provide water, heat, and power "before a long darkness of another polar winter"? Would a man lose his mind if he didn't see the sun? "How far North can one get?" Pick asked. "And live? And work? And operate modern construction equipment?"

Pick's uncertainty was tempered by the knowledge that as he got to work the defense establishment was building a network of research and testing facilities that would help answer these "imponderables." Since the late 1940s, the military had taken a keen interest in the polar regions not only for their clear strategic significance, but also because they were vast unknowns. As scholars have shown, this combination led to a stunning mobilization of funds and institutions devoted to Arctic research. By 1949, each branch of the military had its own cold-climate research facility replete with laboratories, test facilities, and bases. Industry and academic centers were pulled in.[4] To get men and materials to such outposts, and to keep them functioning once there, was going to require a more systematic and coordinated program of study than what had existed up to that point. In building Thule Air Base, as it was ultimately named, Pick could thus increasingly draw on what was becoming a highly coordinated program of military and scientific research aimed at conquering even the most distant and seemingly uninhabitable of places.

The carefully plotted and institutionally embedded systems that the United States military gradually put into place to deal with and get to know extreme terrestrial environments translated rather seamlessly into the extraterrestrial. As the anthropologist Valerie Olson said in speaking of the issues facing contemporary NASA engineers, "Outer space is not considered a unique kind of environment. . . . It is one among a set of environments categorized as *extreme*."[5] The connection is not mere conjecture. The elision took place in institutions and research programs during the Cold War. The Air Force's Arctic, Desert and Tropics Information Center (ADTIC) formed in 1947 to codify best practices for surviving and thriving in environmental extremes. By the 1960s, ADTIC's

3
Paul Siple, preface, *Man Living in the Arctic: Proceedings of a Conference, Quartermaster Research and Engineering Center* (Washington, DC: National Academies Press, 1961). For intriguing comparison with later astronauts operating in space, see Nicholas de Monchaux, *Spacesuit: Fashioning Apollo* (Cambridge, MA: MIT Press, 2011).

4
J. Martin-Nielsen, "The Other Cold War: The United States and Greenland's Ice Sheet Environment, 1948–1966," *Journal of Historical Geography* 38 (2012): 69–80; on tight links between science and military, see Ronald Doel, "Constituting the Postwar Earth Sciences: The Military's Influence on the Environmental Sciences in the USA after 1945," *Social Studies of Science* 33, no. 5 (2003): 635–666.

5
Valerie Olson, *Into the Extreme: U.S. Environmental Systems and Politics beyond Earth* (Minneapolis: University of Minnesota Press, 2018), 20.

multidisciplinary teams evaluated emergency landing sites for space vehicles. In 1961, when Lockheed Aircraft Corporation issued its three-part annotated bibliography of all things lunar, it asserted, "Arctic exploration, including base construction, surface vehicles, clothing and equipment, and environmental effects on man is included because of its applicability to lunar bases and exploration."[6] No one had yet proposed earth-based analogues, but extreme terrestrial places were already being presented as mid-way points between the known and the unknown of outer space. The Arctic, an inhospitable frontier, an unnatural space, was that much closer to the extremes explorers could expect when they soared into the heavens.

Despite the considerable obstacles, Thule Air Base was fully operational by 1953. The *Washington Post* gushed that its completion proved that the word "impossible" was not in the military's vocabulary. Pick was even more enthusiastic. Writing for the *Military Engineer*, he linked the construction of Thule to a long tradition of American exploration and expansion. Engineers had "pushed our railroads out the West," and built the "canal through the Isthmus of Panama." The construction of Thule "broke the world's last great frontier, the Arctic." In Pick's retelling, military engineers and logisticians had displaced explorers and adventurers in mapping out and marking the extremes, in pressing the American project to the edges of what was known. Through hard work and careful planning, Pick concluded, "big-time construction was brought to the roof of the world."[7]

Thule itself quickly became an important node in the national network of research and military centers aimed at understanding the extremes. From Thule, scientists and military parties moved out over and onto the ice sheet. In 1954, Corps of Engineers representatives started an intensive research and development program on Arctic construction techniques, including tunneling. By 1960, they had created an under-the-ice laboratory, Camp Century, where 200 men lived and worked for years before their heat led to cave-ins and ice-wall deformities. The scientists stationed at Camp Century drilled ice cores that would later be important for building climate models. Their scientific work also became an important cover to the military research taking place on a parallel track. For example, Project Iceworm was an effort to design a system for shuttling nuclear missiles around on railcars under the ice cap.[8] Though ultimately a failure, the project remained secret until the 1990s.

Throughout the 1950s, military deployments and research programs transformed the Arctic from a specific location into an abstract environmental designation that could be known and conquered.[9] Specific locations mattered less than general ideas. Indeed, through the burgeoning network of bases and research institutions, knowledge and expertise could be transferred anywhere considered climatically "hostile." Alaska could be Greenland and vice versa. Building a base at Point Barrow would mirror the work at Thule, and so on. Early Cold War base construction and operation provided the military with the experiences and incentive to catalogue the world's environments. The step to extraterrestrial planning was thus incremental; a transfer of focus and funds, not a reorientation of outlook or institutional resources.

The multifaceted approach to both research and operation concerning extreme environments was highlighted in the 1960 symposium "Man Living in the Arctic," held at the Quartermaster Research and Engineering Center in Natick, Massachusetts. The two-day meeting featured papers given by the country's most distinguished polar experts. Their disciplinary fields ranged from military planners and tacticians to physiologists, anthropologists, glaciologists, political scientists, explorers, and more. Panels discussed research on clothing and equipment; on weather and climate;

6
Paul H. Nesbitt, "A Brief History of the Arctic, Desert and Tropic Information Center and Its Arctic Research Activities," in *United States Polar Exploration*, ed. Herman Friis and Shelby G. Bale Jr. (Athens: Ohio University Press, 1970); A. Beltran, J. B. Goldmann, and E. E. Graziano, *Annotated Bibliography of Lunar Properties, Geology, Vehicles, and Bases* (Sunnyvale, CA: Lockheed Aircraft Corp., 1961), i.

7
Lewis A. Pick, "Greenland Base," *Washington Post*, September 20, 1952, 8; Pick, "The Story of BLUE JAY," 278–286.

8
On Camp Century, see Elmer F. Clark, *Camp Century: Evolution of Concept and History of Design, Construction and Performance* (U.S. Army Materiel Command, 1965), https://web.archive.org/web/20110125020712/http://stinet.dtic.mil/cgi-bin/GetTRDoc?AD=AD477706&Location=U2&doc=GetTRDoc.pdf; on Project Iceworm, see Erik D. Weiss, "Cold War under the Ice: The Army's Bid for a Long-Range Nuclear Role, 1959–1963," *Journal of Cold War Studies* 3, no. 3 (2001): 31–58.

9
Matthew Farish, "The Lab and the Land: Overcoming the Arctic in Cold War Alaska," *Isis* 104 (March 2013): 1–29; Farish, *Contours of America's Cold War* (Minneapolis: University of Minnesota Press, 2010).

on the operation of machines; on industry's role in developing new materials; on the ways that scientific research and military outposts worked so fluidly together. Lt. Gen. Arthur Trudeau, chief of research and development for the US Army, announced that only by working together were they all "developing the means to conquer the beautiful but biting environment."[10]

So much had been studied in such a short period of time. Physiologist Steven Horvath lamented the loss of a particular way of seeing the world. Man "has become so familiar with the Arctic that he looks upon it with a certain amount of contempt," he wrote. Instead of treating the environment with a cautious respect and concern, he continued, "man brings his own environment with him" and so cannot experience the true North.[11]

Others at the conference were less discouraged. "Bringing one's environment" along was precisely the point. This migration of technology and temporary settlement would enable more advanced research and exploration. It is partly why Camp Century was buried under the ice, to practice building structures to maximize human comfort in the extreme climates. "It is only when man attempts to conquer his environment that progress is made," insisted the explorer Paul Siple, now part of the Army Research Office. Siple's transition from adventurer to military researcher perfectly encapsulated the broad shift in orientation that had taken place regarding the Arctic. It was no longer up to individuals to overcome the environment, but to well-planned teams, to systems, and meticulously established logistics. This was the realization of the network of military and research facilities established out of Cold War strategic imperatives. Nodding to the work of Pick and other military engineers, Siple wrote that the military was "accelerating" civilization in the Arctic and pushing boldly into new frontiers.

The Canadian geographer Trevor Lloyd agreed. He too singled out the role of the US military in Arctic research progress, though he added a cautionary note about how easy it was to avoid seeing the militarized nature of this work. I "can go in any good library and look up a map of military camps and settlements of the Roman Gaul of 2,000 years ago," he said. But he worried that he was unable to find the US military installations that he knew proliferated across the Arctic in 1960.[12] We would do well to contemplate Lloyd's musings today, particularly as the privatization of space travel, led by companies such as SpaceX, threatens to further mask the military's central and ongoing role in shaping and funding such programs. By truly seeing the military's role in extreme environmental research and planning, we might better imagine what a non-militarized extraterrestrial could look like.

10
Arthur Trudeau, "Significance of Research and Development in the Arctic," *Man Living in the Arctic: Proceedings of a Conference, Quartermaster Research and Engineering Center* (Washington, DC: National Academies Press, 1961), 7–10.

11
Steven M. Horvath, "Summation: Man's Future Conquest of the Arctic," in *Man Living in the Arctic*, 115–118.

12
Paul Siple, "Limitations to Living in the Polar Regions," 14–17; Trevor Lloyd, "Human Society in the Arctic Today," 125–134, both in *Man Living in the Arctic*.

Space Is Not the Final Frontier

JULIE MICHELLE KLINGER

The status of outer space as the final frontier is a cultural fetish. What a given culture fetishizes reveals the blind spots of power in specific times and places. That outer space should even be considered a frontier is a recent historical phenomenon that reflects the fusion of political power with techno-optimism, and it is far from final. But the temporal horizon of finality speaks to the desires felt among putative winners and losers alike under postatomic capitalism to transcend the brutalities of our age while preserving the status quo.

The invocation of the frontier orients political, economic, cultural, and technological power toward a specific sequence of activities: resource discovery, enclosure, devastation, and abandonment. In this, there is an extractivist intention,[1] driven by the need to capture new resources in order to escape or ameliorate crises in the metropole. Therefore, naming a place a frontier sets it up as a problem to be solved: territories to be conquered or resources to be claimed, both processes as markers of a certain kind of "progress" that leaves the old world, and its old problems, behind. In this fantasy, taming "the final frontier" signifies the transcendence of earthly problems. But more important, it exonerates the protagonists of accountability for those problems: war, pollution, poverty, and that suite of brutalities summed up in passive voice as "the Anthropocene."[2]

To be clear, it is one thing for historically oppressed global majorities to fight for a transcendent peace via shared human cause realized through scientific collaboration. But it is quite another for privileged minorities—these descendants of settler colonialists and beneficiaries of 500 years' exclusion of nonwhite peoples and women from the European Enlightenment category of human—to demarcate outer space as the final frontier, as though it were the last place left to conquer in the colonial civilizational project.[3]

The ideal of peaceful, collaborative space exploration that benefits all of humankind motivates thousands of space professionals and scientists around the world. These shared ideals have been a potent political force over the course of the 20th century, culminating in one of the most robust international treaties in history, the 1967 United Nations' Outer Space Treaty (OST), formally known as the Treaty on the Principles Governing the Activities of States in the Exploration and Use of Outer Space, including the Moon and Other Celestial Bodies.[4] But lately, the grotesque alliance between militarism and

1 Extractivism refers to the practice of removing high-value resources—natural or otherwise—to export or sell. The term also characterizes economies that depend primarily on the removal of local resources for sale in nonlocal markets.

2 Most recently, Kathryn Yusoff has critiqued the Anthropocene as a scientifically coded description of the consequences of the Euro-American capitalist legacy of brutally racialized human-environment relations. See Kathryn Yusoff, *A Billion Black Anthropocenes or None* (Minneapolis: University of Minnesota Press, 2019).

3 Patricia Limerick, "Imagined Frontiers: Westward Expansion and the Future of the Space Program," *Space Policy Alternatives*, ed. Radford Byerly (Boulder, CO: Westview Press, 1992), 249–262.

market-driven ambition has co-opted and ensnared even the most idealistic advocates of space sciences.[5]

The alliance between legislative power and private capital is driven by a potent combination of *El Dorado* fever and Malthusian paranoia, which has recast the cosmos as replete with immense untapped resources that are not only free for the taking, but simply must be exploited to avoid a scarcity-induced apocalypse.[6] Wastefulness is confused with scarcity, and elite fears of limited availability of critical resources on Earth lent an air of urgency and legitimacy to the recent legal initiatives to sidestep the provisions of the OST: the 2015 SPACE Act,[7] signed into law by Obama, followed by Trump's 2019 executive order to establish a Space Force.[8] Ongoing processes of exploration and expropriation are now routinely discussed as essential to avoid environmental apocalypse or to escape civilizational collapse.[9]

But we have seen this all before. Frontiers, and particular visions about the resources they hold, are an imagined geography that reflects the fears, hopes, and failures of a given culture at a particular historical-technological conjuncture. When Thomas Malthus wrote his *Essay on the Principles of Population* in 1789, he provided at once an explanation of the existence of the poor and a tidy reasoning against redistributive politics. The poor were poor because there were too many of them and not enough resources to go around, and not because kicking people off their land for elite enjoyment or colonial surplus extraction deprived peasant majorities of their means of subsistence.[10] In Malthus's reasoning, lifting a finger to alleviate suffering would only disrupt the "natural" check that starvation enacts on population growth and would imperil us all. Such a tidy dismissal of responsibility for creating poverty, as well as the dismissal of redistributive justice on moral grounds, must have done wonders to unburden the conscience of colonial elites. The same logics are at work with respect to outer space. Privatizing outer space eases elite fears of having to answer for antisocial policies brutally enacted to enrich a few at the expense of the many while justifying these same brutalities in nationalist and Social Darwinist terms.

The broad cosmopolitan scientific sensibility to explore the cosmos for the benefit of all humankind has been harnessed by an ethos of enclosure that shapes geographies of extractive frontiers on Earth. Although both cosmopolitan science and jingoist accumulation employ frontier imaginaries, the territorial stakes are different. The former espouses a leave-no-trace ethos enshrined in planetary protection protocols and popularized in *Star Trek's* Prime Directive, while the latter champions a conquistador approach to "harvest the heavens"[11] and "terraform new worlds."[12]

Extractive frontiers are characterized by a dynamic of resource discovery, enclosure, devastation, and abandonment. On Earth, Anna Tsing describes extractive frontiers as conjured into being by a view from elsewhere.[13] In the trick of power that leaves the dominant unmarked, that "elsewhere" from which the frontier is conjured is often erased. This is part of the frontier fetish. So when we characterize outer space as a frontier, our perspective from Earth is erased, and with it, all the lessons we might learn from the spaces and outcomes of resource frontiers on Earth.

4
United Nations Office for Outer Space Affairs, "Treaty on Principles Governing the Activities of States in the Exploration and Use of Outer Space, including the Moon and Other Celestial Bodies," http://www.unoosa.org/oosa/en/ourwork/spacelaw/treaties/outerspacetreaty.html.

5
Neil Degrasse Tyson and Avis Lang, *Accessory to War: The Unspoken Alliance between Astrophysics and the Military* (New York: W. W. Norton & Company, 2018).

6
Julie Michelle Klinger, "Extraglobal Extraction," Chapter 6 in *Rare Earth Frontiers: From Terrestrial Subsoils to Lunar Landscapes* (Ithaca, NY: Cornell University Press, 2017), 199–227.

7
H.R. 2262—Commercial Space Launch Competitiveness Act (2015), https://www.congress.gov/bill/114th-congress/house-bill/2262.

8
"President Donald J. Trump Is Launching America's Space Force," 2019, https://www.whitehouse.gov/briefings-statements/president-donald-j-trump-launching-americas-space-force/.

9
See, for example, Philip Metzger, "How Asteroid Mining Could Save the Planet," *The Week*, 2018, https://theweek.com/articles/748563/how-asteroid-mining-could-save-planet.

10
Edward Palmer Thompson, *Whigs and Hunters: The Origin of the Black Act*. (London: Allen Lane, 1975); Mike Davis, *Late Victorian Holocausts: El Niño Famines and the Making of the Third World* (London: Verso, 2017).

11
John S. Lewis, *Mining the Sky: Untold Riches from the Asteroids, Comets, and Planets*, Helix Book Series (Reading, MA: Addison-Wesley, 1996).

12
Martin Beech, *Terraforming: The Creating of Habitable Worlds* (Heidelberg: Springer Science & Business Media, 2009).

13
Anna L. Tsing, *Friction: An Ethnography of Global Connection* (Princeton, NJ: Princeton University Press, 2011).

Mines

A mine marks a conquered frontier. It serves as an immutable "outpost," a surefire sign that unproductive lands have been put to productive use, or in other words, expropriated for nonlocal enrichment. From the perspective of the "New World" mine, the contemporary race to enclose outer space looks particularly familiar. Myths of *El Dorado* drove colonial exploration and justified an erasure of what came before. The wholesale plunder and genocides in Africa, Southeast Asia, and the Americas, not just for land but for the land's geological endowments, was crucial to the colonial project and the rise of capitalism. Accordingly, the agendas of space mining and space colonization share the common elements of identifying and tapping immense mineral wealth as part of the process of characterizing other celestial bodies as new lands to be conquered by the brave. Pop culture is replete with such tropes.

Settler colonial states have responded to demands to preserve landscapes and lives that preceded settler colonial domination by designating reservations and parks. These set-aside places enable the wholesale transformation of the surface of the Earth to proceed everywhere else. A similar ethos has been applied in conservationist interjections in plans to mine the Moon and "terraform" Mars[14]: set aside a few conservation and heritage sites here and there to appease the sentimentalists so that business can get on with mining and colonizing the rest. Conservationism, too, can serve an ethos of abandonment.

Former mining sites, or exhausted frontiers, are the spaces abandoned in the movement of capital, the vicissitudes of the market, and the ambitions of territorial control. In the extractivist move to the cosmos, Earth has been reimagined as a place that can and must be left behind, like an old mine or a toxic waste dump. But this abandonment ethos forgets that frontiers—even mining and waste frontiers—are recursive, doubling back and morphing as technology and cultures change. Tailings from old phosphate mines can become new rare earth mines.[15] The mining frontier can extend in multiple directions, taking extractivism above ground, so to speak. "Flex-mining," wherein mining companies source materials from discarded vehicles and electronics, as well as wastes from existing mining operations,[16] troubles linear notions of the extractive frontier while opening a horizon of resourcefulness. That we've mined Earth to exhaustion is a false premise on which to territorialize other planets, unless to provide a spatial fix to mining behemoths that refuse to innovate. In short, the destruction wrought by large-scale commercial extractive activities is not absolute. There is room for maneuver within the ruins.[17]

Wastes

The notion of absolute resource exhaustion on Earth is absurd. Very few mineral resources, other than materials for combustive fuels, are destroyed through use. We may burn fossil fuels, but other metals are turned into tools, vehicles, technological components, and building materials that do not simply melt into air when they are discarded. Annually, we transfer more metals to waste sites than we extract from the lithosphere. Yet the putative scarcity of certain metals on Earth is upheld as the primary reason to enclose outer space.

In the years between the 2010 rare earth crisis and Obama's 2015 signature of the SPACE Act, which granted to US citizens private property rights over any resource found in outer space, a coalition of billionaire investors, defense commentators, and pundits argued that Earth was running dangerously short of rare earth elements necessary to the technologies of contemporary life. China held the greatest reserves and was unfairly controlling supply while also aiming to colonize the Moon. The only solution for the United States, the story went, was to unleash the power of private enterprise to bring these valuable resources back from outer space, thereby beating China and reclaiming US space dominance.[18]

14
Alice Gorman, "The Archaeology of Space Exploration," *Sociological Review* 57, no. 1 supplement (2009):132–145; I. Stoner, "Humans Should Not Colonize Mars," *Journal of the American Philosophical Association* 3, no. 3 (2017): 334–353.

15
Minpeng Chen and Thomas E. Graedel, "The Potential for Mining Trace Elements from Phosphate Rock," *Journal of Cleaner Production* 91: 337–346.

16
Freyja L. Knapp, "The Birth of the Flexible Mine: Changing Geographies of Mining and the e-Waste Commodity Frontier," *Environment and Planning A: Economy and Space* 48, no. 10 (2016): 1889–1909.

17
On collaborative survival in capitalist ruins, see Anna L. Tsing, *The Mushroom at the End of the World: On the Possibility of Life in Capitalist Ruins* (Princeton, NJ: Princeton University Press, 2015).

18
Julie Michelle Klinger, *Rare Earth Frontiers: From Terrestrial Subsoils to Lunar Landscapes* (Ithaca, NY: Cornell University Press, 2017).

Incredibly, this narrative worked. The story moved from the margins to the mainstream over and above mounting piles of electronic waste. When the latent mineral wealth in discarded electronics was not ignored outright, commentators railed against the incredible difficulties of extracting metals from old cell phones and laptops. NASA signed multi-million-dollar contracts with private enterprises to develop lunar mining robots while researchers at the EPA could not get funding to test their electronics recycling prototypes. We are not so much up to our necks in garbage, longing for a new Eden among the stars,[19] as we are surrounded by mineral wealth that we mistake for waste.

The latent mineral wealth in discarded electronics is a frontier with greater finality than outer space. Where else could we reduce the material content of the frontier to zero while satisfying a host of environmentalist and accumulationist desires? Although perhaps less glorious than pulverizing asteroids, mining the waste frontier creates a circular economy without upsetting the liberal capitalist status quo. The problem remains that concentrations of technology metals in electronic waste are often lower than found in minable deposits; therefore, the energy demands for disaggregating our laptops, cell phones, high-rises, and airplanes into reusable elements are significant. But this is a design problem that can be addressed with a design solution.

The waste frontier could be final in that we have the capacity to eliminate it completely, leaving outer space free from the fetish of finality that legitimates the enclosure and destruction of celestial bodies.

Asteroids

Among the celestial bodies celebrated in popular science and protected under international law, asteroids stand apart as potential threats. Often depicted as barren hazards, asteroids represent the new no-man's-land: flecks of wasteland floating in the heavens waiting to be put to productive use. Here, the frontier sensibility closely resembles its earthly counterpart. Frontiers are seldom as empty as those naming them would claim. Where they are not populated with people, they are imbued with collectively held meanings. Imposing the frontier vision involves discursively rendering places devoid of people, or downgrading their life-forms and other properties as expendable to extractivist ends.

Never mind that tardigrades and other metazoans riding asteroids through the cosmos may have been responsible for the Cambrian explosion of extraordinary genetic variety on Earth,[20] or that asteroids are some of the only celestial bodies that could transfer genetic material between worlds without cataclysmic impact. Contemporary asteroid-related research and development is overwhelmingly geared toward capturing them, grinding them up, and turning them into the machinery of extraplanetary exploration.

Definition is key here. Just as naming a place a frontier orients political and economic power toward conquest, the choice to value an asteroid as a harbinger of life or a dangerous lump of metals mobilizes different processes. NASA's Office of Planetary Protection states that "if the target body has the potential to provide clues about life or prebiotic chemical evolution, a spacecraft going there must meet a higher level of cleanliness."[21] Their greater numbers and apparently freewheeling character position them as a threat to fixed powers on Earth,[22] and this makes their destruction less controversial. There is a reason why asteroid collisions feature in doomsday films more so than planetary collisions. This problematization of mobile objects resonates with Empire's historic unease with nomads and gypsies. Destroying asteroids to preserve order and facilitate surplus accumulation from captured objects readily maps onto state logics to destroy nomadic cultures, thereby consolidating territorial control and faciliating surplus extraction from sedentarized peoples.

It is far less risky and much less energy intensive to pulverize mountains of electronic waste into reusable material than it is to capture an asteroid mid-orbit and tow it back to Earth. But there is a scenario under which pulverizing asteroids makes

19
Lisa Messeri, "Gestures of Cosmic Relation and the Search for Another Earth," *Environmental Humanities* 9, no. 2 (2017), 325–340.

20
See, for example, Annabel Cartwright, "The Venus Hypothesis," *Earth and Planetary Astrophysics*, 2016, arXiv:1608.03074; L. Rebecchi, T. Altiero, R. Guidetti, M. Cesari, R. Bertolani, M. Negroni, and A. M. Rizzo, "Tardigrade Resistance to Space Effects: First Results of Experiments on the LIFE-TARSE Mission on FOTON-M3, " *Astrobiology* 9, no. 6 (2009), 581–591.

21
NASA Office of Planetary Protection, n.d., https://planetaryprotection.nasa.gov/categories.

22
Valerie A. Olson, "Political Ecology in the Extreme: Asteroid Activism and the Making of an Environmental Solar System," *Anthropological Quarterly* 85, no. 4 (2012): 1027–1044.

sense. For extended deep space exploration to be sustainable, missions should be able to meet their equipment and fuel needs without relying on Earth's resources. The capacity to build equipment outside Earth's gravity well reduces the environmental footprint of space activities on Earth. But because this would expand our footprint beyond our atmosphere, care must be taken to ensure that our footfalls do not crush genetic material circulating in the heavens.

Not all space rocks contain genetic material; not all mineral resources are confined to subterranean deposits. There are ways to provision ourselves on Earth and to continue our explorations of space beyond the frontier practice of enclosure, devastation, and abandonment. Within this, as within all daily practices, lies revolutionary potential. Practices in one frontier space inform practices in other frontier spaces.[23] Perhaps an ethos of privileging the biotic preconditions to complex life on asteroids over and above capital's need to pulverize rocks into building materials could have the effect of staying the more destructive frontier tendencies on Earth.

(Extra)terrestrial Extractive Ethics

In resource-driven desires to colonize outer space, earthly environmental destruction and extraterrestrial exploitation provide mutual justification. Space as a so-called final frontier is a potent cultural fetish because at best it promises cosmopolitan transcendence of a terrifying Anthropocene, while at worst it offers an escape for the most privileged from political accountability or economic justice on Earth.

All frontiers are conjured in order to be destroyed. But the only frontiers that have any sort of finality are those that are finite and mutable. In other words, objects as opposed to places. Space is infinite. A place on a planet, even one disastrously plundered of its minerals and nutrients, remains an immutably physical fact. Objects, on the other hand, can be obliterated or totally transformed so as to be effectively reduced to zero. Obsessions with conquering outer space confuse the two.

Although outer space and extractivist ambitions may be infinite, humans are not. This fundamental fact constrains access to the "untold riches from asteroids, comets, and planets,"[24] and even those "untold riches" in our immediate solar neighborhood can be mined only at great cost. By contrast, discarded electronics, vehicles, building materials, and industrial effluent are an untapped abundance here within Earth's atmosphere: readily available, largely unclaimed, finite, and full of promise. They represent a persistent problem we have yet to solve. Their destruction for productive reuse could obviate capitalist claims to the cosmos.

Waste, not space, is the final frontier.

23 Silvia Federici discussed how practices of sexual domination in the New World informed the witch hunts in Europe, effectively describing a relationality of practice and ideas among frontier spaces. Silvia Federici, *Caliban and the Witch: Women, the Body, and Primitive Accumulation* (New York: Autonomedia, 2014).

24 John S. Lewis, *Mining the Sky: Untold Riches from the Asteroids, Comets, and Planets* (New York City, NY: Perseus Books, 1996)

Afterlives of Orbital Infrastructures: From Earth's High Orbits to Its High Seas

RAJJI SANJAY DESAI

As of 2019, the global space industry generates approximately US$350 billion in revenue and is estimated to become a $1.1 trillion industry by the year 2040, with over 500 satellites being launched into Earth's orbit every year.[1] Until recently, national governments had a *de facto* monopoly on orbital space, using it to exercise military prowess and exert hegemonic dominance in the international political sphere. Still dominant within public consciousness, this way of understanding orbital space and its primary actors has in fact become outmoded. Recent extraterrestrial activities have taken on new, more commodified dimensions, with this decade's leading projects being spearheaded by corporate actors from the private sector.

Unlike the "Old Space" era (late 1950s to 1990s), with its state-driven approach to orbital space, this "New Space" movement (post-1990s) is premised upon a historic shift in which orbital space is increasingly controlled by independent corporate institutions that are profit driven rather than security focused.[2] Moreover, the New Space movement primarily involves the exteriorization and externalization of infrastructural systems into a much larger extraterrestrial, vertical domain—that of the hard vacuum of orbital space itself. As a result, Earth's orbital zone—a domain once restricted to the exclusive exercise of military operations in the service of nationalist statecraft—has slowly but steadily become a site for corporate commercialization.[3]

A variety of projects drive this form of commercialization. These include a vast array of privately owned, state-mediated orbital infrastructures that bring satellite technologies into our everyday lives, whether relaying data for cable and network television, rapid video conferencing and telephone connectivity, Global Positioning Systems (GPS), climate and environmental monitoring, or land and air stewardship across a multitude of scales.[4] Now more than ever, all spheres of our lives—material, social, political—are increasingly mediated by the myriad workings of these privately owned, techno-scientific objects circling Earth at different velocities and altitudes.

Despite our massive reliance on satellite infrastructures, we have almost no direct interaction with any of these objects: relatively few of us have ever seen, let alone touched, a satellite, and it is rare that we even acknowledge their presence above us. This is perhaps also unsurprising, since they occupy

1
"Space: Investing in the Final Frontier," Morgan Stanley, July 2, 2019, https://www.morganstanley.com/ideas/investing-in-space.

2
"The Old Space Program and the New Space Movement," Library of Flight, December 10, 2014, https://doi.org/10.2514/5.9871624103223.0099.0106.

3
Jacqui Frost, "Outer Space and Earthly Inequalities—There's Research on That," *The Society Pages* (blog), March 24, 2017, https://thesocietypages.org/trot/2017/03/24/outer-space-and-earthly-inequalities/.

4
"What Are Satellites Used For?" Union of Concerned Scientists, February 13, 2014, https://www.ucsusa.org/nuclear-weapons/space-weapons/what-are-satellites-used-for.

a territory that "most of us will never visit—one that only astronauts have seen—and yet it is a place we cannot afford to overlook."[5] Despite their many profound implications on our lives, satellite systems remain both elusive and peripheral in our understanding of the world. As a consequence, our capacity for democratic evaluation has been greatly inhibited, both as a matter for public debate as well as any general literacy regarding the actual operations of these satellite systems. This is perhaps because even though orbital space is relatively proximate to us, it has long seemed to carry connotations of both "astonishment and anxiety" in popular culture and the media, even continuing to occupy an otherworldly, secluded position in our collective consciousness.[6] This is likely due to the nature of satellites as material objects and their operation in obscure locations. They have assumed a character that is at once "visible yet invisible, evidentiary yet abstract."[7] Additionally, the activities of satellites largely lie beyond human sense-perception and therefore, in some sense, always have to be constructed by means of the human imagination. And yet the seeming obscurity of these privatized satellite infrastructures nevertheless has consequences that are carried back to Earth.

The operation of these orbital objects in peripheral zones of invisibility is not only restricted to their life spans in orbital space but is also maintained in their afterlives. Surprisingly, given the sheer number in orbit, satellites have a relatively short life span—around only 5 to 10 years.[8] But what happens at the end of a given satellite's life span? What starts as a feat of complex engineering and precision craft eventually ends up being decommissioned in two principal ways, both of which are largely invisible. Once a satellite nears the end of its life span, one method of decommissioning is to discard the techno-object in a way that does not interfere with the circulation of global trade and travel routes and that presents a minimal risk to human beings. This first approach is known as the "Graveyard Orbit." It is located at about 22,000 miles above Earth, near the outermost edge of orbital space.[9] This site is routinely stocked with dead and decaying space artifacts, and at present several thousand obsolete satellites in various stages of decay lie suspended above Earth. The Graveyard Orbit, which occupies a band roughly 300 to 400 km in width, has exponentially transformed, from its beginning as a single orbital zone to an ever-expanding space burial region. The practice of sending dead space techno-objects there expanded it so much that it has become a "permanent fixture" around our planet: "unlike the rings of Saturn . . . [which are] made out of dust and debris, the rings of the Earth are made out of dead machines."[10]

The second method of decommissioning involves returning the techno-object to Earth itself. In this approach, which is used by governments and private corporations, obsolete satellites are extricated from their operational orbits and dumped into the depths of the South Pacific Ocean. A remote zone known as the "Spacecraft Cemetery" has been used as the reentry location for several hundred obsolete space objects, which eventually plummet to depths of about two miles below the ocean's surface, where their toxic residue has been accumulating for the past 40 years or so.[11] Following the precedent of the orbital decommissioning zone, it is also in the South Pacific graveyard where one can find several thousands of defunct human-made space objects, with the bulk of them being remainders from the Space Race that began during the Cold War. During a brief span of about 45 years (c. 1971 to 2016), over 190 Russian space objects, 52 American objects, and several hundred more from Japan, China, and various European efforts have all met their untimely ends in this uncharted watery horizon.[12] Most

5
Lisa Parks, "Orbital Ruins," NECSUS, November 8, 2013, https://necsus-ejms.org/orbital-ruins/.

6
Fraser MacDonald, "Anti-Astropolitik—Outer Space and the Orbit of Geography," *Progress in Human Geography* 31, no. 5 (October 1, 2007): 592–615, https://doi.org/10.1177/0309132507081492.

7
Gary Kafer, "Documenting the Invisible: Political Agency in Trevor Paglen's Limit Telephotography," *Contemporaneity: Historical Presence in Visual Culture* 5, no. 1 (n.d.): 53–71.

8
"How Long Should a Satellite Last: Five Years, Ten Years, 15, 30?," SpaceNews.com, May 24, 2018, https://spacenews.com/how-long-should-a-satellite-last/.

9
"Graveyard Orbits and the Satellite Afterlife," NOAA National Environmental Satellite, Data, and Information Service (NESDIS), October 31, 2016, https://www.nesdis.noaa.gov/content/graveyard-orbits-and-satellite-afterlife.

10
Trevor Paglen, Rebecca Solnit, and Aperture Foundation, *Invisible: Covert Operations and Classified Landscapes*, 1st ed. (New York: Aperture, 2010), 8.

11
"Where Spaceships Go to Die: NASA's Watery Graveyard in the South Pacific 1,600 Miles from Land Is Now the Resting Place for 260 Sunken Craft," Mail Online, October 23, 2017, http://www.dailymail.co.uk/~/article-5007681/index.html.

12
Shannon Stirone, "This Is Where the International Space Station Will Go to Die," June 13, 2016, https://www.popsci.com/this-is-where-international-space-station-will-go-to-die/.

significant among these oceanic "splashdowns" was the Russian space station MIR which, upon reentering the atmosphere in 2001, left behind a debris trail of about ±1,500 kilometers (930 miles) along its trajectory and ±100 kilometers (62 miles) wide.[13] Much like the MIR splashdown, several other defunct space objects have left behind an enormous trail of environmentally degrading pollutants that are not just sitting neatly on the ocean floor in one piece or even two pieces but exist as fragmentary remains of once celebrated space missions that are now destroyed beyond recognition.[14] Scattered, dispersed, and strewn across vast distances beneath the ocean's surface, this rapidly expanding oceanic waste field remains minimally visible despite geographically spanning about 3,000 km from north to south, and about 5,000 km west to east.[15]

Originally operationalized sometime in the early 1970s, these extraterrestrial and subterrestrial space graveyards have been used as a waste sink by some of the world's greatest space-faring nations. Salient in the waste exchange between these two extreme sites of waste externalization (i.e., the orbital and oceanic graveyards) has been the "movement of space junk (that) continues to break down geographical boundaries, with waste from one extraterritorial region transforming upon arrival in other extraterritorial and sovereign spaces."[16] In addition, "when satellites or meteorites fall back to earth they draw attention to the extraterritorial domains that extend up from the surface of the planet; through the atmosphere, stratosphere, and ionosphere, into the multiple orbital paths and out to the edges of the super-synchronous or 'parking' orbit, where satellites go to die."[17] More specifically, their waste exchange is marked by the forced internalization of the embedded environmental and socioeconomic ramifications onto less-regulated international, shared spaces that are located beyond the national jurisdiction of any one nation-state.

A key principle that characterizes the present-day workings of satellite systems is "false externalization": despite their apparent status as purely external to Earth, the forms of techno-waste generated by satellite networks are in fact still subject to a material dialectic between externalization and internalization. Although their operational lives unfold in a place more or less external to Earth, these ostensibly externalized toxic wastes are ultimately subject to important processes of (re-)internalization back here on Earth. Crucially, these processes have dire consequences for Earth's environments—whether built or unbuilt, human or nonhuman. Moreover, these so-called externalizations remain internal to Earth's life-supporting and self-sustaining systems, and the ramifications are profoundly destructive, both socially and environmentally. The reason these particular tactics are exploited is directly tied to our present context of the ongoing privatization of orbital space. These tactics of false externalization are advantageous to space corporations, businesses, and other profit-driven organizations like Elon Musk's SpaceX and Jeff Bezos's Blue Origin because they allow such groups to lower their operating costs—and thereby increase their profit margins—mainly by avoiding costly environmental and/or legal regulations. In other words, this is beneficial to the various powerful, economically and politically vested actors not only because it allows them to circumvent their economic and environmental responsibilities—which should be part and parcel of the proper decommissioning and disposing of these hazardous forms of waste—but also by allowing them to evade the legal repercussions that would follow if the real effects of such activities came to light.

Central to the principle of "false externalization" is the "politics of visibility." It helps bring to the forefront the paradoxical ways in which visual discernment both facilitates and frustrates the representation and public knowledge of the sites of satellite operations, as well as the toxic realities that accompany them. More pointedly, it foregrounds the strained interrelationship between scale, visibility, and distance, highlighting the unique trifecta of controlled (in)visibility, extreme geographical distance, and massive extraterritorial scales that serves to dissolve the legal and environmental accountability inherently

13
"Mir Re-Entry—Updated Analysis," http://www.zarya.info/Tracking/Mir/Mir-Re-entry2.php.

14
Kiona Smith-Strickland, "This Watery Graveyard Is the Resting Place for 161 Sunken Spaceships," *Gizmodo*, May 14, 2015, https://gizmodo.com/this-watery-graveyard-holds-161-sunken-space-ships-1703212211.

15
Vito De Lucia and Viviana Iavicoli, "From Outer Space to Ocean Depths: The 'Spacecraft Cemetery' and the Protection of the Marine Environment in Areas Beyond National Jurisdiction," April 17, 2018, https://papers.ssrn.com/sol3/papers.cfm?abstract_id=3153458.

16
Lisa Rand, "Orbital Decay: Space Junk and the Environmental History of Earth's Planetary Borderlands" (PhD diss., University of Pennsylvania, 2016), https://repository.upenn.edu/edissertations/1963.

17
Parks, "Orbital Ruins," https://necsus-ejms.org/orbital-ruins/.

underpinning these private orbital operations. In the first instance, let us consider scale. Because of and despite their massive scale, the sites of satellite operations in Earth's near orbital space as well as their sites of disposal in the orbital graveyard and the oceanic cemetery remain negligibly visible. These sites remain "out-there domains" whose sheer scale escapes our grasp. This unfathomable scale allows them to exist on an unlimited margin, or what is effectively a margin without scale. This is fundamental since it reveals the phenomenological link between invisibility and infinity—or what is an indeterminate boundlessness that makes hiding these multi-scalar operations not only possible but also difficult to discern, despite the highly potent nature of the destructive forms of waste they send away and back to Earth.

Second, concerning visibility, satellites operate in sites of very low visibility, practically obscured from public perception. This willful obscuring from public view means that they take on the quality of invisibility with regard to most everyday activities of human life, both inner- and outer-worldly. It is clear, then, that this invisibility helps not only to obscure but eventually to drive into oblivion the contested nature of these orbital operations, making it easy for space agencies to circumvent their legal responsibility to decommission and dispose of these space vessels properly. This is remarkable given that many of the significant projects of orbital infrastructure are publicly touted to benefit everyone on Earth—a justification made in the public eye. However, in reality, this visibility does not equate to access: many of these same projects are driven by an underlying profit motive, and access is granted only to those who pay.

In addition to scale and visibility, the key to visual politics is the notion of extreme geographical distance and displacement. With respect to the afterlives of satellites, the sites of their disposal "represent places where humans can go, but only by using life-sustaining technologies, and only temporarily. In these places life either does not exist or exists only at the microbial level and at the margins."[18] This is due in large part to their location in "remote, uninhabited, and unruly natural places" whose extreme physical distance from everyday human life makes the operations of satellite dumping invisible—not only physically but also culturally.[19] The further satellites and their sites of operation and disposal are pushed away or "distanced," the less visible and consequently less perceptible they are within the public consciousness. Their owners benefit in two primary ways: first, limited visibility neutralizes and thus normalizes these operations and, second, it depersonalizes their occurrence, since people think of these operations as occurring far enough away to be of no risk to them personally, hence diminishing or reducing the perceived magnitude or threat of these operations. The peripheral location and inaccessible character of these far-flung territories and in particular the "lack of other humans and even biota to resist or conquer ha[ve] translated to a lack of urgency in examining the environmental histories of extreme environments" such as these.[20]

Despite their seeming innocuousness it is essential to bring into focus the obscure—and often invisible—mechanisms through which the current paradigm of the privatization of orbital space immutably transforms transnational territories—such as those of the extraterrestrial Graveyard Orbit and the subterrestrial Spacecraft Cemetery. In this regard, false externalization, when mobilized through the lens of the politics of visibility, is useful in two key ways. First, it allows us to recognize and problematize the increased undertaking of privatized orbital infrastructural endeavors, which, as we have seen, repeatedly externalize their toxic end-products and other forms of waste onto sites outside their own visible spheres of responsibility. Second, if we recognize the phenomenon of false externalization, it can enable systems of public accountability and civic participation, the lack of which, at present, undermines democratic debate and decision making regarding such practices.

Finally, the concept of false externalization can aid spatial thinkers comprehend the transformation of spaces that can and should belong to all of humankind. When understood in conjunction with the politics of visibility, false externalization can also serve as an all-encompassing tool that reveals the indexing logic of the contemporary space race—a race that fundamentally entails the transformation of nascent spaces into environmental sacrifice zones. Such sacrificial zones are ultimately internal to both the actual confines of our planet and the radically tiny region of space we are currently capable of operating in. Ultimately, this fact entails that the very idea of externalization is itself incoherent when applied to the effects that human infrastructures have for any and all entities that remain tied to this planet.

18 Ibid.

19 Steve Pyne, "Extreme Environments," *Environmental History* 15, no. 3 (2010): 509–13.

20 Ibid.

Modern Mundi
DAVID SALOMON

> All natures-cultures are similar in that they simultaneously construct humans, divinities and nonhumans. . . . The presence of the sciences does not suffice to break [this] symmetry.
> —Bruno Latour, *We Have Never Been Modern*

Earth is not alone. It is not isolated. It responds to forces outside itself, including the gravity of the moon and the energy from the sun. The sublime objects of the geological are always in relationship with the sublime spaces of the astrological. A number of architectural types also interact with these seemingly disparate realms. Ancient temples, modern scientific observatories, and Land art can all be understood as axes mundi—devices that attempt to aesthetically, technologically, and theologically link the earth with the heavens. For Bruno Latour, these three modes for understanding and making are not independent from one another.[1] Nor is one more advanced than the others. They are simply inevitable. Objects such as Angkor Wat in Cambodia, the McMath-Pierce solar telescope in Arizona, and Nancy Holt's *Sun Tunnels* (1976) sculpture in Utah engage all three epistemologies simultaneously.

Recognizing this disparate set of axes mundi as equals illustrates Latour's argument that all cultures continue to invent and combine humans, nonhumans, and divinities with one another.[2] This conceptual symmetry echoes the flat ontology of Manuel DeLanda. Built upon the virtual philosophy of Gilles Deleuze and linked with empirical facts established in math and science, DeLanda's work describes a common ground from which specific entities, disciplines, and cultural practices emerge. He maintains that these singularities are "classified not by [their] extensities or [their] qualities, but by [their] affects, that is, by [their] invariants under a transformation (or group of transformations). . . . We need to conceive a continuum which yields, through progressive differentiation, all the discontinuous individuals that populate the actual world."[3] In this "continuum," both physical and social "individuals" manifest the same processes of creation (as either "strata" or "meshworks") which "at every spatiotemporal scale, [exhibit] properties of a whole which cannot be explained as a mere sum of the properties of its component parts, but which emerge from their causal interactions."[4] Such "individuals" are found in physical phenomena such as atoms, molecules, fluids, species, and rocks, but also in cultural ones such as cities, social classes, laws, markets, and architecture.[5] What all forms of axes mundi, as "discontinuous individuals," attempt to do is provide a link between the physical world of mountains, telescopes, and concrete pipes with

1
Bruno Latour, *We Have Never Been Modern* (Cambridge, MA: Harvard University Press, 1993), esp. 91–129.

2
Ibid., 106.

3
Manuel DeLanda, *Intensive Science and Virtual Philosophy* (New York: Continuum, 2002), 69.

4
Ibid., 143.

5
Manuel DeLanda, *A Thousand Years of Nonlinear History* (New York: Zone, 1997).

the cultural realm of imagination opened up by the social practices of science, art, and religion. In other words, they connect the gravity-bound facts of the terrestrial with the ever-expanding reality offered by the extraterrestrial.

The scientific, religious, and artistic axes mundi discussed below are distinct in their forms and functions, yet they share something. How and why the discontinuities between them arise differs dramatically from context to context. But these differences don't undermine the regularity with which they occur or the frequency with which architecture is called upon to describe and embody them. Today, in an age when humans are disproportionately focused on affecting the geosphere, it is productive to widen our lens and look at the multiple ways and the multiple architectural examples where the terrestrial is intertwined with extraterrestrial in the hopes of developing additional ways of understanding, influencing, and modifying the relationship between the two.

Between the Earth and the Heavens

An axis mundi is a datum between the earth and the heavens. For millennia cultures have imagined and attempted to build spiritual poles that connect the earth's primordial and geological underworld with the heavens above it.[6] Tall mounds, pyramids, and domes are the traditional architectural figures used to mark the intersection of the geological/human realm with the celestial/divine one. Their shapes often echo a sacred mountain that appears as a literal meeting point between the earth and the sky, and they function as the terrestrial home of the gods. Such structures often hold relics and serve as sites for sacrifices. Some have acted as astronomical observatories and timepieces.[7] The temple at Angkor Wat efficiently illustrates all of these qualities. More recent examples of axes mundi share its goal of joining worldly objects with otherworldly phenomenon. However, they differ dramatically in terms of their materials, forms, and primary functions. A modern observatory such as the McMath-Pierce solar telescope is a scientific version of an axis mundi. It literally guides the light of the sun into Earth's crust.[8] Certain works of Land art also fulfill the requirements of an axis mundi. A piece such as Nancy Holt's *Solar Tunnels* was specifically designed with the goal of "bringing the sky down to the earth."[9]

No matter when they were built or for what purpose, axes mundi share a set of common characteristics. Their form and location are always aligned with celestial objects and movements. Physically, they combine a hidden, usually underground element with a conspicuous formal component that can typically be seen from a distance. Spatially, they are isolated from their contexts, either through physical barriers, remote locations, or both. They are also somewhat indifferent to the atmosphere. Finally, they are born of and harbor the traces of a historically specific sociopolitical milieu.

The temple at Angkor Wat is a robust example of a building that was designed, and subsequently operated, as a religious structure, a scientific instrument, and a political monument.[10] Begun in the early 12th century by the Khmer king Suryavarman II, it was built as a Hindu temple devoted to the god Vishnu and was subsequently rededicated as a Buddhist shrine less than a century later. As is common in this building type, the peaks of the structure were designed as a representation of Mount Meru, which symbolically marks the center of the Hindu universe and the vertical axis around which all celestial objects orbit. This is reinforced by the central peak that marks the

6
As Rosalind Williams recognized, in the 19th century both real and imagined infrastructural objects like transportation tunnels and mines served a similar purpose. Rosalind Williams, *Notes on the Underground* (Cambridge, MA: MIT Press, 1990).

7
Ivan Šprajc, "Astronomical Alignments at Teotihuacan, Mexico," *Latin American Antiquity* 11, no. 4 (December 2000): 403–415; J. L. Heilbron, *The Sun in the Church: Cathedrals as Solar Observatories* (Cambridge, MA; Harvard University Press, 2001).

8
Reyner Banham, "Marks on the Landscape," in *Scenes in America Deserta* (Salt Lake City: Gibbs M. Smith, 1982), 171–190; Reyner Banham, "Mountain of Modern Icons: The Exhilarating Experience of Kitt Peak," *Architecture* (March 1984): 143–149; Wonne Ickx, "For All the Wrong Reasons: Myron Goldsmith and the McMath-Pierce Solar Telescope," *San Rocco*, no. 14 (Spring 2018): 241–248. On observatories in general, see Marian Card Donnelly, *A Short History of Observatories* (Eugene: University of Oregon Books,1973); Cristiana Dumitrache and Daniel Dumitrache, "Architectural Evolution of Astronomical Observatories," *Romanian Astronomical Journal* 19, no. 1 (2009): 81–97.

9
Janet Saad-Cook, Charles Ross, Nancy Holt, and James Turrell, "Touching the Sky: Artworks Using Natural Phenomena, Earth, Sky and Connections to Astronomy," *Leonardo* 21, no. 2 (1988): 127.

10
Eleanor Mannikka, *Angkor Wat: Time, Space, and Kingship* (Honolulu: University of Hawaii Press, 1996).

site of the small, dark sanctuary. The axis is continued underground to the temple's small sacred treasury. While this axis extends upward into the sky, at Angkor Wat the atmosphere would appear to be a visually and symbolically neutral zone between the sacred realm of the earth and the sacred realm of the gods.

As Eleanor Mannikka's research has shown, the height of the towers, the dimensioning of the courtyards, and the spacing of columns and ornamental motifs are all tied to the quantification, subdivision, and multiplication of accurate observations of solar and lunar movements. These observations are linked to other numerological systems found in Hindu theology which are in turn used to link these religious narratives—outlined in the temple's ornaments—to the political and military history of the Khmer empire.

The temple is physically separated from its surrounds by a rectangular moat that represents the primordial ocean. This serves to establish the temple as a sacred site as well as to protect the holy ones inside it. But the moat, and the causeway that connects it to the rest of the empire, has other functions as well. Angkor Wat was not just a site for kings and priests, it was also for engineers. The moat and causeway were part of a vast transportation and irrigation system that was responsible for the kingdom's wealth. In DeLanda's terms, the temple was a site where the physical, political, and religious realms of the Khmer empire existed along a highly divisible but ultimately integrated continuum.

Observatories are nodes where the physical energy of the cosmos is captured by devices designed to extract information from it. Instead of using the sun's path to organize a building's spatial and symbolic elements, as is the case at Angkor Wat, the McMath-Pierce solar telescope establishes a literal spatial axis with the sun. Its long, diagonal section channels the sun's rays through its optical tunnel down to mirrors and spectrographs literally buried in Mount Kitt.[11] The choice to locate the project on the top of a remote, hard-to-reach mountain in the desert 60 miles outside Tucson, Arizona, was made in order to evade the atmospheric impurities of moisture and light that would interfere with its ability to peer into the universe.

While there is no ornament on the structure recounting spiritual, scientific, or historical facts, it engages these topics in other, more modern, more scientific ways. Telescopes like McMath-Pierce are perpetually transforming energy into data sets and images that enable scientists to understand the universe's past, present, and future. By empirically examining extraterrestrial objects and behaviors, telescopes help humans define our place within the sublime time frame and infinite space of the universe, a task formerly associated with religion.

The social history of the McMath-Pierce instrument has other tales to tell. The commissioning of the Kitt Peak National Observatory (where the McMath-Pierce telescope is located) was part of a large-scale commitment to spending on the hard sciences by the United States government during the Cold War—an era guided in part by a fear of technological, military, and political inferiority. In this context, the value of such large telescopes—and the general will to master the extraterrestrial realm—was as symbolic as it was utilitarian.[12] Big-space-science was both a means and an end to besting our enemy at all costs and in all arenas. As that cultural pressure waned and the McMath-Pierce's technology became obsolete, its value as a scientific instrument decreased. However, its symbolic and use value as an axis mundi remains. It is currently being converted into a simulated telescope that will give the general public more intimate access to work being done by astronomers around the globe.[13] In other words, it will become a virtual axis mundi.

Artists have also been interested in the geocosmic relationship present in axes mundi. The four cylinders of Nancy Holt's *Sun Tunnels* in the Great Basin Desert in Utah are aligned with sunrise and sunset on both solstices. The holes pierced in the top of her cylinders mimic the constellations of Columba, Draco, Perseus, and Capricorn. As Holt describes it, "The sun, being a star, is casting spots of starlight through the star holes, so that when one walks through the tunnels, in effect, one is walking on stars. It's an inversion of the sky/ground relationship—bringing the sky down to the Earth."[14] "Tunnels" is somewhat of a misnomer,

11
"McMath-Pierce Telescope," Kitt Peak Virtual Tour, National Optical Astronomy Observatory, https://www.noao.edu/outreach/kptour/mcmath_sch.html.

12
Leandra A. Swanner, *Mountains of Controversy: Narrative and the Making of Contested Landscapes in Postwar American Astronomy* (Ann Arbor: UMI, 2013). ProQuest, https://proxy.library.upenn.edu/login?url=https://proxy.library.upenn.edu:2174/docview/1417075941?accountid=14707.

13
"National Science Foundation to Fund New Windows on the Universe Center for Astronomy Outreach at Kitt Peak National Observatory," National Optical Astronomy Observatory News, September 25, 2018, https://www.noao.edu/news/2018/pr1803.php.

14
Saad-Cook et al., "Touching the Sky," 127.

as the elements that make up the piece are in fact concrete tubes placed on the ground. However, their large scale, which recalls urban water infrastructural elements, does produce a set of large artificial underworlds in the otherwise sunburnt landscape. Their size and weight anchor them to the ground even though they don't penetrate its surface. These artificial tunnels block out the atmosphere in order for the light of the sun to be perceived directly.

As Holt described it, the desert site was picked in part because "in the desert . . . I really started to perceive the sun. . . . In the desert . . . one is overwhelmed by the sun." The goal of the project is thus to make everything else disappear and for the sun and its effects to be the only things one encounters. This location was also picked because "it is a very desolate area, but it is totally accessible, and it can be easily visited, making *Sun Tunnels* more accessible really than art in museums."[15] This accessibility was made possible by ubiquity of the automobile and by roads. As with Angkor Wat and the McMath-Pierce telescope, *Sun Tunnels* is located in an out-of-the-way place made accessible via large-scale infrastructural interventions. Holt's emphasis on accessibility reveals that she and other Land artists who chose to locate their work in the desert during the 1960s were motivated not only by sunlight and space but also by the opportunity to critique the economic model of the gallery and museum system. Here again is an axis mundi that combines the physical, the experiential, and the political realms.

The three types of axes mundi outlined above (the religious, the technological, and the aesthetic) are each fused with the ground; all rise above their surroundings and become focal points on the horizon; and each is located and oriented in relationship with specific celestial objects and movements. Each example is spatially isolated from its surroundings either by water, height, or distance from other human activities. In all cases, there is an attempt to make the atmosphere "disappear" in order for there to be a more direct connection between the inner spaces of the terrestrial and outer space of the extraterrestrial. For different reasons (political, physical, and phenomenological) but in all instances, a *temenos* is established, a hallowed world within the world; a world with different rules, a different temporality; a nexus that links the now with the eternal, the here with the infinite. But they are far from being the same. They are also far from being just religious or just technical or just artistic. They are not just the home of the divine or of power or of knowledge or of sensations. They engage all of these in different ways and to different degrees. Their function is more to reveal their heterogeneous parts than to reconcile them.

Three at a Time

This raises a question: Does the separation between the geological and celestial, as well as between the religious, scientific, artistic "individuals," really exist? Did it ever exist? As the above examples reveal, our occupation and understanding of the geo/terrestrial is always intertwined with our imaginary and literal access to the astro/celestial. The stars in the night sky were the earliest navigation system. Today satellites make it possible to always know where we are on the surface of the globe, as well as allowing us to study that surface in increasing detail. The same system can also help us to better understand the relationship between Earth's surface, atmosphere, and the creatures that occupy it. Many believe that such an understanding will produce a healthier, more just world. Is the faith in these technologies misplaced?

This question is addressed in projects like Design Earth's *Neck of the Moon* (2015). It would appear to combine the religious, the scientific, and the artistic versions of the axis mundi. In this speculative project, an artificial moon composed of consolidated space junk is tethered to Earth by a space elevator/electrical cord that delivers materials to space and returns energy back to Earth. Instead of spiritual energy, this umbilical cord traffics in solar energy. The Cotopaxi volcano in Ecuador is the meeting point of the two realms. This combination of the fantastical and the mundane, the geological and the astronomic, recognizes the interdependence of the two: "It is with the help of mountains that the project pursues the will to connect the internal, external and aerial layers of the Earth, to articulate cosmic, topographical, climatic and vegetal features of the surface of the Earth, and to analyze the interaction between the features of landscape and the imaginations of people, including scientists and artists."[16] Scientists and artists. No priests, no gods, no myths. What happened to that aspect of the axis mundi? Perhaps it is located in the conical concrete void placed at the tip of the volcano. Part navel of

15
Ibid.

16
Design Earth, *Neck of the Moon*, http://design-Earth.org/projects/neck-of-the-moon/.

the world, part space port, part tomb, this chamber houses a collection of space-age ancestors who started the colonization process that resulted in their obsolete offspring being harnessed and recycled. In other words, it houses the origin story of the species *Homo caelestis*.

The Rough and the Smooth

These examples suggest that a key difference between newer and older axes mundi is that the former are more likely to be elegant objects placed in nondesigned environments, while the older examples are more likely to be made of textured figures positioned in manicured landscapes. This may be a result of their role in well-attended religious rituals, rituals where each shape, space, and surface is scaled to the body and contains a specific symbolic message aimed at that body. In contrast, the remote and rough lands that surround observatories serve to keep human bodies at a distance—a distance that creates a rarified space for the recording, launching, and viewing of objects present in the extraterrestrial realm. In other words, machines and celestial bodies are privileged over human bodies. Holt's *Sun Tunnels* exists somewhere between these two poles. On the one hand, the industrial materials and scale of the tubes are overwhelming. So too is the desert. On the other hand, once inside these cylinders, an intimate relationship between human, machined, and natural bodies emerges. This change in scale is reinforced by the small holes that outline the constellations, which also recall the ornaments at Angkor Wat but without their scripted narratives. Here the focus is on sensations, not symbolism. It is on affect, not representation.

One might conclude from this analysis that only axes mundi with specific religious functions, such as Angkor Wat, completely engage Latour's triad of "humans, divinities and nonhumans," while more recent ones account for only one or two of these categories. This also suggests that they do not exist on DeLanda's continuum but are instead understood as isolated technical or aesthetic objects. However, even if conceived as being independent of one another, at the level of affect there is always an aesthetic response to technical and religious apparatuses and a technical aspect to aesthetic artifacts. Is there a religious facet to the technical and aesthetic axes mundi? If so, it is also present in the affects they create when they bring to our senses the presence of the otherworldly within the worldly, the infinite within specific, and the eternal within the limited.

Roughness and smoothness are also qualities of axes mundi. These physical properties also produce affects. So too does their orientation with planets, moons, and stars. So too do their dark spaces, their conspicuous forms, their isolated locations, and their histories. All of these qualities generate associations, allusions, sensations and perceptions of things that are hard to see or are physically not "there" but are brought into focus by these objects. These in turn produce less physical, more cultural results. The social effects of the sun's rays, the political aspects of aesthetic objects, and the persistent presence of the heavens on the earth are some of the things these axes mundi also make present.

This does not mean that these examples are identical, that nothing changes, or that today's technology and art aren't "progressively differentiated" from earlier eras. However, there are, to echo DeLanda, invariants that persist even after they undergo transformations. We do still share things with previous cultures. We still look to the sky for answers to earthly questions, but we do so with different tools and for different reasons. Today, the advantage of recognizing a temple as a scientific instrument, or a telescope as belonging equally to the earth and to the heavens, or a sculpture as being both a highly engineered object and an uncanny machine is that it allows one to recognize that the divisions we construct between these territories are artificial. An observatory does not seem to be designed to produce emotions, yet it does. A work of art does not look like it is reassessing our economic or environmental priorities, but it can. Temples do not always produce empirical scientific information, but they have.

These axes mundi, these discontinuous individuals that exist on a continuum of religion, science, and art, also remind us that reifying and relying solely on the agency of humans or divinities or nonhumans to address social issues comes with severe aesthetic, environmental, and political costs. Idolatry and isolation are equally dangerous, and the antidotes of integration and differentiation difficult to achieve. Still, there are many intertwined orbits connecting the extraterrestrial and terrestrial realms and many architectural devices for linking them.

Mono Craters, 2006
Lake Lahontan, 2018
MICHAEL LIGHT

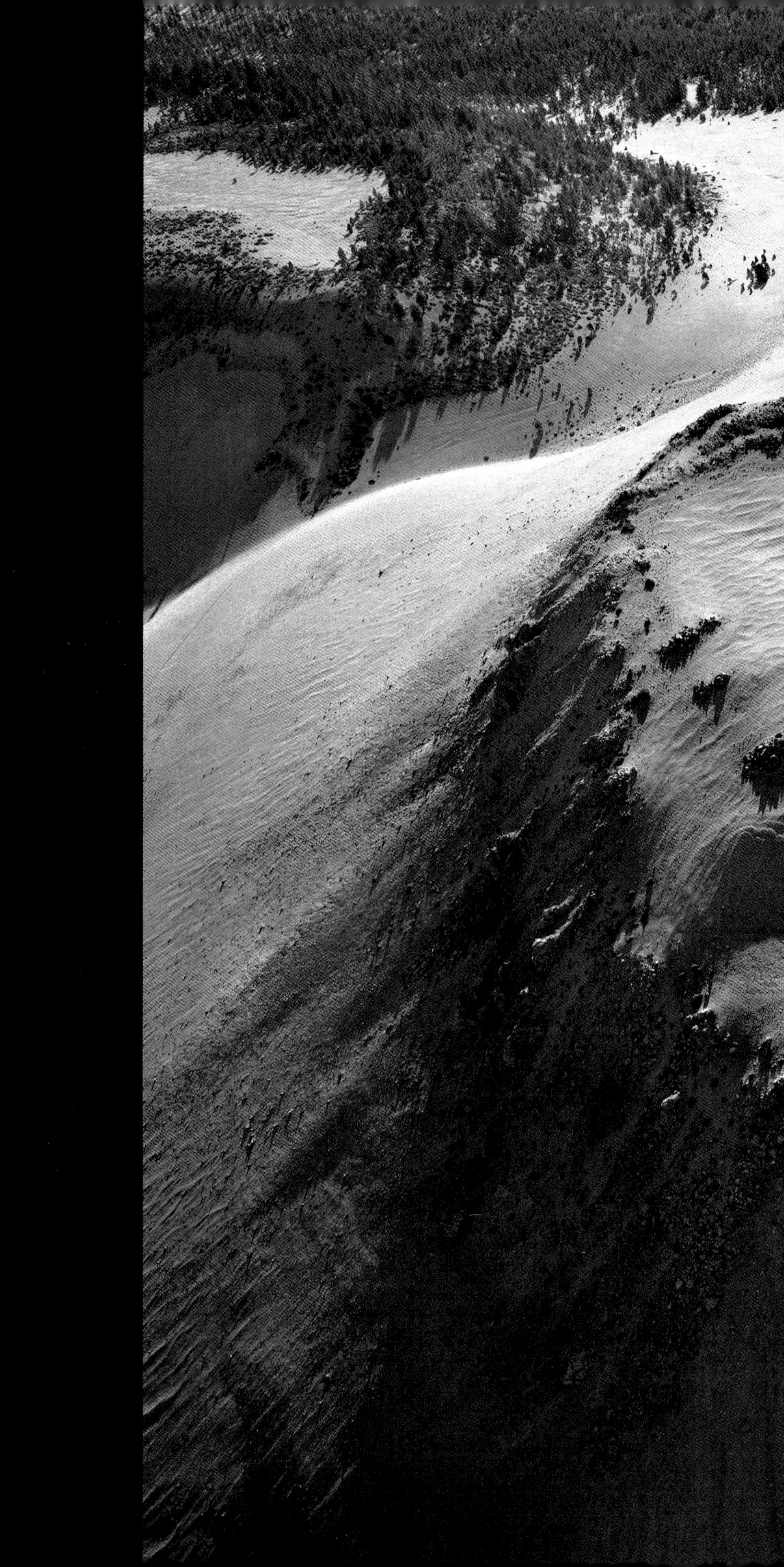

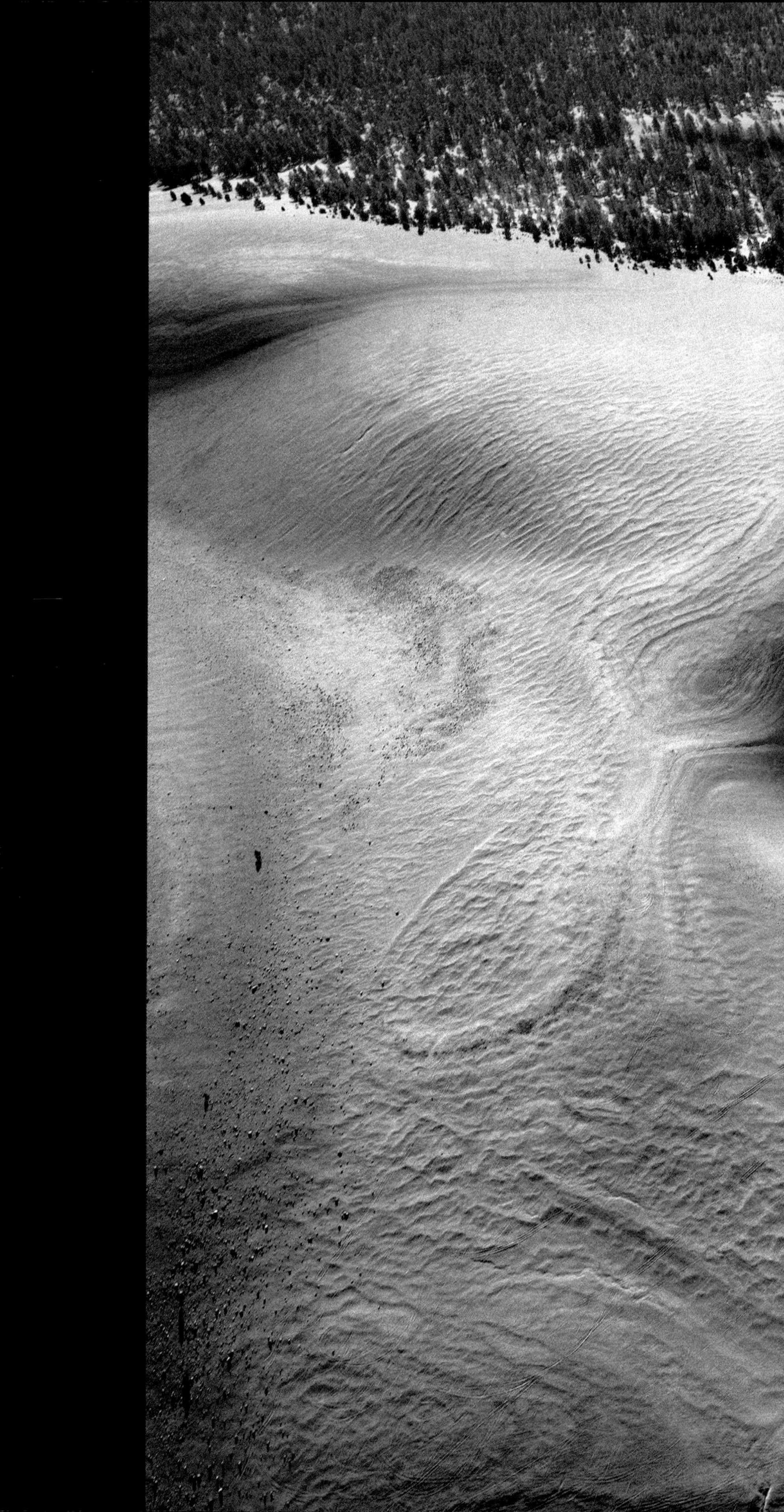

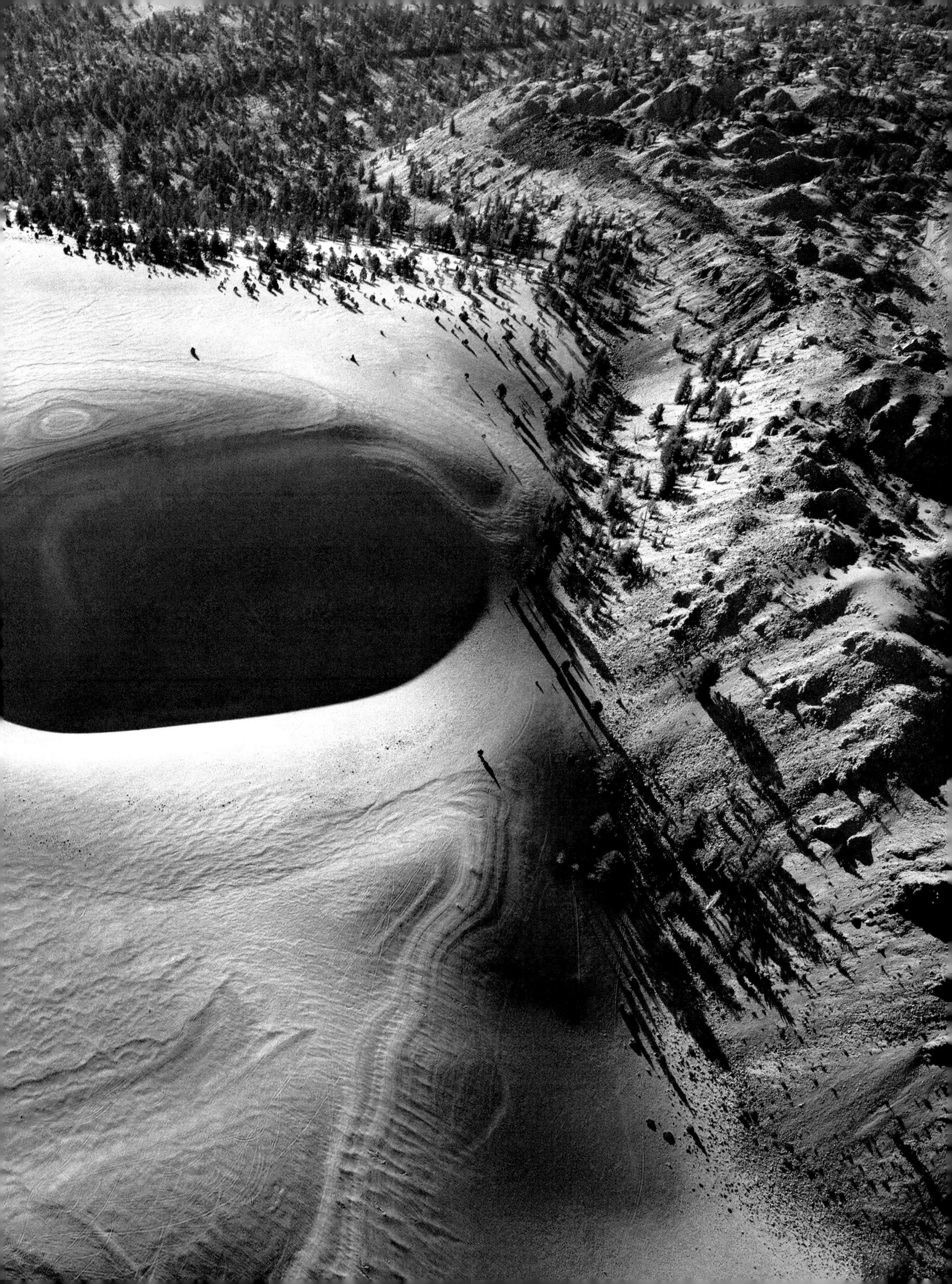

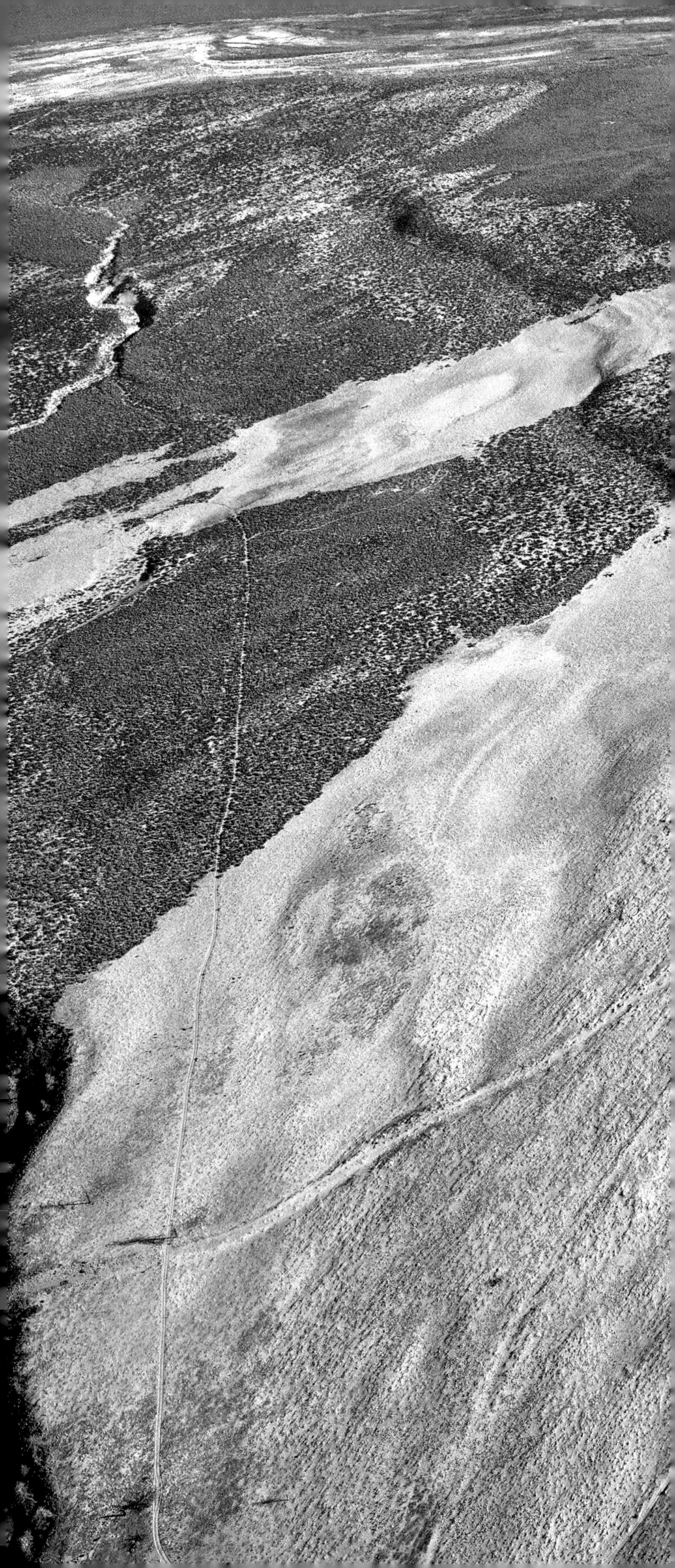

MONO CRATERS

The Mono Craters are the youngest mountain range in the continental United States. The last eruption in the chain, on Paoha Island in the middle of Mono Lake, was in 1894. They consist largely of pumice, and a mine operates on their southeast side.

Looking South over Panum Crater, A Young Plug-Dome Volcano That Erupted in 1375 AD, Mono Lake, CA, 2006

Pumice Erosion Layers on the Summit of Dome #20, Jeffrey Pines Beyond, Looking East, Mono Craters, CA, 2006

Explosion Pit and Pumice Erosion Looking East, South Coulee at Right, Mono Craters, CA, 2006

Pyroclastic Tephra Flow Looking Northwest at Edge of Lake, About 35,000 Years Old, Mono Basin, CA, 2006

LAKE LAHONTAN

12,000 years ago most of the Great Basin was 900 feet underwater, covered by two and now largely evaporated historical lakes, Bonneville and Lahontan. The remnants of Bonneville today are the Great Salt Lake in Utah and its eponymous salt flats, while the best known portion of the former Lake Lahontan is the Black Rock Desert in Nevada, an alkali bed that floods and dries each year, creating the flattest topography on earth and home for the arts festival Burning Man, whose temporary city of 80,000 people rises and falls annually.

Near Frog Pond Looking Southwest, Black Rock Desert, Pleistocene Lake Lahontan, Gerlach, NV, 2017

Carson River Enters Carson Sink, Looking West, Pleistocene Lake Lahontan, Fallon, NV, 2018

Black Rock City in October, Looking Northwest, Pleistocene Lake Lahontan, Gerlach, NV, 2017

Black Rock City in October, Looking Southeast, Center Camp, Pleistocene Lake Lahontan, Gerlach, NV, 2017

Black Rock City in June, Looking Southeast, Pleistocene Lake Lahontan, Gerlach, NV, 2018

Clair de Terre (Earthlight): Paris 1900

ALESSANDRA PONTE

> Nous sommes toujours dans un mauvais point de vue. . . . Il faudrait être simplement Spectateur du Monde, et non pas Habitant.
> —Bernard le Bovier de Fontenelle, *Entretiens sur la pluralité de mondes*, 1686

From 1895 to 1898, the eminent geographer and anarchist Élisée Reclus was enthusiastically absorbed in a project for the construction of a gigantic terrestrial globe for the 1900 World's Fair in Paris. A crowning achievement of his long and distinguished career, the globe was meant to connect Reclus's geographical and political thinking. The epic unity of the terrestrial sphere symbolized at once the triumph of anarchy and the accurate understanding of geography, thus celebrating the role and duties of liberated humans in shaping the earth itself. The project was initially presented at the sixth International Congress of Geography in London in 1895.[1] No plans or drawings illustrated this early proposal, which was accompanied by a description and cost estimate signed by Reclus's nephew, Paul Reclus, who was at the time living under the name of Georges Guyot first in London and later in Edinburgh. Escaping France for political reasons, Paul Reclus had joined the biologist, sociologist, and town planner Patrick Geddes, a great admirer and supporter of Élisée Reclus and of his fellow geographer and anarchist Peter Kropotkin. For Geddes, and under the guidance of Élisée, Paul Reclus was developing models, maps, and instruments to expand the growing collections of Earth-visualizing tools gathered at Outlook Tower, the "world's first sociological observatory,"[2] which Geddes and his Scottish colleagues had begun to shape in 1892 as the headquarters for their "civic" activities in Edinburgh.[3] Together with Paul Reclus, Geddes was involved from the beginning in the plan for the terrestrial globe, actively participating in the campaign to fund the imposing scheme.

To be erected next to the Eiffel Tower on the hill of Chaillot, the project envisioned the construction of a glass-and-steel sphere 160 meters in diameter with the profiles of oceans and continents painted from the inside. Supported by four pillars, the building would be 200 meters high, representing Earth on the scale of 1/80,000. Inside the first sphere, a second revolving globe, made of plaster and with a diameter of 127.5 meters, would display the accurate and constantly updated contours of Earth at a scale of 1/100,000. The space between the two spheres would be occupied by a spiral ramp bringing visitors near the surface of the globe, thus permitting a close analysis of Earth's features. The residual volume, as

1 Elisée Reclus, *Projet de construction d'un Globe terrestre à l'échelle du Cent-millième* (n.p.: Édition de la société nouvelle, 1895); see also Élisée Reclus, "A Great Globe," *Geographical Journal* 12, no. 4 (October 1898): 401–409.

2 Charles Zueblin, "The World's First Sociological Laboratory," pamphlet, reprinted in *American Journal of Sociology* 4, no. 5 (1899): 577–592.

3 See Federico Ferretti, "Globes, savoir situé et éducation à la beauté: Patrick Geddes géographe et sa relation avec les Reclus," *Annales de Géographie* 6 (2015): 681–715.

well the hollow interior of the second globe, would contain visual displays, such as panoramas and dioramas, together with libraries and auditoria. Neither a conventional attraction nor a museum, the entire project was conceived by Reclus as a study center, a pedagogical and political tool, an intellectual laboratory for scholars and visitors of all nationalities.[4] In its intentions the scheme rather resembled or, better, complemented what Geddes was trying to promote at the Outlook Tower in Edinburgh, and it would resurface in just such a guise. The construction of the first version of the terrestrial globe, Paul Reclus estimated, would require 20 millions francs, an exorbitant sum considering that the Eiffel Tower was built for only 8 million in 1889. Moreover, Reclus's project encountered an unexpected obstacle: the wish of Alfred Picard, commissioner of the Exposition Universelle of 1900, to combine the terrestrial globe with the scheme for a celestial globe proposed for the same site and at the same time by architect-astronomer Paul Louis Albert Galeron.

In December 1895, Galeron had delivered a lecture in the hemicycle of the École des Beaux-Arts to promote his grand project for a cosmorama. The presentation was complemented by superb projections displaying the revolutions across the skies of Saturn, Jupiter, Earth, and its Moon. The intention was to impress the public with stunning, state-of-the-art optical technologies to be employed in the cosmorama, bringing to Earth, so to speak, a phantasmagoric image of the cosmos. While Galeron explained the project for the celestial globe on a blackboard, the famous Molteni stage-managed the projections. Scientist, optician, and inventor, Alfred Molteni was a manufacturer of precision instruments, specializing in projection systems. The prospectus advertising the activities of his company attested to the curious status of "scientific" projections during the second half of the 19th century: they could be equally employed to animate social occasions, illustrate lectures, enliven popular educational programs, or actually contribute to the staging of phantasmagorias. Scientific, authoritative, and eerie, the technology offered by Molteni perfectly fitted Galeron's scheme for building an attraction in which the educational function was ancillary to the spectacular.

Galeron's cosmorama combined the geometries of the sphere and the cone to orchestrate a ride that transported visitors on an astronomical journey organized in three stages. A steep mechanical escalator first conveyed sightseers inside a revolving globe eight meters in diameter, representing Earth. From a series of windows, or "observatories," carved on the surface of the globe and located at different levels, the viewers would discover a glittering celestial vault. A geocentric, immersive view of the cosmos was achieved thanks to lamps and scintillating devices masked behind a perforated blue cloth suspended from a gigantic concrete hull. The zodiac was speckled by brilliant planets and traversed by an electric sun, while the Moon, between Earth and sky, slowly completed a revolution. The mechanical ballet of celestial bodies could also be seen from a viewing platform installed at the North Pole or from a spiral ramp rising from the foot of the conical volume to the base of the rotating planet. The lower portion of the cone was hollowed out to enclose a hemispherical, heliocentric space; here the uncanny technology of Molteni was deployed at its best. A partially luminous globe situated at the center supported a number of projectors. Supplemented by mirrors, the projectors reproduced on the white hemispherical surface the movements of the solar system at the scale of one minute per year. Finally, on the ground floor, visitors were invited to enter the "stereoscopic universal panorama" conceived by Paul Moëssard, lieutenant colonel in the corps of engineers. From an aerial belvedere simulating the view from the basket of the balloon, sightseers equipped with apposite binoculars could contemplate at leisure the overlaid double projections of the stereoscopic panorama. Galeron's first scheme was abandoned because of the aforementioned, fairly surreal request of Commissar Picard to combine the celestial with the terrestrial globe.[5]

Meanwhile, in December 1897, a group of entrepreneurs representing a company called Le Grand Globe Céleste de Paris offered Camille Flammarion, titan of popular astronomy in fin-de-siècle France, the scientific direction of an astronomy

4
See Soizic Alavoine-Muller, "Un globe terrestre pour l'exposition universelle de 1900. L'utopie géographique d'Élisée Reclus," *Espace géographique* 32 (2003): 156–170.

5
With the exception of most of the events involving Camille Flammarion, the projects proposed for the construction of celestial and/or terrestrial globes at the Paris 1900 World's Fair are described and illustrated under various entries in *Globes: architecture et sciences explorent le monde*, ed. Yann Rocher (Paris: Éditions Norma/Cité de l'architecture et du patrimoine, 2017). Exhibition catalogue.

Phases de la Terre vue de la Lune.

« Phase de la terre vue de la lune »
Camille Flammarion, Les terres du ciel : Voyage astronomique sur les autres mondes, Paris :
G. Marpon et E. Flammarion Éditeurs, 1884

« La pleine terre vue de la lune »
Camille Flammarion, Astronomie populaire,
Paris : G. Marpon et E. Flammarion Éditeurs,
1890 (first edition 1880)

pavilion for the Paris World's Fair of 1900. The project was initially named *Panorama des Mondes* (Panorama of the Worlds), possibly in homage to Flammarion's 1862 spectacular debut in the field of astronomy: *La pluralité des mondes habités* (The Plurality of Inhabited Worlds). Like most of the works of Flammarion, *The Plurality of Inhabited Worlds* was translated into several languages and had multiple editions lavishly illustrated. It opened with images of Earth and Mars and included chapters on history, physiology, descriptions of the planets and of the skies, together with philosophical reflections about humanity in the universe and pictures of Earth seen from the Moon and other planets. Images of Earth seen hovering in space or from the perspective of the inhabitants of distant worlds appeared also in *Astronomie populaire*, perhaps the most illustrious of Flammarion's literary efforts. Published for the first time in 1880 (translated into English in 1894), the volume was dedicated to François Arago, astronomer, physicist, statesman, close friend of Alexander von Humboldt, and director of the Paris Observatoire. Arago had been the first to inaugurate in 1813 a series of lectures on astronomy open to the lay public, a challenging endeavor for a science centered on mathematics and calculus and given the limited resources available at the time to visualize celestial bodies and their motions. Arago was keenly interested in technological advances in optics and photography: memorably he pronounced a "Discourse on the Daguerreotype" (1839) in support of the successful attempts to fix images in the camera obscura, conducted in collaboration with stage designer Louis Daguerre and the inventor Nicéphore Niépce. A staunch Republican, Arago considered the mechanical reproduction of images and texts necessary not just for the advancement of science itself, but also for the dissemination of scientific knowledge to all classes of society, from cultured bourgeois to artisans and laborers. An outstanding orator, Arago, using only a blackboard, managed to attract such large audiences that an 800-seat auditorium had to be built next to the observatory to host his adoring public. Arago's lessons ran until 1846, when illness limited his public appearances, but his courses were collected in the four volumes of *Astronomie populaire*, published posthumously in 1854.[6]

In the Paris of the first half of the 19th century, Arago was not the only scientist, scholar, or political figure promoting the teaching of astronomy as matter of public concern: for 17 years, beginning in 1831, the founder of positivism, Auguste Comte, taught Sunday lessons in astronomy devised specifically for working-class men. Comte's lectures and his theses on the relevance of astronomy as a philosophical, more than a scientific, educational tool for all classes were collected in the *Traité philosophique d'astronomie populaire*, published in 1844. For Comte, astronomy was the only science free from all theological and metaphysical influences and therefore represented the best introduction to positive philosophy. Astronomy, next to mathematics, which occupied a place apart, figured first in Comte's classification of the sciences. Ranging from the simplest to the most complex, the taxonomy culminated with sociology, the new discipline unifying history, psychology, and economics, whose object was the study of the laws of aggregation and interaction of humans in societies.[7]

If Arago and Comte pioneered and initially led the cause of popular astronomy as the foremost

6
On François Arago's astronomy, technology, and popular science, see John Tresch, *The Romantic Machine: Utopian Science and Technology after Napoleon* (Chicago: University of Chicago Press, 2012).

didactic approach to public education, chief among the many followers and imitators was indisputably the commanding figure of Camille Flammarion. Invited by the Société des conferences, he offered a course in popular astronomy in 1866 and from the inception adopted oxy-hydrogen light projections during his lectures. He later proclaimed to have been the first to project astronomical images and related how he commissioned the optician Alfred Molteni to manufacture 30 slides, delicately hand colored replicas of the illustrations in Flammarion's book *Merveilles célestes* (1866). However, images of skies projected by magic lanterns had been in use in Paris since 1864 in the spectacles of *physique amusante* (amusing physics) of the most famous French illusionist, Jean Eugène Robert-Houdin. Certainly Flammarion had been part of Robert-Houdin's audience and had expressed his passion for and knowledge of the technology and apparatuses employed in magic, illusionism, and phantasmagoria in an homage paid to the master of phantasmagorias, Étienne-Gaspard Robertson, in his 1867 *L'Optique*. The career of Robertson—beyond the sensation provoked by the ghostly apparitions he conjured amid swirls of smoke with the help of hidden magic lanterns and ventriloquists—must have fascinated Flammarion, also because of the meteorological studies conducted by the Belgian physicist and stage magician during highly publicized balloon excursions. Flammarion would follow in his footsteps, building his name as an astronomer and scientist thanks to the accounts of the atmospheric observations gathered during intrepid flights at high altitude published first serially and later in a volume, *L'Atmosphère* (1871).

The correlation between magic lanterns, projections, astronomy, specters, and psychic emanations was reinforced in the mind of Flammarion and other popular-science militants of the time by two orders of assumptions altogether acceptable in the techno-scientific milieu of the time. First, phenomena recently discovered and yet imperfectly known—from animal magnetism to chemical spectral analysis and electricity, together with advances in photography and the invention of X-rays—generated untold expectations about new technologies capable of visualizing and capturing hidden natural wonders like thought-forms or life on distant planets. Flammarion, for example, believed in a Darwinist form of reincarnation (the inhabitants of far-away worlds were the reembodiment of chosen specimens of humans), hosted séances with famous mediums, and advocated a "scientific" instead of religious form of spiritism as he memorably explained in his 1869 eulogy at the death of Allan Kardec, president and founder of the Société spirite. Moreover, the mechanisms of the transmissions of images linking lanterns to screens was perceived to connect luminous rays in general to the traveling of astral light projected by celestial bodies. In the case of Flammarion, light rays were carriers of images or, more precisely, following his own analogy, light rays were transmitters of successions of snapshots, and the cosmos a sort of colossal cinematic apparatus and archive where long-forgotten histories of countless stars, together with the vagaries of untold planets and their inhabitants, could be retrieved.[8]

As scientific adviser for the Panorama of the Worlds, Flammarion proposed a spherical building and listed among the attractions an exhibition on the ages of the earth, a spherical celestial panorama, a Flammarion museum, a concert hall (with an orchestra directed by Camille Saint-Saëns), auditoria, and, notably, stereoscopic and cinematographic panoramas.[9] It has been suggested that a possible inducement to the venture was the success of Urania, an analogous public grouping of exhibition halls for scientific experiments and technical tests, astronomical observatory, and theater that had existed in Berlin since 1888.[10] A superb commercial scientific institution, Urania was inspired by the legacy of Alexander von Humboldt and came about as a result of the collaboration between astronomer Wilhelm Foerster and popular scientific writer Max Wilhelm Meyer. Under the direction of Meyer, the scientific theater of Urania inaugurated in 1889 the performance of two literally spectacular productions: *The History of the Primeval World* and *From the*

7
On Arago, Comte, and other authors of popular astronomical texts, see Carole Christen, "Les leçons et traités d'astronomie populaire dans le premier XIXe siècle," *Romantisme* 166, no. 4 (2014): 8–20; Juliette Grange, "Le rôle social des sciences: l'astronomie dans l'histoire de la modernité," in Angèle Kremer-Marietti, *Auguste Comte et le rôle social des sciences. L'exemple de l'astronomie* (Paris: L'Harmattan, 2007), 85–100.

Earth to the Moon. The first reenacted the birth of Earth from primeval chaos; the "biological" epochs followed, culminating with the flourishing of Greek civilization and the attuning of humans to the "music of the spheres." The second reconstructed a highly anticipated total eclipse that disappointed an eager audience because cloudy skies shrouded Berlin. In the course of the show, spectators were mysteriously transported to the Moon to witness, among other wonders, the apparition of a full, radiant Earth projecting an enchanting light on the stark landscape of its satellite. The two productions were an international triumph: after four years in Berlin, thanks to a recommendation from Thomas Edison and sponsorship by Andrew Carnegie, they were performed in New York, Philadelphia, and Boston.[11] Images from the shows, including details of the apparatuses deployed for the "special effects," appeared in *Scientific American* in 1892 and, not so surprisingly, also occupied an entire chapter of Albert A. Hopkins's book *Magic: Stage Illusions and Scientific Diversions, including Trick Photography*, published in London in 1897.

For the Panorama of the Worlds, Flammarion anticipated the cinematographic projection of an even more heroic form of astral voyage that involved visits to Jupiter, Saturn, Mars, and the Moon together with sequences of eclipses and images of Earth shining on the moonscape. Flammarion, as early as 1898, had penned an article on the results of his experimental use of cinematography to represent Earth's rotation,[12] while in his archive is conserved a script for the *Cinématographe Flammarion*, envisioned for the World's Fair of 1900. Thus, the sidereal voyage imagined by Flammarion preceded the famous film *Voyage dans la lune*, produced in 1902 by Georges Méliès, illusionist and heir to the magic theater of Robert-Houdin. The architect responsible for the realization of Flammarion's cosmographic techno-utopia was the ubiquitous Albert Galeron, who at the same time was also feverishly supplying schemes merging Reclus's terrestrial globe with his own cosmorama. However, in 1898 both Flammarion, alarmed by the uncertainty of the financial situation, and Reclus, discouraged by inadequate funding, abandoned the venture, and it was left to Galeron to realize a slightly sober version of the celestial globe that finally opened near the Eiffel Tower in 1900. In the meantime, the commission for a terrestrial globe at a smaller scale (1/500,000) had been given to well-known architect Louis Bonnier by Reclus, who was unhappy with the scientifically compromised and overtly commercial projects proposed by Galeron. The exquisite art nouveau design by Bonnier included a stunning spiral ramp, which permitted close inspection of the internal terrestrial globe, and space for a chronophotographic panorama on the intellectual ages of humanity by Étienne-Jules Marey.

Despite the distress expressed by Reclus about the less edifying aspects of Galeron's treatment of the cosmos as popular attraction, it was with a project signed by Albert Galeron that Patrick Geddes attempted to revamp and reconfigure the efforts deployed by both parties in Paris in 1900. In an article published in 1902 in the *Scottish Geographical Magazine*, Geddes proposed a grandiose scheme for the construction of a national institute of geography. Introducing the plan drafted by Galeron, Geddes explained that the genesis of the project was but the latest of several attempts to harmonize various lines of geographical and educational activities:

> The accumulation and arrangement of maps, reliefs, and illustrations, the presentment of descriptive and general geography is primarily centered around the Great

8
See Danielle Chaperon, *Camille Flammarion. Entre astronomie et littérature* (Saint-Estève: Éditions Imago, 1997); Lynda Nead, *The Haunted Gallery: Painting, Photography, Film c. 1900* (New Haven: Yale University Press, 2007).

9
This account is based on documents from the archive of Camille Flammarion that we have not been able to consult but are discussed in an important essay by Danielle Chaperon, "Le cinématographe astronomique. Camille Flammarion: un parcours de 1864 à 1898," *1895, revue d'histoire du cinéma* 18, no. 1 (1995), *Images du réel. La non-fiction en France (1890–1930)*, 52–65. However, a sectional drawing for a spherical building titled "Panorama of the Worlds," signed by Albert Galeron and dated October 1897, names Camille Flammarion as scientific director. The drawing presents quite a different scheme and suggests an earlier date of involvement of Flammarion in the venture: Archives Nationales: CP/F/12/4352 pièce 2.

10
According to Danielle Chaperon, one of the founders of a *Société du Panorama des mondes*, M. J. Mesmin, secretary general of the Société populaire des Beaux-Arts, after a trip to Berlin in 1889 had written a memorandum and presented a project inspired by the activities at Urania. See "Le cinématographe astronomique," 56.

11
See Oleg Molvig, "The Berlin Urania, Humboldtian Cosmology, and the Public," in *The Heavens on Earth: Observatories and Astronomy in Ninenteenth-Century Science and Culture*, ed. D. Aubin, C. Bigg, and H.O. Sibum (Durham, NC: Duke University Press, 2010), 325–343.

12
Camille Flammarion, "Le mouvement de rotation de la terre représenté par le cinématographe," *Bulletin de la Société astronomique de France* (January 1898): 33–35.

Relief Globe of M. Élisée Reclus . . . all but realized in the imposing architectural design of Bonnier for the Paris Exposition of 1900. With this is associated as its complement the Celestial Globe already partly realized by M. Galeron. Around this should be placed astronomical collections, together with photographs, star maps, models and so on. Rooms are provided for the concrete, and, as far as may be, the experimental illustration of the physical phenomena of the universe, as already attempted at the "Urania Museum" of Berlin, and in some measure also at South Kensington, and in the "Palais de l'Optique."[13]

The cosmic presentation, explained Geddes, would be crowned and complemented by a monumental tower where knowledge and exhibits where arranged following the ordering in progress at the Outlook Tower at Edinburgh: "proceeding from the visible and immediate prospect, and its study by the help of all sciences of observation. Thence we descend, storey by storey, through City and Province and Region or State to Nation and Empire, and thence again to the larger Occidental Civilization, of which these form a part, and finally to the Oriental and Primitive sources."[14]

The monumental scheme was never realized, but allusions to techno-amplified visions of a glorious Earth drifting across the universe were spread among the Outlook Tower educational tools. Philip Boardman, one of the first biographers of Patrick Geddes, describing the beginning of a visit to the Outlook Tower, explains how, after contemplating the panorama of the city from the prospect roof and looking at the reflection of its animated life in the famous camera obscura, guests were invited to "turn to the octagonal room and discover that it contains apparatus which can extend the visitor's observations to the widest extent of human comprehension. There are devices to show the earth's path through the seasons, and its relation to the sun and polar star. There are models of a celestial sphere and a larger cosmosphere to relate the earth to this universe and others."[15] Among these apparatuses was Galeron's prototype for a rotating hollow celestial sphere. Fortuitously, together with a black-and-white photograph, a blueprint remains of the curious prototype. Outlined in three different positions in relation to a male figure, the hollow sphere seems to be designed as a wearable, personal, immersive cosmos.

The 1900 debacle of the terrestrial globe caused no real regrets for Éliseé Reclus: undeterred, he concluded the six volumes of the geohistorical encyclopedia *L'homme et la terre* (Man and the Earth), published posthumously between 1905 and 1908. For the illustrations, including the cover and promotional image, Reclus commissioned František Kupka, one of the pioneers of nonobjective, or abstract, art. Kupka's involvement with the Parisian anarcho-communist milieu justified the decision together with his reputation as a graphic artist. Kupka arrived in Paris in 1894 and settled there permanently a year later, supporting himself as an illustrator for magazines and periodicals specializing in political satire. Introduced to spiritualism at an early age in eastern Bohemia, Kupka supplemented his income by practicing as a medium. He was quite successful: adept at going into trances and talented in directing the fluid discharges of animal magnetism, he also managed to pay for his art classes in Prague and Vienna and his studies in alchemy, astrology, and theosophy. In fin-de-siècle Paris, amid flourishing investigations of animal magnetism, electromagnetism, cosmic magnetism (Flammarion's contribution), and psychic research conducted by neurologists, scientists, and parapsychologists, Kupka found a congenial environment. The enthusiastic concern with magnetic and psychic phenomena and new, techno-scientific ways of manifesting or controlling them overlapped with spiritualism (or spiritism), theosophy, neo-Lamarckian transformism, Bergsonian vitalism, and the anarcho-communism promulgated by Reclus and Kropotkin. Specifically, Kupka embraced Reclus's and Kropotkin's theses on cooperation and mutual aid, founded on neo-Lamarckian evolutionism, supporting a decentralized economy (a doctrine endorsed also by Geddes). Reclus and Kropotkin, applying the anarcho-communist concept of "propaganda of the deed" to the arts, assigned to the artist the ultimate manifestation of individualism, the crucial double tasks of denouncing the iniquities and horrors of modern society

13
J. G. Bartholomew, "A Plea for the National Institute of Geography. With Plan and Note by Professor Geddes," pamphlet reprinted from *The Scottish Geographical Magazine*, March 1902, 5.

14
Ibid., 6.

15
Philip Boardman, *The Worlds of Patrick Geddes: Biologist, Town Planner, Re-educator, Peace-warrior* (London: Henley; Boston: Routledge and Kegan Paul, 1978), 141.

16
See Fae Brauer, "Magnetic Modernism. František Kupka's Mesmeric Abstraction and Anarcho-Cosmic Utopia," in *Utopia: The Avant-Garde, Modernism and (Im) Possible Life*, ed. D. Ayers and B. Hjartarson (Berlin: De Gruyter, 2015), 135–163.

while prefiguring an anarcho-communist cosmic and naturist utopia.[16] The arresting illustrations realized by Kupka for *L'homme et la terre* responded to this second call to arms.

At the beginning of the first volume, the image of a sky twinkling with stars functions as a backdrop to two human hands holding the terrestrial globe over the inscription *L'homme est la nature prenant conscience d'elle-même* (man is nature becoming aware of itself). The sentence, which has been translated in contemporary parlance as "humankind is nature achieving self-consciousness,"[17] summarized Reclus's geopolitical philosophy, which Kupka transfigured in cosmographic utopia. For the cover and the prospectus publicizing the *L'homme et la terre*, Kupka composed an enigmatic tableau. Its equipoise uncertain, the image wavers across fields of knowledge, adrift in time and space. It represents Reclus's belief that geography was nothing but history in space, just as history was geography in time, while also revealing the cosmic future of a liberated humanity. Framed by a portico, which appears to soar above a vast expanse, a naked virile figure sits in contemplation of starry skics and thc Milky Way. Two caryatids face the spectator: the first, holding a globe in the left hand and what appears to be the model of a city in the right, symbolizes geography; the second, captured in the act of writing, embodies history. A luminous sphere is suspended among the stars. At first glance, the observer imagines that the man is looking at the Moon but soon realizes that he is actually beholding a radiating Earth. Following his gaze, the viewer begins to discern profiles of seas, oceans, and landforms on the glowing surface of the planet.

In 1905 Kupka enrolled at the Sorbonne to study the physics of electromagnetism, and the following year he moved to Puteaux, a quiet town near Paris. His house and studio shared a garden with the cottage of Marcel Duchamp's brothers, the artists Raymond Duchamp-Villon and Jacques Villon. Marcel, at the time living in Neuilly, was a frequent guest, and together they formed the nucleus of the Puteaux Group, a community of painters, writers, mathematicians, and scientists seeking connections between arts and sciences and finding inspiration in various currents of modern art such as Orphism, Futurism, Cubo-Futurism, and Rayonism. Quite possibly Duchamp saw a copy of the poster advertising *L'homme et la terre* hanging in Kupka's atelier, but this was not the only source of Duchamp's obvious fascination with fin-de-siècle geographies and cosmographies, nor was he the sole member of the Surrealists enchanted by the bizarre apparatuses deployed to portray and reveal their visions. For example, the poet, novelist, and playwright Raymond Roussel, mentioned by Duchamp as a major influence for his *Grand Verre*, was a passionate reader of Jules Verne, author of *From the Earth to the Moon* (1865) and *Around the Moon* (1869). Verne's work, in turn, inspired Georges Méliès's legendary film *A Trip to the Moon*, which captivated the Surrealists, as did the rest of the filmic oeuvre of Méliès, which they rediscovered in the late 1920s. For his part, Jules Verne keenly admired the astronomy of François Arago and faithfully used as reference for his "extraordinary voyages" the works of Élisée Reclus. Jules Verne was also a literary rival of Camille Flammarion, the other great passion and inspiration of Raymond Roussel. In July 1923, Roussel returned from a lunch and visit at Flammarion's observatory in Juvisy with a small biscuit shaped like a star. Roussel preserved the broken little biscuit in a silver box of a similar form protected by a crystal lid and fastened by a diminutive lock. To it was attached an inscription, signed by Raymond Roussel, stating the nature, date, and provenance of the biscuit. Later, Georges Bataille commented uneasily that with the shaping of the extraordinary object Roussel had satisfied the dream of eating a star from the sky.

At the beginning of 1923 a troubled André Breton suspended the experiences of hypnotic sleep, commenced in 1922, for fear of harming the mental health of the "sleepers." At the same time, he confided to friends he was going to stop writing because the situation was desperate: he had no more faith in poetry. Yet at the end of the year Breton published a collection of poems, *Clair de Terre* (1923). The title signaled the poetic overturn of the act of illumination. As an epitaph to the volume, Breton quoted, without citing date or author, the manual *Nouvelle astronomie pour tous*: "*La terre brille dans le ciel comme un astre énorme au milieu des étoiles. Notre globe projette sur la lune un intense clair de terre.*" (The earth shines in the sky like a huge star. Our globe projects on the Moon an intense earthlight).

17
James Housefield, *Playing with Earth and Sky: Astronomy, Geography and the Art of Marcel Duchamp* (Hanover, NH: Dartmouth College Press, 2016), 48.

The Moon's Earth
LISA MESSERI

On December 25, 1968, hours after the crew of Apollo 8 captured the remarkable photograph *Earthrise*, astronaut Frank Borman was chatting with mission control. Still stunned at seeing Earth from the Moon, he commented on the surprise accompanying every glance out the capsule window: "I keep expecting to be seeing the Moon." Instead, he was seeing Earth floating in the inky night sky. A bit later, Borman asked Ken Mattingly back on Earth how the weather was at the site where the crew would splash down. Mattingly replied, "They told us there is a beautiful Moon out there." Borman responded, "Now, I was just saying that there's a beautiful Earth out there."[1] This linguistic inversion, just like the photographic inversion offered by *Earthrise*, draws our attention to the Earth-Moon relationship. What do we learn in seeing this relationship differently; how does the perspective of a planet from its moon shape how we think about extraterrestrial geographies?

The experience of seeing our planet from its satellite must indeed have been strange for the 24 American men who flew to the Moon. For the rest of us, we have only photographic postcards. In the stillness of the image, the strangeness melts away and we are left with an eerie but familiar kinship. We recognize the relationship between two celestial bodies because though we have not been to the Moon, we have had the experience of being emplaced and looking up at the faint glow of a crescent companion. Looking at *Earthrise*, we—like Borman—expect to see the Moon but there instead floats a world.

This essay presents three different views of a planet from its moon: Chesley Bonestell's pre–Space Race paintings of Saturn as seen from its moons, the first photographs circulated by NASA of Earth seen from the Moon, and early 21st-century digitally crafted exoplanet moonscapes produced by artist Lynette Cook. What understandings of being in the cosmos do these images draw out? Bonestell's art primed readers for human space flight, establishing the solar system as a place for human exploration and expansion. *Earthrise* illustrated how Earth is not only a world but also a planet among others. Exomoons help make the invisible planets that fill our galaxy into places; a step, so say astronomers, toward ending

1 Transcript available at https://history.nasa.gov/afj/ap08fj/20day4_orbit8.html.

cosmic loneliness.[2] Each image accomplishes what we anthropologists state as our goal; each image makes the strange familiar. Referencing the experience of looking up from the surface of Earth and seeing the Moon grounds each of these strange geographies in a familiar, terrestrial sensibility even as they simultaneously challenge us to imagine a cosmos filled with places, destinations, and relations.

Titan

In the May 29, 1944, issue of *Life* magazine, amidst articles about World War II's impacts at home and abroad, there is a piece of touristic escape inviting American readers to imagine journeying through the solar system. Alongside grainy black-and-white photographs of the nine planets, a two-page color spread presents six realistically painted views of Saturn from its various moons. "The pictures show the changing aspect of Saturn and its satellite family as it would appear to a traveler hopping toward the planet from moon to moon." Saturn and its iconic rings hang in the sky of each of these paintings, each moon providing a landscaped foreground reminiscent of the stark, imagined wildness of the American Southwest. As we moon-hop, Saturn looms progressively larger, and in the last image we float above the gaseous planetary surface. Created by Chesley Bonestell (described in the article as a "Hollywood miniature-set designer and amateur astronomer" and referred to by many since as the "father of space art"), the images are praised for being astronomically accurate and "enlivened by no more than reasonable fancy in the detail of satellite landscapes which show in their foregrounds."[3]

One of these paintings, *Saturn as Seen from Titan* (1944), is Bonestell's most iconic work. It takes up two-thirds of a page and is notable because Saturn, rather than hanging in a black sky, hovers low in a sky whose blue hues evoke dusk. As the caption in *Life* explains, the pigmented sky is due to Titan being the only Saturnian moon with an atmosphere. Saturn itself is not "full" but depicted mostly in shadows as a thin crescent. Jagged rock formations jut from Titan's surface, framing the planet and its rings. The ground is covered in ice and snow; it is a crisp and clear winter's night. Saturn might be our focus, but Titan is made fully a world for us to stand upon.

Even as this image makes Saturn strange, the progressive movement closer to the planet gives the outer solar system a sense of familiarity. This is a travelogue, establishing Saturn—and by association other planets and moons in the solar system—as a site of potential human experience.[4] Bonestell tries to make gaseous Saturn a relatable place, depicting fluffy clouds in the high atmosphere from where, in the final painting in the series, we look up to see the magnificent band of rings stretching across the sky like a white rainbow. And yet this composition seems more similar to geometric abstraction than the preceding romantic landscapes from which we view Saturn at a distance. Indeed, Bonestell draws directly on a motif of 19th-century Romantic painters, who placed miniscule, nearly invisible human figures against their sublime landscapes.[5] Inspecting more closely the foreground of the paintings from Saturn's moons Mimas and Iapetus, one sees tiny space travelers, all in white, traversing the rugged terrain. This human presence, apparently within Bonestell's "reasonable fancy," is easily missed by the viewer, whose eye is drawn upward to Saturn and its rings.

To see Saturn from its moons is to make sense of a planet otherwise incomprehensible. While Saturn seems to have little in common with Earth, its rocky satellites relate to both our planet and its moon. It is from the lunar surface that we are shown a familiar landscape. Bonestell is making the solar system a site of human expansion (quite literally by placing humans in these spacescapes) and thus providing a visual aesthetic for the coming Space Race. As one essayist has suggested, Bonestell opened up "worlds within worlds, inviting adventure, converting those abstract points of light into real places."[6]

Luna

Bonestell became a prolific illustrator of potential celestial futures. He returned to the pages of *Life* in 1946 with a series of illustrations titled *Trip to the Moon*. We travel with Bonestell's rocket men from Earth to the Moon, and upon reaching the

2
Lisa Messeri, *Placing Outer Space: An Earthly Ethnography of Other Worlds* (Durham: Duke University Press, 2016).

3
"Solar System: It Is Modeled in Miniature by Saturn, Its Rings and Nine Moons," *Life*, May 29, 1944, 78.

4
This sense of movement was a first for the new field of "space art," argues Catherine Newell, "Without Having Seen: Faith, the Future, and the Final American Frontier," *Astropolitics* 12, nos. 2–3 (2014): 148.

5
For the influence of Romanticism on space art in general and Bonestell in particular, see Elizabeth Kessler, *Picturing the Cosmos: Hubble Space Telescope Images and the Astronomical Sublime* (Minneapolis: University of Minnesota Press, 2012); Ron Miller, "The Archaeology of Space Art," *Leonardo* (1996): 139.

Saturn as Seen from Titan by Chesley Bonestell.

surface, we have an opportunity to look back. "On the Moon's surface the tiny figures of the rocket's occupants view their earth, shining brilliantly in the lunar night."[7] Bonestell was not the first to imagine or depict what Earth might look like from the Moon, but in this brief caption the power of seeing Earth from the Moon is provocatively articulated—travelers see "their earth" and experience a sense of human-planetary connection that, for the Western imagination, is more easily felt at a distance.

Earthrise.

Seeing Earth from the Moon was not a positive experience for all mid-century thinkers. One of the first circulated photographs of Earth taken with the lunar surface prominently in the foreground was a black-and-white image from the Lunar Orbiter I mission of 1966 (two years before *Earthrise*, 20 years after Bonestell's illustration). A month after this photograph appeared, Martin Heidegger sat down for the famous *Der Spiegel* interview addressing his complicity with Nazism in Hitler's Germany. Heidegger made passing reference to this photograph when explaining his concern over the increasingly technical character of Western culture: "Technology tears people away and uproots them from the earth more and more. I don't know if you are scared; I was certainly scared when I recently saw the photographs of the earth taken from the moon." Heidegger articulates the stakes of this uprootedness: "Everything essential and great has only emerged when human beings had a home and were rooted in a tradition."[8]

This regressive philosophical interpretation of the journey to the Moon in the lead-up to the Apollo program is at odds with the legacy of the moon photo. When rendered in color, the view of Earth from the Moon was stunning and sublime, not scary. The transcript from Apollo 8 captures the moment when astronaut Bill Anders became the first human to see Earth rise over the lunar surface: "Oh my God! Look at that picture over there! Here's the Earth coming up. Wow, that is pretty!" He snaps a quick, unscheduled shot with the black-and-white film loaded in his camera and then asks Jim Lovell to hand him a roll of color. From the transcript we feel the excitement of the astronauts fighting over the camera to snap the iconic picture.

As foreshadowed by the Bonestell image caption of "their earth," *Earthrise* is a study of relations, humankind's relationship to the planet and the planet's relationship to the Moon. To think of Earth *in relation* is to dispel the fear Heidegger saw in the uprooting of humans and to instead understand the journey to the Moon as reconnecting with Earth. We see the Moon, Earth, and the humans both on Earth and behind the camera as part of a system, both gravitationally and cosmologically.[9] Earth is not an isolated world but a planet connected to a broader solar system. Earth's planetary nature, made legible when looking back from the Moon, draws our thinking to the other planets that Earth might be in relation to.

Exomoon

This trope of seeing a planet from its moon links the pre–Space Age imagination of human space flight to the peak of Project Apollo and extends into the 21st century and the rise of exoplanet astronomy (exoplanets are planets in orbit around other stars). In an alien solar system, a purple volcano spews orange lava from its craggy peak. Like a mountain stream, the lava braids down the ashen sides of the volcano and joins an ocean of melting rock. In the foreground, islands of solidified debris float in the molten sea. Surfaces glimmer, reflecting the light of a distant star. This molten vista of an imagined exomoon, dynamic and threatening, serves as a frame for the focus of the painting: an exoplanet. A gas giant, half in shadow just like Bonestell's Saturn, rises above the melting moon's surface. The atmosphere of the planet is filled with swirls of orange and white clouds and, reminiscent again of Saturn,

6
Wyn Wachhorst, "The Dream of Spaceflight: Nostalgia for a Bygone Future," *Massachusetts Review* 36, no. 1 (1995): 13.

7
"Trip to the Moon: Artist Paints Journey by Rocket," *Life*, March 4, 1946, 74.

8
Martin Heidigger, Interview, *Der Spiegel*, Nr. 23 (1976), 193-219.

9
See Valerie Olson, *Into the Extreme: US Environmental Systems and Politics beyond Earth* (Minneapolis: University of Minnesota Press, 2018).

47 Ursae Majoris by Lynette Cook.

the planet is adorned with a system of rings, at a slight angle from the moon's horizon. A second and third planet, mere dots in the night sky, create a trail between this mammoth planet and its host star.

This is a painting of the planetary system 47 Ursae Majoris by Lynette Cook. In 2001, when this detection was made, exoplanet hunting was a relatively new endeavor, the first exoplanets confirmed just six years earlier. Today, scientists know of over 4,000 exoplanets. Back in 2001, there were around 70. The first detected exoplanets were all gas giants like Jupiter and Saturn. The yellow dwarf star 47 Ursae Majoris was host to the first multiplanet system in which both exoplanets had near-circular orbits and were located at distances from their star on scale with our solar system. The 2001 discovery strengthened the possibility that there existed elsewhere a planetary system like our own. Might we then also find another Earth? The hope that such a planet exists is evident in Cook's painting. Lingering close to the star, hardly visible to the viewer, is an illuminated speck representing where a rocky, Earth-like planet is fantasized to be.

The purpose of this painting, for the scientists who commissioned it, is to showcase the exoplanet, not the moon whose existence is speculative. The moon is there to offer context for what would otherwise be an indistinct gaseous planet. By placing the exoplanet in relation to a fictive exomoon, the host planet can be understood from a new perspective.

I met Cook at her home in the Bay Area in 2010. We sat in her living room, where her walls were adorned with her art. There were several paintings of exoplanets, often, like the one described above, with a rocky landscape of a moon in the foreground and a gas giant suspended in the sky. Cook was one of the first artists to paint exoplanets. She was approached in 1995 by Frank Drake, famous for his equation predicting the number of planets in the Milky Way existing at present that have communicative life; he asked her to depict 51 Pegasi b, the first exoplanet known to orbit a Sun-like star. From there, Cook collaborated with the first American planet-hunting team, producing artist interpretations for press releases and other public-outreach needs. She described for me the process of painting an exoplanet. She begins by meeting with the astronomer, who tells her the type of star the exoplanet orbits, the distance between the planet and star, and the mass of the planet. From there it's an iterative process, a negotiation between her artistic license and the scientist's devotion to fidelity. Sometimes the astronomer instructs Cook to depict just the planet and its star, but she much prefers it when she has the liberty to include a moon.

Especially in those early days, scientists sought artistic representations that did not stray far from the known data. Cook leveraged this logic, agreeing to be faithful in her depiction of the exoplanet but offering moons as a compromise—since a moon is completely fictional (the data simply aren't good enough to identify a companion to an exoplanet), she could be more imaginative. This was also helpful for Cook in conveying to the viewer what kind of world the exoplanet might be. Since they were mostly gas giants, Cook could use the moon to indicate attributes it and the exoplanet shared, like temperature, by including ice or pools of lava. Cook explained how including an imagined moonscape "tells the viewer what could be there."

When Cook paints moonscapes, she draws on familiar geological formations: snow-capped mountains, volcanoes, buttes, clouds, and craters. With these forms, her paintings make imaginary moons relatable. While many of Cook's colleagues in astronomical art agree that this landscape tradition pays homage to both Bonestell and to Romantic paintings, Cook personally does not identify with any such tradition other than scientific illustration. She did, however, allow the comparison to American landscapes insofar as "space artists are showing worlds that the rest of society cannot see, that we cannot travel to." Her depictions bring exoplanets into the common vernacular: "It makes the distant worlds in our universe seem more real and close and more a part of our lives." A familiar landscape that frames an alien exoplanet offers an entry point from which to comprehend an invisible and distant world.

Lunar-Planetary Kinship

Putting planets in relation to moons humanizes these extraterrestrial geographies. Not only does it evoke the experience any one of us might have had of looking up at a crescent celestial body, but it also envisions a planet in a pack, giving it a companion or even a whole kin network. Even as I have described a series of images in which moons are pictorially in the foreground, the cultural meaning remains attached to the planet floating in the distance. Earth, Saturn, and exoplanets become part of a connected cosmos in which moons enrich our imaginations of these cosmic places. Returning to the edge of our solar system, we see another example of the supporting role imaginatively granted to moons in a song written by folk satirist Jonathan Coulton to comfort

Pluto following its demotion from planet to dwarf planet. This upbeat song of solace is presented from the viewpoint of Charon, a celestial body that used to be classified as Pluto's moon but whose status also changed after Pluto's demotion. Suddenly on equal footing with Pluto, Charon comforts Pluto by reframing their relationship:

> I'm your moon
> You're my moon
> We go round and round
> From out here, it's the rest of the world that
> looks so small
> Promise me
> You will always remember who you are.

Thinking about a moon and its relationship to a planet, reimagining as I do a closeness or kinship, is to presuppose an emptiness, distance, or outsideness between them—the "extra" of extraterrestrial. This is a specifically Western cosmology, and I'd like to end by gesturing to other cosmologies where lunar-planetary relations are already embedded in human geographies. Folklorist Jane Young has described the Native American understanding of space and the Moon in order to critique the frontier mentality. For Zuni and other Native American communities, space is not "outer" but rather "inner." Instead of the view of the universe as comprising inanimate objects in mathematical motion, many Native American cosmologies teach of intimate relations between people, stars, and the Moon. Kinship abounds throughout the universe. It is a way of knowing, Young demonstrates, that facilitates travel to the Moon by means other than a rocket ship. She tells of one anthropologist who, when working with the Inuit in Alaska, recorded the following response to being told about astronauts walking on the Moon: "We didn't know this was the first time you white people had been to the Moon. Our shamans have been going for years. They go all the time."[10]

More recently, scholars writing about and producing indigenous futurisms[11] illustrate how indigenous cosmologies and scientific knowledge are not relegated to the past but inform our present and future thinking about earthly and multiplanetary relations. The animations of Elizabeth LaPensée, an Anishinaabe, Métis, and Irish scholar and artist, depict the complex entanglements between people, other living things, Earth, sky, and Moon. She illustrates travel between Earth and Moon via canoes and intimacies between moon women and earth men.[12]

Thinking about moons and their planets as part of a continuous geography reminds us that the cosmos is neither universal nor empty. From the Moon's surface, we see a cosmos structured by relations made meaningful by different people in different ways. These relations pattern what geographies get imagined as places and destinations. As we step back onto Earth's surface, how do we hold on to the various connections, commitments, values, and practices that enliven and complicate our understanding of Terra and her kin?

10
M. Jane Young, "'Pity the Indians of Outer Space': Native American Views of the Space Program," *Western Folklore* 46 (1987): 272.

11
Grace L. Dillon, ed., *Walking the Clouds: An Anthology of Indigenous Science Fiction* (Tucson: University of Arizona Press, 2012); William Lempert, "Decolonizing Encounters of the Third Kind: Alternative Futuring in Native Science Fiction Film," *Visual Anthropology Review* 30, no. 2 (2014): 164.

12
See "Along the River of Spacetime," "The Path without End," and "Returning," http://www.elizabethlapensee.com/#/animations. Thanks to Zoe Todd for telling me about this work.

Brick Moon, Glass Moon
FRED SCHARMEN

Near the end of the 19th century, two fiction writers unknown to one another, independently conceived the idea of the space station. In the United States, a Unitarian minister named Edward Everett Hale published a story entitled, "The Brick Moon" in The Atlantic Monthly (1869). The tale involves a group of industrialists and their proposal for an aid to navigation. They would place a moon—made of brick—into polar orbit over the Greenwich Meridian, giving sailors a stable reference to find their position in the Atlantic Ocean between England and America, thereby solving the problem of how to accurately determine longitude. In Hale's story the Brick Moon, with workers (and their supplies) still inside, launches too soon. What would have been the first navigation satellite instead becomes the first place where humans live in outer space. In 1896 a Russian author, Konstantin Tsiolkovsky, started work on a novel imagining what life would be like in space. Tsiolkovsky, in Beyond the Planet Earth (1920) envisioned the construction of great glass greenhouses in Earth's orbit. These two early fictional depictions illustrate permanently inhabited places in extraterrestrial space. Previous writers had speculated about the possibility of space ships. Tsiolkovsky's work on thrust and orbital mechanics later established him as "the father of the Soviet space program."[1] The idea that humans could use ships to fly to, and live on, other planets, was not new. But Hale's Brick Moon and Tsiolkovsky's glass moon were the first attempts to think through the technical, social, and political consequences of life entirely away from planets, in free space.

Brick Moon (I)

The production of the eponymous brick moon in a story by Edward Everett Hale is an act of speculation. The Board of Longitude, an advisory group in the British government, awarded cash prizes for technologies that could accurately indicate longitude at sea. But in 1828 this board was disbanded, and margins of uncertainty in location for navigation persisted. Hale's story tracks a group of men who begin dreaming of solutions to the problem of longitude in their college years. They come back together later in life after they've found success in transportation and business. To nail down the particulars of their scheme—complete with detailed estimates of cost and material needed—they take to the road seeking potential funders. The technical questions have been settled. The brick moon will be a solid sphere 200

1
For a sketch of Tsiokovsky's life and influence, see B. N. Vorobyev, "Konstantin Tsiolkovsky and his Work on Interplanetary Travel," in Konstantin Tsiolkovsky, *Beyond the Planet Earth*, trans. Kenneth Syers (New York, NY: Pergamon Press, 1960), 1-16.

feet across with several void spheres nested within it to save on weight. When complete, it will launch into orbit with flywheels accelerated by hydropower. The three speculators deliver a three-pronged pitch to an audience of shipping magnates, bankers, and other interested parties. The first speaker appeals to order and intention: the brick moon is meant to be in the sky, and these men are meant to build it. "And I said that whenever a man knew his place in this world, it was always likely all would go well."[2] The second appeals to virtue, "for he believed, on his soul, that the success of this enterprise promised more for mankind than any enterprise which was ever likely to call for the devotion of his life. 'And to the good of mankind,' he said, very simply, 'my life is devoted.'"[3] And the third would-be entrepreneur appeals to the potential investors' vanity and cleverness "till, as their mouths dropped a little open in their eager interest, and their lids forgot to wink in their gaze upon his face, and so their eyebrows seemed a little lifted in curiosity,—till, I say, each man felt as if he were himself the inventor, who had bridged difficulty after difficulty; as if, indeed, the whole were too simple to be called difficult or complicated."[4]

But despite these seeming simplicities, things indeed become both difficult and complicated. The pitch works, and the audience of businessmen see the value of investing in infrastructure to protect their previous investment in shipping, preventing loss and wreckage. The group's detailed cost estimates, though, show that their best fundraising efforts still fall short. The narrator credits the start of the American Civil War, catalyzed by Jefferson Davis and P. G. T. Beauregard, as the unintentional turning point in the story and in their fortunes: "But at last Jeff Davis was ready. 'My preparations being completed,' wrote General Beauregard, 'I opened fire on Fort Sumter.' Little did he know it,—but in that explosion the BRICK MOON also was lifted into the sky!"[5] The Civil War caused interest rates on their existing balance to rise much faster than projections, and the first artificial satellite launch would proceed similarly—up, and to the right—paid for by war profiteering.

And this is not the last unexpected circumstance. Like the currency spike, the satellite launch would come as a surprise. After spending a mild winter completing the construction of the brick moon early, one of the three entrepreneur founders moves his family into the interior of the structure. To stay warm and dry, several of the immigrant workers on site likewise set up family households inside the moon, bringing their grain stores, chicken coops, and cattle with them. The late-winter rains fill the stream and soften the ground just enough. One night, as everyone inside is sleeping, the moon slips on its bearings, slides down the valley into the flywheels, and is flung into orbit.

Glass Moon (I)

Like Hale, Konstantin Tsiolkovsky was a writer, a bit of a scientist, and a bit of a mystic. Tsiolkovsky was a self-taught physicist who developed the mathematics necessary to calculate a spacecraft's exhaust velocity, its speed, and its changing mass as fuel was consumed for thrust. This breakthrough made possible the multistage rocketry schemes that followed in the Soviet Union and in the United States. Tsiolkovsky was also a disciple of Nikolai Fyodorov, whose cosmist doctrine taught that the "Common Task" of all effort, science, and technology should be the restoration of all past wrongs and an infinite expansion of human existence. Fyodorov suggested scientific knowledge and application could and would reverse engineer the existence of the dead from the traces they left behind, resurrecting them from their graves. Humanity, he predicted, would eventually need to leave Earth for other planets, to make room for the rapidly expanding population of everyone who ever lived.[6]

In Tsiolkovsky's book *Beyond the Planet Earth* (1920), a group of reclusive scientists make a breakthrough. They create powerful and lightweight combustible fuel, providing them with the means to reach escape velocity in rockets large enough to house several men, with enough food and other supplies to stay in space for long periods of time. They soon realize they can't stay indefinitely, though. Once they've left Earth their thirst for exploration exceeds their capacity for living on their stores. They design and construct a greenhouse in space, with an environment inside perfectly tuned to encourage prodigious

2
Reprinted in Edward Everett Hale, "The Brick Moon," *The Brick Moon and Other Stories* (New York: Astounding Stories, 2017), 11–12.

3
Hale, "The Brick Moon," 12.

4
Ibid.

5
Ibid, 16.

6
There is an effective brief description of Fyodorov's ideas and of Russian cosmism in Boris Groys, "Introduction: Russian Cosmism and the Technology of Immortality," *Russian Cosmism*, ed. Boris Groys (Cambridge, MA: MIT Press, 2018) 1–16.

plant growth, supporting an abundance of food. This enables them to fly to the Moon (the original stone moon), Mars, and the asteroid belt. But they cannot occupy their greenhouse themselves; given its high temperatures, stifling humidity, and carbon dioxide atmosphere, humans need space suits to enter. This is a heaven for plants but a hell for people. When they signal information about their success back to Earth, a new wave of humans comes to live in space. This requires an even larger orbital greenhouse, an orbiting glass moon, with a milder climate based on compromise, allowing people to live among the plants that produce their air and food.

This harmony in orbit is underscored by the corresponding disruption on Earth. The potential for a completely new kind of existence—built from the ground up, but without ground—leads directly to questions about how life should be structured. Who are these new worlds off the planet for? What should the temperature be? What is the optimum length for the day/night cycle? Will people still wear clothes? "'Men and women practically naked! Impossible!' thundered the moralists." The argument raged, "'They'll get used to it!' . . . . 'If there are people who don't, it means that they are not pure-minded enough, and such people had be better left on Earth. Not everyone will go! Some people will have to stay here. Earth will have to be looked after just as before, even more strictly than before, or it will turn into a hell.'"[7]

Glass Moon (II)

Astrophysicist and astronomer Lucianne Walkowicz spent the year 2017–2018 as the Baruch S. Blumberg NASA/Library of Congress Chair in Astrobiology in the John W. Kluge Center at the Library of Congress. Their research topic focused on the ethics of exploring and living in space. As an observer of space science's role in culture and politics, Walkowicz posits, "What happens in space happens on Earth."[8] Scenarios of control, technology, and social life are often rehearsed in the popular imagination, in the future, and in space. Space science and science fiction offer ways to project into other times and other places. This allows us to speculate on how life might be transformed in the world we live in here and now.

Tsiolkovsky's imagination offers a vision of technical precision, rendering a world specifically tuned for a certain kind of human subject not limited to outer space. In an extended pamphlet, "The Future of Earth and Mankind" (1928), he describes how the controlled environments necessary in space habitats might return to our home planet. Tsiolkovsky assumes the inevitability of "homes in the ether"—glass greenhouse space stations in orbit. The tectonics and techniques rehearsed in these glass moons might also remake the surface of the Earth—lest it be turned into "a house of agony." He proposes to redesign and rebuild the unused deserts on Earth and wants to remake areas where ideal tropical climatic conditions exist but whose native peoples, he writes, "are unable to make use of the paradise bestowed on them and lead pitiful, impoverished lives."[9] The question of the optimal use of a given area of planetary surface runs through this pamphlet. Land is not being used optimally, in Tsiolkovsky's scenario, so it must be put under common ownership. People are not making their time and effort useful, he hints, so they must be enlisted. This "multimillion man voluntary army and all the technological means at our disposal" would address the common task of maximizing Earth's useful output.[10]

This transformation would take place step by step, starting with the organization of the territory into 10-meter-wide strips. A moving front of action (1,000 kilometers long) mobilizes this "volunteer army" to clear the first strip of all plant and animal life. Following removal, a series of layered surfaces, each performing a different function, are built up in successive steps. First, a metal mesh grid keeps unwanted insects and other creatures from returning, and then the cleared ground is planted with "the purest varieties of the plants most beneficial to man."[11] The next step in this series of control layers is glass in frames, equalizing the climate from the

7
Konstantin Tsiolkovsky, *Beyond the Planet Earth* (Oxford, UK: Pergamon Press, 1960), 122.

8
Lucianne Walkowicz, "What Happens in Space Happens on Earth," *Slate*, June 22, 2018, https://slate.com/technology/2018/06/trumps-space-force-has-a-lot-to-do-with-the-u-s-border-crackdown.html.

9
Konstantin Tsiolkovsky, "The Future of Earth and Mankind," in *Russian Cosmism*, 113–131.

10
Tsiolkovsky, "The Future of Earth and Mankind."

11
Ibid.

temperate region to the tropics. Finally, this interior climate would be regulated by the same tectonics that Tsiolkovsky proposed for his orbital greenhouses. Tsiolkovsky's army would install another layered system of slats and surfaces that could be alternately matte black or super-reflective, depending on whether energy was meant to be absorbed into the structure or reflected away. This scheme would provide each person on Earth with housing and 100 square meters of productive soil for food production. The people who would live in this space might not necessarily be the ones who built it. Until this interior climate could be totally controlled, work inside the structure, he writes, "could be done by natives, who are more accustomed to the climate, and suffer from it less."[12]

Tsiolkovsky's scheme is a totalitarian modernism, encompassing the Earth with a glass grid not unlike one of the critical speculative projects of the Italian design group Superstudio, who wrote of their 1971 project *The Continuous Monument*, "Architecture is one of the few ways to realize cosmic order on earth, to put things to order and to above all affirm humanity's capacity for acting according to reason."[13] This is also a kind of supercolonialism, in which any relationship between people and land is controlled and measured in terms of use value produced for a technological subject. The oceans would be covered with rafts and glass roofs to extend the human population to 400 billion and beyond. The endgame of this grid is total enclosure—an extreme environment in which even the atmosphere, both inside and outside this world-encompassing glass house, would be designed. In a final stage, engineers would revert the air above the glass to vacuum. A premonition of Buckminster Fuller's Spaceship Earth concept, Tsiolkovsky's plan would make Earth itself into a space station, circling the Sun.

Brick Moon (II)

Hale's brick moon has its own implications for life on Earth. The narrator emphasizes not the disrupting effects of new technology like inhabited satellites, but rather their tendency toward normalization: "It is indeed astonishing to think that we so readily accept a position when we once understand it."[14] Once the two entrepreneurs left on Earth establish communication with the third who has been accidentally launched—along with his family, several other worker families, and their stores—into orbit while aboard the brick moon, they realize that a new independent existence off the Earth has been established. Instead of perishing, this new society has survived and even thrived. The moon has dragged along its own atmosphere, the snow that fell into it over the winter has melted to plentiful water reserves, and their supply of plants and animals is alive, reproducing, and even, astonishingly, evolving: "Write to Darwin that he is all right. We began with lichens and have come as far as palms and hemlocks."[15] Just as Tsiolkovsky relied on an imaginary fuel source to create his story on living in outer space, Hale applies artistic license to some technical details about evolution in order to make a point.

In a sequel story, "Life on the Brick Moon," Hale elaborates on normalization and evolution. An attempt to send books on governance and culture to the brick moon fails. The partner on the moon signals back to Earth they don't need to remain politically connected to their home planet anyway. "Go to thunder with your old law-books," and "We have not had a primary meeting nor a justice court since we have been here."[16] The inhabitants of the brick moon live in relative leisure, based on socialization and ritual, with little work. Gradually, their concerns diverge from Earth's, and the narrator suggests cultures on our planet could learn a lot from this situation. He imagines how nice it might be if some benign cataclysm broke the planet Earth itself into dozens of independent moons: "Gradually people and despatches came in, who said that they had parted company with some of the other islands and continents." Rather than a cause to lament, this parting of company is an occasion for levity: "But, as I say, on each piece

12
Ibid.

13
Peter Lang and William Menking, *Superstudio; Life without Objects* (Milan: Skira Editore, 2003), 122.

14
Hale, "The Brick Moon," 27.

15
Ibid., 24.

16
Ibid., 30.

the people not only weighed less, but were much lighter-hearted, had less responsibility."

> Now will you imagine the enthusiasm here, at Miss Hale's school, when it should be announced that geography, in future, would be confined to the study of the region east of the Mississippi and west of the Atlantic,—the earth having parted at the seams so named. No more study of Italian, German, French, or Slavonic,—the people speaking those languages being now in different orbits or other worlds.[17]

If Tsiolkovsky returns to Earth with a grand project of the space station, Hale brings a grand accident to ground, with semi-Utopian consequences. The brick moon, and the story of its subsequent fate, has context in common with the glass moon. The entrepreneurs who make the brick moon are, like Tsiolkovsky's engineers, obsessed with utility. When they discover a pristine landscape with a river, all they can think of is to dam the flow of the water for energy and dig up the yellow earth for bricks. Both stories, the American one in 1869 and the Russian one in 1920, were published only a few years after their countries' revolutions. The Russian Revolution of 1917 seemed to offer a chance to remake the world. Tsiolkovsky's vision of a Spaceship/Space Station Earth is in resonance with that opportunity. In the American Civil War, the kind of schism imagined by Hale's narrator had just been averted, and Hale, who was an abolitionist and outspoken supporter of the Union, used his two stories to address questions of separatism and secession in a counterfactual narrative.

The glass moon is assembled additively, with glass and frame, and is designed to optimize certain conditions, engendering a certain mode of life. The brick moon has a different structure. It is made—at least conceptually made—through subtraction, with voids hollowed out from solid material *poché*. In Gottfried Semper's system of architectural elements, the heavy weight of masonry precedes the lighter tectonics of frame and skin, and in the 19th and early 20th centuries, ponderous brick construction was giving way to the same glass and iron that characterizes Tsiolkovsky's orbital greenhouses. But the cultural and historical resonances of these two stories complicate that order. If the glass moon is the apotheosis of an extended modernist paradigm, then the brick moon, even though it came before, is a kind of postmodern response to that totalistic logic. Instead of making one environment optimized for one kind of humanity, the narrator of the brick moon stories imagines that living in space would enable more difference and perhaps more difficulty. The brick moon was not designed for habitability. This is not an artifact made for humans, but they nevertheless adapt themselves to its accidental affordances.

These postrevolutionary stories from Russia and the United States precede the Cold War and the Space Race. To put these stories beside one another, though, is to open up a conflicted territory—in politics and design—with several axes. The range between the provisional and the precise, the subtractive and the additive, the multitude and the unity—this is the socio-technical arena of the 20th and 21st centuries, for architecture as much as for society. These 19th-century stories provide a unique orbital perspective from beyond the fray. They are embedded in that arena but are also distant from it, in space and time. What happens in space happens on Earth, and vice versa. Although these two moons differ, they illustrate a general principle—to think about change in a world, whether that change is totalization or fragmentation, it is often necessary to get outside of it.

17
Ibid., 28.

The Postlunar Imaginary through Inflatable Architecture

KATARZYNA BALUG

> The membrane of the [inflatable] structure becomes an extension of one's skin, seen from inside the body, as it indents, sweats and changes shape, as the person inside moves over and through various locations. . . . We are all part of an energy continuum throughout the universe. . . .Understanding of energy processes is reaching the point where the wave emissions of the body and brain can be registered and measured, opening up the possibility of ultimate environmental control. . . . We are not alienated by technological hardware, but freed by technological forecasting, control and simulation of the elements.
> —Graham Stevens, "Pneumatics and Atmospheres," *Architectural Design*

The artistic exploration of bodily enmeshment with technology and environmental control is emblematic of the changing conceptions of human subjectivity that occurred throughout the 1960s. In his 1972 article for *Architectural Design*, English artist Graham Stevens claimed that an existential extension of the body becomes coterminous with its environment—a body that, like its environment, is fully quantifiable, its mysteries decoded and controlled. NASA's 1960s Apollo missions made explicit the case of human dependence on technology as they transformed the lunar voyage from long-standing fiction to reality.[1] This article explores how the existential questions prompted by the Space Race manifested through inflatable structures, an often overlooked mode of experimentation in architecture. Inflatable constructions, made in the United States and Western Europe in the 1960s, appropriated the physical materials, iconography, and narrative of the NASA Apollo program to produce the imaginary of a new world not in outer space but firmly grounded on Earth. Deploying the materials of the Space Race, these structures expressed possible meanings of lunar conquest for humankind.

1 Though, as Nicholas de Monchaux and David Mindell have shown, human physiology and psychology tend to resist total control, so that the most efficient techno-rational systems leave some room for human autonomy. De Monchaux's analysis reveals, for example, how the logic of cybernetics influenced a brief consideration of the human body in space as a cyborg whose responses to the pressures of air space could be adapted not by external prosthetics, but by chemical, mechanical, and biological changes to its internal control systems. While this did not endure, it illuminates how the new technology-enabled age was an environment to which the human mechanism, thoroughly integrated into a global technology network, was expected to adapt. Here, technology tended to displace the human body from the center of achieving a feat the systems technicians saw as technological, rather than human, as the pilot astronauts saw it. Mindell shows that it was only through arguments that Wernher von Braun, head of the Apollo program, conceded to allow lunar flights to be manned. Though it seems difficult to imagine Apollo 11 without Neil Armstrong's "small steps," this attitude is an important scientific precursor of the posthuman philosophies that are discussed in the rest of the article. See Nicholas de Monchaux, *Spacesuit: Fashioning Apollo* (Cambridge, MA: MIT Press, 2011) and David A. Mindell, *Digital Apollo: Human and Machine in Spaceflight* (Cambridge, MA: MIT Press, 2008).

NASA, Representation and Affect

When the Soviet Union successfully launched the Sputnik I satellite in 1957, Americans were reminded of the potential dangers of advanced technology in the hands of an ideological enemy. Amidst President Kennedy's call for the race to the Moon in 1962, the American space agency launched the NASA Art Program, whose mission was to "interpret the space program in terms already understood."[2] In other words, the goal of the program was to condition the American public to identify with the pursuit of the lunar frontier, to at once naturalize the technology and make palatable the expense that the feat entailed. What would be directly experienced by only two men needed to reverberate as a feat for and by the West.[3] Art was chosen as the most relatable means by which to connect with the public imaginary. NASA recognized that "space travel started in the imagination of the artist," and the program invited young and established painters and illustrators to serve as "witnesses and recorders of our efforts in this field."[4] Dozens of artists attended launches from 1963 through all of the Apollo missions. They had full access to the astronauts and the infrastructure required to reach space. In return, NASA widely published their sketches, drawings, and paintings, which depicted raw, emotional responses to the human-machine spectacles that the artists witnessed.[5] The artworks leading up to and including the 1969 Moon landing mission of Apollo 11 projected a heroic link between technology and man in anticipation of the lunar event. They tended to emphasize the technological apparatus, the astronauts, and, more rarely, imagined vistas of the Moon. Few, if any, depicted the potential view of Earth from the Moon or considered the return back to Earth.[6] This suggests that the focus of participating artists and of NASA was on the pursuit of the frontier, not on what might come after.

Historian Benjamin Lazier examines the unanticipated existential transformation via German philosopher Hans Blumenberg: "If one tries to relate the centuries of imaginative effort and cosmic curiosity to the event [of the lunar landing], then the both unexpected and heart-stopping peripety of the gigantic departure from the Earth was this one thing, that in the sky above the Moon one sees the Earth."[7] Seeing Earth surrounded by the vastness of space revealed that man has no realistic alternative to the planet; one result of this was a new sense of rootedness, often accompanied by a deep sense of oneness. The overwhelming response of astronauts who witnessed this view exemplifies Blumenberg's notion of reenchantment with Earth. For example, Apollo 9 astronaut Russell Schweickart recounts that seeing Earth in the profound silence of a spacewalk occurring at thousands of miles an hour made him feel like a "sensing element for man," that it was as if life itself were having the experience rather than Schweickart as an individual.[8] The astronauts' images brought this extraplanetary perspective of Earth to the public and in the *Earthrise* moment transformed notions of Earth.[9] The planet appeared as a "world picture": fully knowable and representable.[10] However, understanding Earth as a closed-loop system in an infinite array of space also made visceral its limits, including the imminent ecological consequences of unfettered expansion.[11, 12]

2
Anne Collins Goodyear, "The Relationship of Art to Science and Technology in the United States, 1957–1971: Five Case Studies" (PhD diss., University of Texas at Austin, 2002), 44.

3
Ibid.

4
James Dean, "The Artist and Space," *Interdisciplinary Science Reviews* 3, no. 3 (1978): 244–259.

5
Ibid.

6
All the works of the NASA Art Program from 1963 to 1969 are compiled in Hereward Lester Cooke, *Eyewitness to Space* (New York: Harry N. Abrams, 1971).

7
Hans Blumenberg [1975] in Benjamin Lazier, "Earthrise; or, The Globalization of the World Picture," *American Historical Review* 116, no. 3 (2011): 602–630, 619.

8
Russell Schweickart in Frank White, *The Overview Effect: Space Exploration and Human Evolution* (Boston: Houghton Mifflin, 1987),12–13.

9
Patrick McCray argues that the *Earthrise* image, which was taken on the Apollo 8 mission on Christmas, 1968, was especially instrumental in making the notion of "Spaceship Earth" a much less abstract concept. Patrick McCray, *The Visioneers: How a Group of Elite Scientists Pursued Space Colonies, Nanotechnologies, and a Limitless Future* (Princeton, NJ: Princeton University Press, 2013).

10
Lazier addresses Heidegger's ideas of Earth as world picture in Benjamin Lazier, "Earthrise; or, The Globalization of the World Picture," *American Historical Review* 116, no. 3 (2011): 602–630.

11
Lazier, "Earthrise."

12
McCray, *The Visioneers*.

Space Colonies, on Earth

Habitable, inflatable structures were part of the space imaginary long before the founding of NASA. As early as the 1950s, human space colonies were depicted as tightly regulated, enclosed, inflated environments shaped like large tori. Flexible, light nylon and plastic forms, which could inflate with pressurized air to recreate Earth's atmosphere, were commonly envisioned as the exterior shells of the satellite dwellings.[13] In response to the recognition of Earth's bounded form in the late 1960s, inflatable space colonies were reinvigorated as emblems of an idealized mode of ecological living. The lunar landing inspired Gerard O'Neill, among others, to explore their viability as liberators of humanity from the home planet.[14]

However, another source of the postlunar imaginary was an ever-present but understudied form in Earth-oriented architecture. The inflatable articulates a blending of the two contradictory responses to space travel: rootedness and desire to leave Earth permanently. Just as the idea of human space colonization appeared closer to fruition with the race to the Moon, a number of architects in the US and in Western Europe began to experiment with inflatable forms. Inflatables had appeared earlier in art linked with kinetic sculpture, and in architectural experiments in housing or defense. Yet it was not until the 1960s that experimentation with grounded inflated forms contained social and sensory experiments self-aware of the earthly context. Many of their authors were in dialogue with one another across the two continents and have often been associated with countercultural collectives distinct from, and critical of, mainstream modernism and modern life more generally. At the same time, these architects found inspiration in NASA's inflatable technologies and space aspirations, and they embraced Buckminster Fuller's technocratic views, idolizing him despite his engagement in government commissions.[15] Fuller unceasingly pursued technological visions to sustain life on Earth rather than away from it; inflatable works combined his ecological concerns with efforts to make strange the familiar of the planet so that it could be experienced anew. During the 1960s, publications like *Architectural Design* featured modernist architecture, conceptual designs for space habitats, and inflatable architectural experiments with equal gravity.[16] By the late 1980s, however, inflatable projects, like other countermodernisms, were relegated to the margins as postmodernism consolidated. Caroline Maniaque-Benton poignantly demonstrates that the 1982 edition of Charles Jencks's *Architecture Today* included a chapter on "alternatives" by William Chaitkin that contained a section on inflatable, or "soft," architecture, a section missing by the 1988 edition.[17] Two of the creators of inflatable architecture featured in Chaitkin's chapter are the collective Ant Farm and the artist Graham Stevens, whose quote opens this essay.[18] In the subsequent section, we revisit both of these entities to consider how the inflatable form helped to usher in a postlunar imaginary.

Blurring the Boundary between Body and Environment

Ant Farm was formed in San Francisco by young architects Chip Lord and Doug Michels, who were soon joined by artist Curtis Schreier, among several more transient members. The beginning of their decade-long practice in late 1968 just preceded the Apollo 8 mission, which brought home the famous image of Earth rising over the lunar horizon. Their

13
See, for example, Chesley Bonestell's illustrations of Wernher von Braun's articles on space colonization in *Collier's* magazine from the 1950s, particularly March 22, 1952, "Man Will Conquer Space Soon."

14
McCray, *The Visioneers*.

15
Felicity Dale Elliston Scott, *Architecture or Techno-Utopia: Politics after Modernism* (Cambridge, MA: MIT Press, 2007); Caroline Maniaque-Benton, *French Encounters with the American Counterculture, 1960–1980*, Ashgate Studies in Architecture (Burlington, VT: Ashgate, 2011).

16
For example, the article by Graham Stevens, cited at the start of this essay, appeared in the March 1972 issue adjacent to work on and about modernism. A special issue of the magazine, *Space 2000+*, from February 1967, featured extensive contributions by Fuller and John McHale that concerned life on Earth and in space in the year 2000. Another special issue, *Pneu World*, from June 1968, was dedicated to inflatable structures.

17
Maniaque-Benton, *French Encounters*. For more on the counterculture's paradoxical embrace of both cybernetics and resistance to modern politics and practices, see Fred Turner, *From Counterculture to Cyberculture: Stewart Brand, the Whole Earth Network, and the Rise of Digital Utopianism* (Chicago: University of Chicago Press, 2006).

18
Charles Jencks and William Chaitkin, *Architecture Today* (New York: Harry N. Abrams, 1982).

earliest projects often featured inflatables and borrowed liberally from NASA iconography and materials. In their own words, an ongoing shift from car culture to communications media underscored a rapid exchange of ideas independent of place, which in turn facilitated nomadism.[19] Felicity Scott analyzes Ant Farm as reflexive about the passage to an information economy made possible by cybernetics and about new experiential conditions of space and time.[20] In addition to this analysis, I suggest that their inflatables activated new relationships between humans and their surroundings.

The group was based largely in San Francisco but had a strong presence in Houston between the Apollo 8 mission in late 1968 and the Apollo 11 Moon landing in the summer of 1969. At sunrise on the morning of July 20, 1969, the day that Neil Armstrong and Buzz Aldrin set foot on the Moon, Ant Farm was perched in front of NASA headquarters with an inflatable called *Space Egg* designed by Ant Farm collaborator Charley Tilford. Tilford waved a large American flag in front of the egg-shaped black inflatable, which was covered in parachute fabric. In an interview with curator Constance Lewallen, they claimed that their goal was to attract media attention.[21] While a suspicious reading may interpret this work as a desire to both distract and benefit from the momentous occasion, it can also be intuited as an impulse to amplify earthly existence at the moment of man's arrival on another celestial body.[22] During their time in Houston, the group produced several performances using space memorabilia and astronaut-inspired costumes and began to deploy enormous inflatable forms and parachutes in experimental social events. With inflatable "pillows" large enough to accommodate dozens of people inside and on top of the structures, they would soon return to California and combine heightened bodily experience with politically engaged performances of ecological protest. The media-sensitive collective absorbed the Apollo hype in late 1960s Houston, then used the materials of the Space Age to reflect on a shift in perspective underscored by space travel. Ant Farm's and others' inflatable forms captured the essence of the term "Spaceship Earth" as popularized by Fuller: as an ineluctable limit, not to be abandoned for space colonies, but to be reinhabited in a more thoughtful, enduring way.

Though Ant Farm's projects regularly utilize the semiotics of NASA and the Apollo space program, their inflatable structures underscore and reaffirm the grounded condition of earthly residence. To understand the subtlety of their operations, it is helpful to contrast Ant Farm's inflatable work with the NASA Art Program. Contrary to the Art Program, Ant Farm's inflatable architectures do not attempt to translate or interpret the otherworldliness of a human departure from Earth through representation. Instead, they "actually enact and perform the worlds they imagine," a fundamentally different act from representation.[23] Through this differentiation, a significant rift emerges between inflatable practices like Ant Farm's and the intended orientation of artworks produced under the NASA Art Program. Writer Frank White captures the difference: "Landing on the moon was a goal that was part of a vision, but it never made sense as an end in itself."[24] Rather than illustrate the journey, the ambition, or the technological apparatus of getting to space, Ant Farm's inflatables appear to grapple with new existential dimensions opened up by space travel as they appear here, on Earth.

An additional aspect of this existential dimension is suggested within Andrew Pickering's concept of performance as outlined by Salter.

19
Ant Farm and Chip Lord, *Automerica: A Trip down U.S. Highways from World War II to the Future* (New York: E. P. Dutton, 1976).

20
Felicity Dale Elliston Scott, *Living Archive 7: Ant Farm; Allegorical Time Warp: The Media Fallout of July 21, 1969* ; plus the *Complete Ant Farm Timeline* (Barcelona; New York: Actar, 2008).

21
Constance Lewallen and Steve Seid, *Ant Farm, 1968–1978* (Berkeley: University of California Press; Berkeley Art Museum and Pacific Film Archive, 2004).

22
I thank Stephanie Cannizzo at UC Berkeley Art Museum & Pacific Film Archive for the reference for this project and Ant Farm member Curtis Schreier for further elucidating it.

23
Chris Salter, *Alien Agency: Experimental Encounters with Art in the Making* (Cambridge, MA: MIT Press, 2015), xii. Salter makes this distinction in analyzing contemporary art projects; I find his framework useful in reading the earlier work. Salter borrows the concept of performance from Andrew Pickering, examined in Andrew Pickering, *The Cybernetic Brain: Sketches for Another Future* (Chicago: University of Chicago Press, 2010), as cited in Salter, *Alien Agency*, 8.

24
Frank White, *The Overview Effect: Space Exploration and Human Evolution*, 2nd ed. (Reston, VA: American Institute of Aeronautics and Astronautics, 1998), 44.

Pickering argues, as do others, that materials engaged in a particular activity have agency equal to that of the humans involved in the arrangement. In other words, the human and nonhuman actors together produce reality through mutually informing interactions.[25] Frameworks that depose the human as the central agent on the planet have become increasingly present in academic literature, from science to critical theory, in recent decades. Ant Farm and other inflatable practices remarkably preceded them in envisioning and putting into momentary play worlds in which humans and nonhumans coexist, communicate, and thrive on the limited resources of the planet. Adjacent to the influence of the Space Race, interest in these dimensions is further evidenced by the group's ties to the budding ecological movement and by self-authored texts in which they question man's capacity to control technology's domination of nature.[26]

Inflatable forms are generally temporary, yet video footage of Ant Farm's installations captures the essence of performance.[27] The plastic membrane is flaccid until inflated via a blower or wind, at which point it becomes difficult to tame. The suddenly enormous plastic bubble comes to life as it fills with air. Its human occupants pull it and get pulled by it in turn; the object has a mind of its own, balancing the urge to billow out its insides with the human tugging on it and with the ever more powerful wind that jolts it about from the outside. The 50-foot structure is tethered by crisscrossing ropes. This limits the bubble's movement across the ground and allows the suddenly light human the experience of being weightless atop the air-supported surface. In the process, the state of earthly weight is momentarily suspended—just around the time that freedom from gravity is attained by the Moon-jumping astronauts streaming via pixelated videos on television. While the surfaces bulge about, the helpless human bounces along, holding on to the rope structure for the illusion of balance. Underneath, more human bodies occupy the bubble, pushed from side to side as the walls cave in and expand on them.

This larger-than-life, gravity-defying balloon itself is not new: balloons have facilitated new visual perspectives and scientific discovery in flight since the late 18th century. Once in flight, however, balloon occupants depended on maintaining the vehicle's state of equilibrium, using ballast but avoiding direct interaction with the form. With the 1960s grounded inflatables, the form itself is playable, pliable for maximum experience of the subject, who can be immersed inside or on top of it. In confronting inflatable structures, one cannot frame the subject as a distanced observer perceiving passive objects as in representation; nor as a passenger tending the machine to remain in the elements' good graces; nor as in control of the constructed object. The inflatable invites active encounters between humans, the plastic mass, and the wind, blurring the boundary between subject and environment.

Graham Stevens similarly experimented with body limits and environmental control through inflatable structures. In his projects, the body became physically enmeshed with the inflatable form as he explored the material limits of plastic in both containing a particular body and in sustaining life in general. For example, his 1972 *Desert Cloud* was a large solar balloon that filled at sunrise with gradually warming air and floated low above the Arabian desert. The balloon form produced much-needed shade and, as the air in it condensed, extracted potable water from the desert atmosphere. His 1970 project, *Hovertube*, was a quarter-mile-long inflated pedestrian tunnel extended to the middle of a lake in Cornwall, allowing the experience of walking on water. In both of these inflatables, as in Ant Farm's, air defines both the form and the structure. The envelope, made of a two-dimensional polymer such as plastic sheeting, fills with air that gives form to the continuous surface. The form's coextensive structural integrity is immediately graspable despite being largely invisible. It is continually conditioned by outside forces, whether these are elements such as wind or water, or human occupants.

The inflatable structures of both entities exhibit a certain freedom from the burden of progress, relieved of the techno-rational utopia of the lunar frontier to reengage with earthly existence. This disposition was made physically possible by the

25
The concept of nonhuman agency is certainly not new, but it has become more commonly explored by theorists since the 1970s, starting with Gilles Deleuze, Felix Guattari, and Bruno Latour, and more recently by movements like Object-Oriented Philosophy, New Materialism, or Speculative Realism. For more on these ideas, see Gilles Deleuze and Felix Guattari, *A Thousand Plateaus: Capitalism and Schizophrenia* (Minneapolis: University of Minnesota Press, 1987); Levi Bryant et al., *The Speculative Turn: Continental Materialism and Realism, Anamnesis* (Melbourne: re.press, 2010); Diana H. Coole and Samantha Frost, *New Materialisms: Ontology, Agency, and Politics* (Durham, NC: Duke University Press, 2010); Jane Bennett, *Vibrant Matter: A Political Ecology of Things* (Durham, NC: Duke University Press, 2010), among many others.

26
Curtis Schreier (member, Ant Farm), conversation with Katarzyna Balug in Berkeley, CA, March 18, 2019; Ant Farm, *Automerica*.

27
See, for example, *Ant Farm Inflatables*, 16 mm film to dvcam transfer. Filmed by Kelly Gloger, 1969–1970/2006.

material form of the inflatable bubble. As alluded to earlier, it was made thinkable by the existential gap produced when humans first saw Earth outside themselves. The Copernican Revolution had technically proven that Earth revolved around the Sun; seeing Earth in its celestial context in the late 1960s made this scientific fact resonate anew. Earthly departure created a new perspective that undermined Enlightenment anthropocentrism.

Philosopher Elizabeth Grosz explains the capacities of art to produce a similar gap, without leaving Earth's orbit. Grosz, following Gilles Deleuze, explores art's capacity to frame the forces of chaos existing in the universe, rendering them sensible so that the body can directly experience them through its nervous system rather than representationally.[28] Similarly to Salter, Grosz posits that art is neither representational nor metaphorical. In her view, it is a mediation, an opening—or momentary gap—between the experienceable and the concealed. Darwin's concept of sexual (as opposed to natural) selection allows her to posit that art is not limited to the human but is an animal quality. Art acts directly on the body's nervous system, rather than on its sensing apparatus, which requires rational consciousness to process, as it momentarily brings into focus the forces acting and existing on Earth. Artist László Moholy-Nagy suggested in 1947 that art-making is itself a subconscious, intuitive act that both captures and conditions its cultural and social setting.[29] The inflatable, through immersive experiences inside or on top, produced such precognitive affects and suggested new, more lateral relations of existence on the planet. Cary Wolfe further helps to connect Deleuze's momentary enframing to a posthumanist ontological framework by underscoring that, once made (or in our case, inflated), an artwork is responsive to the forces acting on it and is ambivalent toward the human subject as such.[30] The comingling of dependency and resistance is prevalent throughout 1960s inflatable practices, as architects blurred the boundary between the human body and the plastic bubble's capacity to keep it afloat, as in Stevens, or elevated, as in Ant Farm.

Romantic writer Victor Hugo, writing at the end of the ballooning era in the 19th century, likened the flying balloon to a cloud, with no navigational capacity. Instead, he foresaw an embrace of the "bird" for flight, a steerable helicopter.[31] The 20th century attested to this foresight, as humans perfected environmental control. However, historians of space have convincingly shown that the social imaginary had no apparatus to receive the image at the pinnacle of technological achievement: the 1968 view of the planet in its totality. Understanding this suggests a different analytic lens for 1960s inflatable practices: beyond critiques of modernism, technology, or the relationship of politics and praxis, the fundamental concern is to find the human back on Earth, via architecture. Part of that, inflatable practices suggest, is learning how to work Hugo's cloud and bird together, to balance control with collaborative assemblages in considering the survival of not just the human but all other forms of life and matter on the planet. Tuned in to their historic moment, the two practices explored here, Graham Stevens and Ant Farm, examined new possibilities of existence on Earth through encounters between human and nonhuman forms, an existence that theory has continued to address in the decades after the lunar landing. In the seriousness of the Space Race, the playful medium of inflatable architecture provided an imaginary from which to imagine life in which humans could alternate floating with flying.

28
Elizabeth Grosz, *Chaos, Territory, Art: Deleuze and the Framing of the Earth, Wellek Library Lectures at the University of California, Irvine* (New York: Columbia University Press, 2008).

29
László Moholy-Nagy, *Vision in Motion*, ID Book (Chicago: Paul Theobald, 1947).

30
Cary Wolfe, "Lose the Building," in *What Is Posthumanism?* (Minneapolis: University of Minnesota Press, 2009). Wolfe describes the Blur Building by architecture firm Diller Scofidio + Renfro to illustrate his point in this chapter.

31
As cited in Richard Holmes, *Falling Upwards: How We Took to the Air*, 1st US ed. (New York: Pantheon Books, 2013), Hugo's 1863 Letter on Flight included the following: "Let us deliver mankind from the ancient, universal tyranny! What ancient, universal tyranny, you cry. Why, the ancient, universal tyranny of gravity! . . . Today the balloon has been judged, and found wanting. . . . To be torn from the ground like a dead leaf, to be swept along helplessly in a whirlwind, this is not true flying. And how do we achieve true flight? With wings! . . . What do you see above you? You see clouds and you see birds. Well then, these are the two fundamental systems of aviation in operation. The choice is right in front of your eyes. The cloud is the balloon. The bird is—the helicopter!"

The Lunar Receiving Laboratory: Apollo 11 and the Possible Beginnings of the End of Life (on Earth)

EDWARD EIGEN

> Here rests his head upon the lap of Earth
> A youth to Fortune and to Fame unknown.
> Fair Science frown'd not on his humble birth,
> And Melancholy mark'd him for her own.
> —Thomas Gray, "Elegy Written in a Country Churchyard"

The still relatively recent history of the Apollo space program typically takes as its starting point the challenge issued by John F. Kennedy during his "Special Message to Congress on Urgent National Needs" (May 25, 1961): "This nation should commit itself to achieving the goal, before the decade is out, of landing a man on the Moon." Less often cited is the concluding clause of the president's bold—indeed, designedly incautious—fiat: "and returning safely to the Earth." It is this perilous homecoming that provides the crux of the present investigation, focusing as it does on a built structure, really a techno-managerial dream of a comprehensively controlled artificial environment that was designed to manage the unknowable risk of contamination posed by the return of Apollo 11.[1] And therein lies the still-present but displaced (because anthropogenically induced) sense of urgency: the more recent recognition that the urgent call is coming from within the house or, rather, from the leaky compartments of Spaceship Earth.

If ever there were a situation to test the unsettled metes and bounds of the inseparable verbal predicament that is hospitality/hostility, mutually born of the root word *hos*, then it is the Lunar Receiving Laboratory (LRL) at the Manned Spacecraft Center (MSC).[2] What the facility was meant to receive, in addition to weary astronauts kept there under strict quarantine, were moon rocks and samples of the regolith. According to plan, the specimens were to be borne homeward by the Columbia command module in two vacuum-sealed containers (total weight: 36.2 kilograms, 23 of which accounted for the samples and the rest specialized packaging). Separate "lunar-environment" samples were to be stored in containers designed to maintain the best possible vacuum and transport the specimens under pressure conditions similar to those of the lunar atmosphere.[3] The crucial question was what this material bore evidence of, even—or especially—in undetectably minute quantities. Did these unprecedentedly rare bearers of "new knowledge" present signs of extraterrestrial biomatter, which might threaten the continuity of life on Earth? The LRL was a precautionary site for the homebound delivery of constitutively exogenous pathogenic agents.

In July 1964, almost exactly five years prior to the liftoff of Apollo 11, a two-day Conference on

1 This paper draws upon the careful documentary research presented in Susan Magnus and William Larsen, *Lunar Receiving Laboratory Project History* (NASA/CR-2004-208938).

2 For a comprehensive "official" history of the MSC, see Henry C. Dethloff, *Suddenly, Tomorrow Came: The NASA History of the Johnson Space Center* (Houston, TX: NASA, 1993).

3 James C. McLane Jr., Elbert A. King Jr., Donald A. Flory, Keith A. Richardson, James P. Dawson, Walter W. Kemmerer, and Bennie C. Wooley, "Lunar Receiving Facility," *Science* 155, no. 3762 (February 3, 1967): 525.

the Potential Hazards of Back Contamination from the Planets was convened at the National Academy of Sciences in Washington, DC. Given Kennedy's urgent timeline, the duly empaneled experts were to discuss the possibility of "returning space missions' bringing back to earth organisms that might prove harmful."[4] Without any "direct experience" of extraterrestrial life, the interagency panel based their assumptions on known terrestrial biological events, including pandemics, plague, smallpox, and yellow fever. The assembled biologists, epidemiologists, zoologists, and public-health officials came to an inconclusive conclusion: "The existence of life on the moon or planets cannot . . . rationally be precluded. At the very least, present evidence is not inconsistent with its presence."[5] Balanced between presence and the present, matters of fact are left in a state of suspension, wafted involuntarily in the sort of irregular, random motion Robert Brown once observed of pollen seeds. The conference attendees, on whom the fate of life on Earth potentially depended, were themselves unsettled passengers in an aborted flight of arguably fanciful reasoning. Yet the existence of life on the Moon or planets, in the experts' collective opinion, could not at that time "rationally be precluded."

In the subsequent planning of the Apollo program, every manner and method of precaution was thus seen to be called for, if for no other reason than to remain in compliance with the Treaty on Principles Governing the Activities of States in the Exploration and Use of Outer Space, Including the Moon and Other Celestial Bodies (United Nations General Assembly Resolution 2222 XXI). Ratified on January 27, 1967, the Outer Space Treaty addresses Levitically "matter out of place," as Mary Douglas termed it in her magisterial *Purity and Danger*, published a year earlier. Article IX reads in part:

> States Parties to the Treaty shall pursue studies of outer space . . . and conduct exploration of them so as to avoid their harmful contamination and also adverse changes in the environment of the Earth resulting from the introduction of extraterrestrial matter and, where necessary, shall adopt appropriate measures for this purpose.

The terms of the treaty notably did not contemplate an advantageous change in the environment (say, from some species of volunteer seed that might penetrate the slowly descending cloud of so-called rainbow herbicides—Agent Orange and others—then covering ever more remote regions of conflict and angrily dividing people on the home front). The main distinction drawn by the treaty was between "forward contamination," or the introduction of alien biological matter into presumably pristine outer space, and "back contamination," or that which returns to Earth along with the astronauts and their craft.

It was the return of the Apollo astronauts, and the threat of adverse changes to the environment, that was the great unknown, the final, final frontier. "We set sail on this new sea because there is new knowledge to be gained, and new rights to be won," Kennedy proclaimed of the incipient space program. We might, in another setting, speak of *nostalgia*, a term concocted by the Swiss student Johannes Hofer in his medical dissertation of 1688 from the Homeric *nóstos* (return home) and *álgos* (longing, a sorrow or grief, painful enough in kind to become a sort of sickness).[6] But the sickening—due to rational yet unconfirmed—fear the Lunar Receiving Laboratory was meant to mediate was that homecoming was itself the vector of contamination unto sickness. If the Odyssean voyage that ultimately inspires these terms was characterized by narratively alluring peripeteias, the techno-scientific logic applied to lunar samples—the evidence newly at hand, around which multiply redundant barriers were erected to prevent any contact by human hand—was scripted in advance, anticipating a prophylactic path from the moment of removal from the airless lunar surface to encapsulated entry into the administrative domain of NASA.

The conference made a qualified virtue of putting things off. "Conclusive answers may not be obtained for some time. In the interim, however, negative data will not prove that extraterrestrial life does not exist; they will merely mean that it has not been found."[7] So what ultimately was the conference's indecisive, but nonetheless unanimous, conclusion? "Extraterrestrial life and the concomitant possibility of back contamination must be

4
Allan H. Brown, *Conference on Potential Hazards of Back Contamination for the Planets, 29–30 July 1964* (Washington, DC: National Academy of Science, 1965): i.

5
Ibid., 4.

6
See Carolyn Kiser Anspach, "Medical Dissertation on Nostalgia by Johannes Hofer, 1688," *Bulletin of the Institute of the History of Medicine* 2, no. 6 (1934): 376–391.

7
Conference on Potential Hazards of Back Contamination, 4.

presumed to exist. To presume otherwise could lead to inadequate planning of precautionary measures and failure to foresee a danger which might be avoided."[8] What was called for were preliminary measures, a threshold of elaborate description with recesses opening only into other still more secluded points of entry, delaying perhaps indefinitely the moment of possibly fatal contact. The LRL was built for a state of indeterminacy, awaiting resolution. It was not a matter of clarifying perception or principle, of bringing matters into view, but of receiving the available evidence into its intricate and anxious confines. The LRL was an incubator of consciousness about the presumed limits of self and other, from the scale of the cell to the still unknown universe. A scene of guarded expectancy, it was designedly undramatic.

"The famous Christmas Eve snapshot took 90 seconds to make and kicked off five decades of awareness of our planet's beauty and fragility," *National Geographic* wrote in commemoration of the globally perception-changing *Earthrise* photograph (NASA image AS08–14–2383) made by Apollo 8 crew member William A. Anders. The command module audio transcript records the hectic moment of exposure as the spiritually arresting visual constellation shifted between the spacecraft's narrow view portals. Anders: "Wait a minute, just let me get the right [camera] setting here now, just calm down. Calm down, Lovell." By whatever not-so-silent channels the image seeped into the burgeoning ecological consciousness of a pre–Earth Day nation—a print was accorded pride of place in President Nixon's Oval Office—at MSC it was but an excited blip on the screen, a welcome break from programmatically desirable managerial monotony.[9] Seasons and mission cycles keep and tell their own time; life goes on, except when it does not. As Bernard Weinraub of the *New York Times* reported of his visit to MSC: "Behind the gray plate-glass windows . . . closed-circuit television sets flicker mutely everywhere with a continual live color shot of men sitting or walking or standing in the mission control room. Watching this screen for five minutes has the same numbing effect of an Andy Warhol movie of the Empire State Building."[10] It is a slow cinematic march to sunrise; the unbidden arrival with the returning astronauts of something truly new under the sun—or, rather, within the far narrower but still unescapable ambit of Earth's biosphere—was threat enough to remain wakefully vigilant.

Stage Two

Unlike the wastelands of Cape Canaveral, punctuated with sublime technological assemblies of rocket-launch armatures, the planning and control elements of the Apollo program gave rise to the horizontal sprawl of the campus-like Manned Spacecraft Center.[11] Early issues of *Space News Roundup*—the organization's house organ, or "vehicle"—featured boosterish items describing the move westward of the Space Task Group, from Langley Air Force Base, in Virginia, to Houston. Anticipating the change in scene—and at the same time rewriting constitutive narratives of American territorial self-possession—President Kennedy said in his September 12, 1962, address at Rice University that "what was once the furthest outpost on the old frontier of the West will be the furthest outpost on the new frontier of science and space."[12] The task—or, rather, the Puritan "errand into the wilderness," to use the imagery deployed by Kennedy's speechwriters—had become the image. Space City, USA, as it came to be known, was no "shining city on a hill" but instead a multi-integrative command-and-control post. "Now . . . [/] . . . And Later" is how *Space News Roundup* adverbially encompassed the move. Under "Now" (to be read proleptically as "before") appear two photographs, looking as if they had been taken from the Farm Security Administration's files on rural desolation, their captions written in seeming emulation of James Agee's *Let Us Now Praise Famous Men* (1941).[13]

8
Ibid., 4–5.

9
For the scene in the mission control room on the day of December 24, 1968, see Samuel C. Phillips, "The Shakedown Cruises," in Edgar M. Cortright, *Apollo Expeditions to the Moon* (Washington, DC: NASA, 1975), 178–182.

10
Bernard Weinraub, "MSC-H, USA: 13,000 Make Moon Project Go," *New York Times*, May 23, 1969, 22.

11
On the choice of the site, see Francelle Pruitt, "Congressman Albert Thomas and NASA's Coming to Houston: A Study in Legislative Effectiveness, 1936–1966," *Southwestern Historical Quarterly* 105, no. 4 (2002). For a compelling study of the cultural politics of the space program's installations, see Neil M. Maher, *Apollo in the Age of Aquarius* (Cambridge, MA: Harvard University Press, 2017).

12
"Kennedy Makes MSC Third Stop in 'Space Tour,'" *Space News Roundup* 1, no. 24 (September 19, 1962): 6.

13
"Now . . . And Later," *Space News Roundup* 1, no. 12 (April 4, 1962): 2.

An abandoned shack, its door inviting in errant winds, sheds pieces of corrugated tin onto the surrounding weeds and remembered dreams of better days, when an old era of want was to have given way to a new time of plenty. Corrugated metal, rusty and rattling, the rough surface of rural poverty, was recast in the "space age" as the high-performance, corrosion-resistant Alcoa aluminum V-Beam sheets of the Launch Complex 39 Vehicle Assembly Building. The sheets were treated to resist all weather conditions, materials for a structure that was said to create a weather system of its own. This was the architectural superstructure where spacecraft were delivered. At Rice, Kennedy had spoken prophetically of a "giant rocket" made of "new metal alloys, some of which have not yet been invented." These new materials would be used in the ablative heat shield of the command capsule that bore the astronauts back to Earth. Other means were required to keep stowaways out of the capsule.

The second photograph shows a "lonely windmill." A decade earlier, in his paper on "some prairie inventions," the historian Walter Prescott Webb likened the windmill to "a flag marking the spot where a small victory had been won in the fight for water in an arid land."[14] When Cape Canaveral was rededicated as Cape Kennedy following the president's assassination, the installations there were described as a "center and symbol of our country's peaceful assault on space." As for the flag that Buzz Aldrin cumbrously implanted on the Moon, a congressional bill, written in accordance with the 1967 Outer Space Treaty, specified that it was "intended as a symbolic gesture of national pride in achievement and is not to be construed as a declaration of national appropriation by claim of sovereignty."[15] Assault, but do not claim. This former marker of progress, the windmill, was now merely in the way (of progress).

Below these images, along with the tease " . . . And Later," appeared the "architect's conception," showing "the future, expressed in the long, low lines of the Auditorium-display building," and still more prominently on the horizon, the Project Management Building with its "glass-and-steel honeycomb façade." Here was a "monument to an age when man looks up for his future instead of out across the flat landscape."[16] The "Now . . ." and " . . . Later" derive their specific loco-temporal sense only from one another, related by a small constellation of ellipses. The ellipsis itself is more than double in meaning—referring to an oval-shaped Keplerian orbit, as depicted on the NASA insignia—and, like the *lunulae* (little moons), or parentheses, they set things apart in a sentence. Ellipses indicate that something has been left out, drawing attention to an intentional void.

The dramatically compressed time frame in which the Manned Spacecraft Center was conceived is enumerated by Charles Luckman in his memoir *Twice in a Lifetime* (1988). Luckman claims that *Time* magazine ran a feature story with the headline "Forty-Nine Buildings in Forty-Eight Days, a Super-Human Effort."[17] (This historian can find no evidence of it.) In the span of those 48 days (November 15, 1961–January 3, 1962) Luckman produced a masterplan for the center. According to a refreshingly straightforward technical appraisal offered by *Architectural Record*, the "repetitive use" of materials, structural systems, and architectural details served "to unify and speed construction."[18] The result, as it appeared to the visiting reporter from the *New York Times*, was a "complex of white metal and marble chip concrete buildings that resembles . . . a clean futuristic city whose residents had suddenly fled."[19] A new nowhere, irrecusably clean.

In his account of the Apollo program, serialized in *Life* magazine from 1969 to 1970 and published as the book *Of a Fire on the Moon* (1970), Norman Mailer spoke of the buildings as "architectural fungoids," which were "as sinister to him as the arbitrary growth of ugly species of mushrooms in the middle of nowhere."[20] To Mailer's eye, the MSC resembled nothing so much as a "college campus, one of those miserable brand-new college campuses with

14
Walter Prescott Webb, "The Story of Some Prairie Inventions," *Nebraska History* (December 1953): 232.

15
PL.91-119, November, 18, 1969, 83 Stat. 202.

16
"Now . . . And Later," 2.

17
Charles Luckman, *Twice in a Lifetime: From Soap to Skyscrapers* (New York: W. W. Norton, 1988), 396.

18
Architectural Record Magazine, January 1963, Issue 1 (Vol 133, No 1), 149.

19
Weinraub, "MSC-H, USA: 13,000 Make Moon Project Go," 22.

20
Normal Mailer, "A Fire on the Moon," *Life*, August 29, 1969, 28.

21
Ibid., 26.

22
Ibid., 28.

23
Norman Mailer, "Superman Comes to the Supermarket," *Esquire*, November 1960, 120.

24
Ibid.

buildings white as toothpaste."[21] Melvillean whiteness is here turned into something still more sinister because detached from the surface of "that wall" (the white whale), the mask of inscrutability that so vexed *Moby-Dick*'s Captain Ahab. "'Recognize'"—here Mailer has the "windowless walls" speaking for themselves—"'that something is taking over from you, kid.'"[22] Whiteness is made familiar and readily available at the drugstore or grocery in tube form or as pill or powder. "Superman Comes to the Supermarket" was the title of Mailer's dispatch from the 1960 Democratic National Convention held in Los Angeles, which for him was symptomatic of the "interchangeable, geographically unrecognizable" sprawlscape of "postwar SuperAmerica."[23] In his report Mailer charted the unnatural but inevitable evolution of what Henry James called the "advertising aesthetic." The presidential election of 1960 was a contest between "ugliness" (Nixon) and "glamour" (Kennedy or "Superman"); the deciding factor was the "spirit of the supermarket."[24]

This was explicitly the domain of Luckman. Unable to find work as an architect during the Depression, Luckman took a job as a draftsman in the advertising department of the Colgate-Palmolive-Peet Company before moving to the Pepsodent Company, where he proved himself to be a "great packager."[25] Pepsodent was later acquired by Lever Brothers, or what Luckman described as "a world of fats and oils." This was not the rock oil (kerosene is one of its distillates) drilled on the ranch where the MSC rose or, rather, spanned out horizontally. Rather, it was the vegetable oil used in Lever's Imperial brand margarine, but also the whale oil used in its Lifebuoy brand of antiseptic soap. Advertisements placed in *Life* and elsewhere produced and preyed on fears of "B.O." (body odor). The whale oil was not, however, used in Lever's upmarket Sunlight brand (later renamed Lux), where its strong odor, without the carbolic acid masking agent in Lifebuoy, would have been objectionable to discriminating consumers.[26] The people who worked for NASA, Mailer wrote, were WASPs, altogether untinged, "and it was part of the folklore of New York that Wasps were without odor." Thus, they were already "halfway to the moon."[27]

The Lunar Receiving Laboratory, located on Avenue B and Fifth Street in the southwest corner of the Manned Spacecraft Center, was designed by Smith, Hinchman & Grylls Associates, of Detroit, in conformity with Luckman's masterplan. The facility is a particularly unexpressive agony of Earth-preserving sterility, far beyond the cosmetic sheen of cleanliness expressed by the curtain wall of the Lever House, for which Luckman himself was the client. Yet what captured the attention of Dora Jane Hamblin, writing in *Life* magazine, was what she described as the "incredibly complex interior arrangements."[28] Replete with multiply redundant, hermetically sealed microenvironments, designed to manage and contain the incalculable threat of unwanted things in the air, the LRL was a monument to prescience—a scrupulously alert encounter with its own limits, architectural or otherwise. To wit, the title of Hamblin's article: "After the Moon Flight, a Wall against the Unknown." Thus, a two-way containment system was devised, both to protect laboratory scientists and technicians "on the outside" from contact with possible lunar biological materials and to protect the samples "on the inside" from terrestrial biocontamination.[29] The wall was in fact a series of portals, thresholds, and zones of pressurization. Among the techniques for sorting out environments were the underground low background radioactive assay area, sterilizing ultraviolet locks, negatively pressurized work rooms, and positively pressurized nitrogen glove boxes for processing lunar samples. The technicians worked on the specimens inside, recorded findings orally on tape while their hands remained in glove ports. The specimens arrived in the laboratory in the form of an environmental riddle wrapped up in an enigma, the opposite of the forms of legibility promised by packaging research.

Hamblin's article appeared in a special July Fourth issue of *Life* devoted to Apollo, published a little more than two weeks before the Lunar Modular was scheduled to reach Mare Tranquillitatis. Serving as an extended epigraph, James Dickey's poem "The Moon Ground" is a puzzling musing on an astronaut who collects moon rocks while recalling words from Thomas Gray's "Elegy Written in a Country Churchyard" (1751). The astronaut and his lone

25
John Kobler, "The Great Packager," *Life*, May 2, 1949, 112. On NASA's own marketing program, see David Scott and Richard Jurek, *Marketing the Moon: The Selling of the Apollo Lunar Program* (Cambridge, MA: MIT Press, 2014).

26
Charles Wilson, *The History of Unilever* (New York: Praeger, 1968), 130.

27
Mailer, "A Fire on the Moon," 27.

28
Dora Jane Hamblin, "After the Moon Flight, a Wall against the Unknown: A Close Watch on the Men and Their Prizes," *Life*, July 4, 1969, 54.

29
McLane et al., "Lunar Receiving Facility," 528.

companion survey the surface while a third member of the mission remains suspended "overhead" in the lunar-orbiting command module. "He is reading the dials he is understanding / Time, to save our lives." The poet anticipates the return home, the astronauts carrying back with them "the very stones / Of Time."[30] Where Gray described the mournful scene of a coffin borne "Slow thro' the church-way path"—his annotators seeking to determine whether this path was *in* the churchyard or rather led from the high-road *to* the church—the final leg of the astronauts' journey, as well as the rocks they brought with them, was scrutinized step by step, one form of containment and transition making way for another, some portable, until they reached final quarantine (and release) at the LRL.[31]

Stage Three

The interpretive gesture here is to consider the Apollo mission, for all its undeniable capacity to expand the bounds of human imagination and ingenuity, as nothing but a spectacular intermission in a longer-form story about Earth's habitability. How to tell this story, which does not commence with a countdown and end with a splashdown. How does one, even an astronaut, enter into a discourse of unbounded atmospheres and ecosystems and come to interpret the relevant vital signs? Perhaps not incidentally, 1967, the year the exterior envelope of the LRL was completed, saw the publication of Frank Kermode's *Sense of an Ending*. In this study of narrative closure, Kermode writes "Men, like poets, rush 'into the middest,' *in medias res*, when they are born; they also die *in mediis rebus,* and to make sense of their span they need fictive concords with origins and ends, such as give meaning to lives and to poems."[32] We muddle in the middle without understanding our beginning and end. Is there a remedy for this protracted crisis? "Into the middest" evidently comes from Edmund Spenser, his prefatory letter to Sir Walter Raleigh expounding the design of his *Faerie Queene* (1596). But the sentiment reverts further to Philip Sidney's contention, in *An Apology for Poetry* (1595), that "if they" —poets— "will represent an history, they must not (as Horace saith) begin *ab ovo*, but they must come to the principal point of that one action which they will represent."[33]

So, let us finally consider the question of confinement, or in some specially qualified sense, the condition of being *in medias res*. In his 1913 discussion of antiseptic and aseptic practices, Joseph Bolivar DeLee, the so-called father of modern obstetrics, who has also been polemically associated with the pathologization of modern pregnancy, explains that the "child is delivered *inter feces et urinas*," between shit and piss.[34] (The phrasing might be familiar to readers of Freud's *Dora* (1905), who put it in the mouth, or throat, of St. Augustine, but it was invented by the Austrian anatomist Josef Hyrtl, who attributed it to a "Church Father.") To navigate this passage, to ensure the safe reception of the passenger (the newborn) is to remain within the very narrow boundaries between *eutocia* (normal labor) and *dystocia* (abnormal or pathological labor), from the Greek *tókos*, "childbirth." In terms of clinical practice, this means establishing and maintaining a system of antisepsis. The bed is dressed with sterile sheets, the patient in a sterile nightgown and leggings; another sterile sheet covers the belly, but nothing is draped near the birth canal, which is frequently sponged with 1 percent Lysol and 1:1500 bichlorid solutions. The accoucheur too wears a sterilized gown and sterilized rubber gloves, which are kept so by very frequent dipping in actively antiseptic solutions.[35] If the protocols are followed, DeLee observes, "one can conduct the most difficult and prolonged obstetric manipulations in the dirtiest hovel with brilliant results."[36]

According to DeLee, the word *obstetrics* comes from the Latin *ob* and *stare*—"to stand before," "to protect." DeLee's art had to do with managing and monitoring barriers involving both aseptic and

30
James Dickey, "The Moon Ground," *Life*, July 4, 1969, 16.

31
D. C. Tovey, ed., *Gray's English Poems* (Cambridge: Cambridge University Press, 1922), 162.

32
Frank Kermode, *The Sense of an Ending: Studies in the Theory of Fiction* (1967; repr., New York: Oxford University Press, 2000), 7.

33
Geoffrey Shepherd and R. W. Maslen, ed. *An Apology for Poetry (or The Defence of Poesy)* (Manchester: University of Manchester Press, 2002), 111.

34
Joseph Bolivar DeLee, *Principles and Practice of Obstetrics* (London, UK: W.B. Saunders Company, 1921), 318. On DeLee's controversial legacy see Carolyn Herbst Lewis, "The Gospel of Good Obstetrics: Joseph Bolivar DeLee's Vision of Childbirth in the United States," *Social History of Medicine* 29, no. 1 (2015): 112–130.

35
De Lee, *Principles and Practice of Obstetrics*, 330.

36
Ibid., 331.

37
Ibid., 117.

38
See Michael Meltzer, *When Biospheres Collide: History of NASA's Planetary Protection Programs* (NASA SP-2011-4234) (2011), 213.

antiseptic practices, to which he himself was subject. "Without doubt the physician carries the greatest danger of infection to the confinement room," he notes. But the carefully controlled conditions of confinement are in the service of parturition, a laborious process with distinct "stations," in which living bodies undergo transit/transition. According to DeLee, these include: (1) the *powers*, by which the expulsion of the ovum is accomplished; (2) the *passages*, which represent the road and the resistance met; (3) the *passengers*, the child and its adnexa (placenta, etc.); (4) *external complications*, which may disturb the course of the function. The last-named factor, he explains, is the pathological one, which, within the space of his own text, he chooses to omit "for the present."[37] For now, let us suggest that these pathological factors are as boundless as space itself.

Here is an abbreviated outline of the prophylactic measures attendant upon the delivery of the earthbound astronauts, with overall recovery operation directed from Mission Control Center, MSC Building 30.[38] On July 24, 1969, command module Columbia splashed down in the Pacific Ocean 812 nautical miles southwest of Hawai'i and less than 13 miles from USS Hornet, the Apollo 11 prime recovery ship. "Helo 66," a Sikorsky SH-3D Sea King helicopter, its crew attached to Anti-Submarine Squadron 4, was dispatched from the aircraft carrier and rendezvoused with the capsule. Working from an inflatable raft dropped to the sea's surface, the recovery team delivered biological isolation garments (BIGs) to the astronauts through the hatch of the bobbing spacecraft; the team members were also wearing BIGs. After the astronauts exited the capsule, its hatch and upper deck area were sprayed with Betadine, a water-soluble iodine solution, for contamination would have resulted from matter leaving the capsule. Any contaminants on the surface, it was assumed, would have burned during reentry. After the operation, the men and the life raft were wiped with a solution of sodium hypochlorite. (Sensing an unparalleled marketing opportunity, the Clorox Company's Bureau of Bleaching Information trumpeted that "NASA borrowed a page from the housewives' laundry book to help guard against 'Moon Germs.'")

After landing on the USS Hornet, the helicopter was lowered to the hangar-bay level, where the astronauts entered the Mobile Quarantine Facility (MQF), a modified aluminum-bodied Airstream trailer.[39] The astronauts' footsteps on the deck of the ship were swabbed with a disinfectant glutaraldehyde solution. Entry into the Airstream, where Armstrong, Collins, and Aldrin removed their BIGs, "completed the voyage of Apollo 11."[40] Through its rear-facing picture window the now quarantined astronauts were greeted by President Nixon, who was aboard the prime recovery ship. When the Hornet reached port in Hawai'i, the MQF was hoisted off the ship and put on a flatbed truck and taken to Hickam Air Force Base, where it was then loaded on an USAF C-141 for the flight to Ellington Field in Houston. Transshipped again to a flatbed truck, at the MSC the MQF was backed up to the LRL, where a "special airtight plastic transfer tunnel" was attached to the spacecraft and the mobile unit" to facilitate the astronauts' entry into the facility.[41]

Final Stage

"Next Stop: Home" read the heading of *Space News Roundup*'s coverage of Building 39, which was to be the "final stop for Apollo crewmen following their lunar journey." But for the moon samples they brought back with them, it was to be "the first stop in a series of scientific investigations."[42] Upon the immediate outcome of those investigations—that is to say, the detection, or not, of extraterrestrial life—depended the release of the astronauts from their Sears-furnished quarantine within the LRL.

39
NASA, MSC, news release, June 14, 1967.

40
Apollo Mission Report (Houston, TX: Manned Spacecraft Center, 1969), 4–20. (MSC-00171)

41
Bob Gordon, "Where the Moon Meets the Earth," *Space News Roundup* 6, no. 18 (June 23, 1967): 4.

42
Ibid.

43
DeLee, *Principles and Practice of Obstetrics*, 270.

44
DeLee, *Principles and Practice of Obstetrics*, 900. "The term probably is derived from the Latin *partus cesareus*, from *cedere*, to cut. The term section, therefore, is really a redundancy. There is no evidence to show that Julius Caesar was thus delivered. *Cesones* (children delivered by section from their dead mothers) were known long before Caesar's time, and the operation was not performed on the living. Caesar's mother was alive at the time of his wars, as is proved by his letters to her."

45
"First 'Astromice' Shipped for Lunar Testing," *Town Crier, Wilmington, Mass.*, October 26, 1967, 2; Richard C. Simmonds, et. al., "Animal Maintenance for Biomedical Evaluation of Lunar Material," *Journal of the American Veterinary Medical Association* 161, no. 6 (1972): 720–727; on the theory and practice of gnotobiology, see Robert G. W. Kirk, "'Life in a Germ-Free World': Isolating Life from the Laboratory Animal to the Bubble Boy," *Bulletin of the History of Medicine* 86, no. 2 (2012): 237–275.

"Cheers but No Handshakes," the AP aerospace correspondent Paul Recer wrote of the astronauts' dubious welcome. "They'll be locked away" in a laboratory "which looks more like a plush college dormitory than a building of science." When were they fit to leave?; Under what conditions would it be safe for the people of Earth to receive them? How to detect signs of (extraterrestrial) life? In his *Principles and Practice of Obstetrics*, DeLee had addressed the uncertainties of identifying a viable pregnancy: "Without positive evidence to the contrary, a fetus is considered alive. While we can easily assert that the child lives, we can less readily be sure that it is dead."[43] Considering the air of hushed expectancy in which these evidences—auscultatory in nature—were to be interpreted, the difficulty of parsing DeLee's statement produces its own source of anxiety. How, then, to definitively ascertain the absolute absence of unwanted life?

The evidence the LRL was meant to produce—the answer to the question, did lunar specimens bear signs of life?—involved cesarean section. As originally practiced, the obstetrical procedure was performed to save viable children "from their dead mothers."[44] To establish or disavow the threat of back contamination, which would have entailed the permanent quarantine of the lunar samples (and the astronauts), required exposing gnotobiotic subjects to lunar samples. The astronauts' experimental proxies were to be cesarian-originated, barrier-sustained Astromice. These gnotobiotic organisms (from *gnosis*, known, and *bios*, life) were model laboratory specimens either germ-free or bearing only previously identified passengers (pathogens, parasites, etc.).[45] Creating Astromice meant returning, if not *ab ovo*, then at least to the moment prior to their entry into the realm of the pathological (where we all live). In originating a nucleus stock for a pathogen-free animal, the mother was scarified to deliver the pup in an axenic state. According to Henry Foster, founder of the Charles River Breeding Laboratory, which mass-produced experimental animals, "this initial freedom"—not of movement or volition but simply from pathogens—depends entirely on the erection and maintenance of obstacles (to freedom) as variously conceived. It "can be breached if no provision exists for the maintenance of animals within a structure and with a mode of operation which affords a protective barrier against their ordinary pathogens."[46] The method described by Foster is to remove the intact uterus, its own space capsule, and transport it into a sterile plastic isolator maintained under positive pressure. Once inside the isolator, the uterus is opened to remove the pups, which are cleaned free of the placenta and amniotic fluids before being placed with the lactating germ-free females.[47] According to Foster, however, "the most important single factor in establishing healthy colonies is a clean start, for if this is not initially possible, all subsequent efforts are in vain."[48]

Terminal Stage

Clean starts, untouched lands, new frontiers, all have their place in the imaginary of the space program; all were, at least in part, vain aspirations. In his address at Rice, Kennedy offered the planning for the MSC as evidence of "how far and how fast we have come." The first issue of *Space News Roundup* featured a story on the imminent move of what had been known as the Space Task Group to Houston, from Virginia's Langley Air Force Base, named for the aviation pioneer Samuel Langley. The publication's masthead fit the genius of the place. The title was bordered by the loop of a cowboy's catch-rope (lasso) used in rounding up and driving cattle, with the letter *O* replaced by the NASA insignia, and at the end of "Roundup," a rocket silhouette extending beyond the border.[49] With its stylized bolus of exhaust fumes, it was meant either to be read as an exclamation point or to signify that the rope's knot had no chance of reining in the extraterrestrial mission underway.

The cultivated image of astronauts as a new breed of cowboys, solitary and free-ranging, was as

46
H. L. Foster, Sumner J. Foster, and Erving S. Pfau, "The Large Scale Production of Caesarean-Originated, Barrier Sustained Mice," *Laboratory Animal Care* 13, no. 5 (1963): 711.

47
H. L. Foster, "A Procedure for Obtaining Nucleus Stock for a Pathogen-Free Animal Colony," *Proceedings of the Ninth Annual Meeting of the Animal Care Panel* (1958): 136.

48
Ibid., 135.

49
Fay E. Ward, *The Cowboy at Work* (New York: Hastings House, 1958), 155–156.

50
David Mindell, *Digital Apollo: Human and Machine in Spaceflight* (Cambridge, MA: MIT Press, 2008), 74.

51
Amy Bacon, "The West Ranch: From Cattle to Space City," *Houston Review* 17, no. 2 (1995): 68.

52
Dorothy M. Hoskins, "An Italian Villa of Today," *Houston Gargoyle* 3, no. 19 (May 11, 1930): 10.

53
Bacon, "The West Ranch: From Cattle to Space City," 71.

unfaithful to the communal and hierarchical work of the roundup as it was to the constrained forms of autonomy the corps of pilot-astronauts were trained to assume during their stay at the MSC both prior to liftoff and following splashdown.[50] The campus was developed on land donated by Rice that was once part of the 30,000-acre "ranching kingdom" of the self-made lumber, banking, and oil tycoon James M. West.[51] Situated on a wooded waterfront site near where the Armand Bayou flows into Clear Lake, the West Ranch was itself less the sort of *western* outpost imagined by Kennedy than it was a *villa urbana* of appropriately distant classical inspiration. Designed by the Jewish-Austrian émigré architect Joseph Finger, of Houston, West's 17,000-square-foot stucco-clad Renaissance Revival villa was provided with "fully landscaped grounds," including fountains within a "formal Italian garden" framed by an exedra of Serlian inspiration.[52] Beyond the ornamented foreground was a large barn and rustic houses for the foreman and ranch hands, and then, forming the off-skip, the vast prairie chosen as the site for the planning and ground control of the manned space missions that would blast off from Cape Canaveral. As one local resident described it, the desolate land was dotted with "lots of oil wells and cattle."[53] West's success in drilling ultimately led to the sale of his ranch property to the Humble Oil and Refining Company, which in turn ceded it to Rice University for the purpose of attracting the MSC to this wasteland where "cows and even foxes roamed."[54]

This was not the "virgin land"[55] that lies beyond the frontier of settlement, its providential existence the founding and fatally flawed tenet of the American ideology of territory and space. Clear Lake was much like the rest of the benighted landscape, to be found everywhere, that President Johnson (for whom the MSC was renamed in 1973) and the wildflower-loving Lady Bird Johnson sought to beautify by executive fiat. Martin Byrnes, who had served on the site survey team that selected Clear Lake—for its "outdoors type" climate, access to a seaport, and connection to New Orleans and Huntsville—recalled that when the first official NASA delegation made landfall in Houston, on September 22, 1961, spending the night in a motel, the humid night air was "heavy with the odor of the Houston channel, [and] industries blowing downwind from petroleum and chemical facilities."[56] To draw a lesson from the John Constable landscape that hung in the dining room of Villa West, these seemingly discordant elements, cattle and oil wells and computer laboratories and refineries, were all part of what has been called an "open-air factory," a productive landscape governed by forms of management that the planning of the MSC campus served to make only more explicit.[57] As for the area around the Villa West, with its new address NASA Road 1, the Armand Bayou became a protected nature center in 1974, when the explosive growth of sprawling suburban "space communities"[58] in the Clear Lake area, spurred by the MSC, where 13,000 were employed in 1969, threatened to overwhelm its delicate ecosystem and scenic beauty.

Byrnes was subsequently put in charge of overseeing operations at the new center, or as announced in *Space News Roundup*, "Center Mgr. Marty Byrnes 'Keeps the Place Running.'"[59] In that there might be a lesson to be learned from Michael Crichton's novel *The Andromeda Strain*, published a month before the Apollo 11 liftoff. The novel tinkered with the (unintended) consequences of Project Scoop, a secret Army/NASA project to collect organisms that "might exist in 'near space'" for potential biological weapons of war. The Scoop satellite crashed upon reentry. But failure to contain the spread of the deadly Andromeda microbe stemmed from the endemic faultiness of structural means and measures of containment. "All isolation units break down after a certain time," one of the scientists explains of the underground pathogen laboratory in which the researchers themselves were trapped. "So many seals, so much rubber, of such-and-such a thickness. They'd all break, given time." Yes, as it is proverbially said, reality is stranger than fiction, but it was the literally mundane nature of the threat, the inevitable breakdown of (household) maintenance, that made urgent and eerie the question of who or what was along for the ride of a lifetime. Or as Pogo would have it: 'We have met the enemy and he is us.'

54
Weinraub, "MSC-H, USA: 13,000 Make Moon Project Go," 22.

55
For a contemporary response to Henry Nash Smith's influential *Virgin Land: The American West as Symbol and Myth* (1950), see Bruce Kuklick, "Myth and Symbol in American Studies," *American Quarterly* 24, no. 4 (1972): 435–450.

56
Henry C. Dethloff, *Suddenly Tomorrow Came . . . : A History of the Johnson Space Center* (Lyndon B. Johnson Space Center: NASA, 1993), 41 (NASA SP-4307).

57
Ann Bermingham, *Landscape and Ideology: The English Rustic Tradition, 1740–1860* (Berkeley: University of California Press, 1989), 142.

58
Weinraub, "MSC-H, USA: 13,000 Make Moon Project Go," 22.

59
"Center Mgr. Marty Byrnes 'Keeps the Place Running,'" *Space News Roundup* 2, no. 1. (October 31, 1962): 6.

Cratered Landscapes
SCOTT KIRSCH

When Neil Armstrong took his "small step" to the lunar surface, did the landscape seem familiar to him? Surely not—Armstrong himself described the experience as one of spectacular desolation. Still, in some ways evidently it did, at least by analogy. The Moon could be perceived *as* a landscape, through formal components of perspective, horizon, vanishing point, and terrain, as remarkable photographs and grainy televised backdrops have revealed.[1] It could be understood as "land" and opened to practices of survey, expedition, naming, and representation. It contained rocks of different shapes, sizes, and origins, which could be collected and carried home. To these ends, four years before the July 1969 landing on the Sea of Tranquility, Armstrong and his fellow Apollo astronauts undertook training exercises in preparation for their lunar fieldwork at the US nuclear test site in Nevada, the "continental proving grounds" located 65 miles northwest of Las Vegas, which was taken as a reasonable simulacrum of the Moon for geological purposes. The astronauts spent three days of field training at the site, learning about what kinds of rocks to look for and how to collect them during the landing, in which they would be limited to packing away 50 pounds of lunar rock samples. Later, the program in Nevada was expanded to more fully incorporate the test site's natural and artificial terrain. From 1970 to1972, NASA based seven training sessions at the 13,500-square-mile test site facility, featuring the nuclear-blasted Sedan, Schooner, and Danny Boy craters that were the products—and remains—of "nuclear excavation" experiments under Project Plowshare, the Atomic Energy Commission's program for developing "peaceful nuclear explosives," where astronauts trained for the emerging practice of lunar survey by collecting rocks and scrambling over craters, on foot and in new lunar rover vehicles.[2]

Figure 1.
The Apollo 17 crew and lunar rover at Shorty Crater.
Courtesy of NASA.

1
Michael Light, *Full Moon* (London: Jonathan Cape, 1999). See Denis Cosgrove, "Cultural Geographies in Practice: Anti-Ecumene," *Ecumene* 8 (2001): 108–111, 108, 111. The 32,000 handheld and automatic photographs produced under the Apollo program between 1968 and 1972 constitute a visual record of the program that is, for Cosgrove, "complete, defined, and strangely disturbing," the "first true landscapes of an other world."

2
Henry Brean, "Nevada Test Site Gave Astronaut Trainees Taste of Lunar Landscape," *Las Vegas Review-Journal*, July 19, 2009, https://www.reviewjournal.com/news/nevada-test-site-gave-astronaut-trainees-taste-of-lunar-landscape/; National Nuclear Security Administration, "Apollo Astronauts Train at the Nevada Test Site," *Nevada National Security Site* (newsletter), August 2013, DOE/NV-772-REV 2, US Department of Energy.

Whatever the similarities in terrain, the astronauts, not surprisingly, found the rovers to function quite differently on the Moon than in Nevada, operating under conditions of one-sixth the gravity. The lunar landscape differed markedly as well. Geographer Denis Cosgrove describes the singular Apollo photographs: "In the absence of atmosphere, light and shadow etch across the Moon's monochrome surface landscapes of such crystal clarity and incised intensity that color itself becomes the symbol of a softer, gentler other" (see Figure 1).[3] But while objects such as cables and machinery, along with the vaporous astronauts in their space suits, reflect a curious warmth in the photographs, the landscape, reduced to bare elements of light and form, with its undulating, monochrome topography giving way always to close horizons (reflecting the lunar curvature), is profoundly disorienting in terms of distances, direction, elevation, and scale. More than landscape, for Cosgrove, the surface resembles magnified human skin.[4] Given these differences, it is fair to wonder whether other—less radioactive—places might have been of equal utility in replicating the lunar landscape for training purposes, unless the inhospitable (while remaining within an hour's drive of Las Vegas) was in a sense what program planners were after. While additional settings would also be incorporated into NASA's training program, 11 of 12 Apollo astronauts to leave their footprints on the Moon had participated in the Nevada training exercises, in which the militarized high desert nuclear blasting zone had served, for a few days at a time, as proxy for the lunar surface.

This essay is about heaven on Earth, but only the barest and most modest heavens of the cratered landscape. It explores the extraterrestrial, but only as it has been imagined, constructed, and "realized" as a laboratory and training ground for extraterrestrial futures. Of course, whether any place within the envelope of Earth's atmosphere is actually more "extraterrestrial" than another is a different question, but it is hard to deny the appeal of desert environments, in their geophysical qualities as well as cultural associations, as places with special access to the heavens. For early Christian ascetics, the desert was a site of abstinence, fasting, and prayer, constituting "the external landscape for an inner spiritual journey."[5] Yet if the perceived insignificance of human life against the vastness of desert spaces, expanded (especially with urbanization) by the relatively heightened visibility of the night sky, provided a template for sublime understandings of God and nature, in modern contexts the association of deserts with a cosmological sense of place has also been outward looking and technological. Desert mountains, with clear skies and minimal light pollution, emerged as key sites for astronomical observatories, even as astronomy itself began to shift from a field-based science of observation into an "image processing laboratory science."[6] For others, the arid lands offered morphological models against which more speculative "geographies of Mars" could be validated, or so it was argued.[7] While by no means necessary or inevitable, in other words, the affinities between arid lands and "outer space" have been practical, historical, and artifactual; and deserts have remained, along with other real and imagined settings, among the key sites where the extraterrestrial has been socially, culturally, and geographically produced. As geographer Robert Kopack has shown for the ongoing reproduction of rocket "fall zones," strewn with engine parts and toxic heptyl, in central Kazakhstan around the Baikonur Cosmodrome, the world's busiest space complex (operated by the Russian space program), the association of arid lands with the extraterrestrial is by no means a thing of the past.[8] This apparent paradox—the terrestrial production of the extraterrestrial—offers a standpoint from which to reengage with the otherworldly figure of the cratered landscape, the site of sudden, explosive impact, and a physical form that is in fact shared among countless planetary and interstellar bodies.

Prior to the astronauts' arrival, the Nevada Test Site had been the setting for more than 100 atmospheric and near-surface nuclear explosive tests between 1951 and 1963, when compliance with

3
Cosgrove, "Anti-Ecumene," 110.

4
Ibid., 109. For a rethinking of both landscape and the human body as objects of gendered vision, see Catherine Nash, "Reclaiming Vision: Looking at Landscape and the Body," *Gender, Place and Culture* 3 (1996): 149–170.

5
Roslynn D. Haynes, *Desert: Nature and Culture* (London: Reaktion Books, 2013), 171.

6
Karin Knorr-Cetina, "The Couch, the Cathedral, and the Laboratory: On the Relationship between the Experiment and Laboratory in Science," in *Science as Practice and Culture*, ed. A. Pickering (Chicago: University of Chicago Press, 1992), 113–138.

7
K. Maria D. Lane, *Geographies of Mars: Seeing and Knowing the Red Planet* (Chicago: University of Chicago Press, 2011).

8
Robert A. Kopack, "Rocket Wastelands in Kazakhstan: Scientific Authoritarianism and the Baikonur Cosmodrome," *Annals of the American Association of Geographers* 109 (2019): 556–567; and for an ethnography of space's earthly infrastructures from a different latitudinal and postcolonial setting, see Peter Redfield, *Space in the Tropics: From Convicts to Rockets in French Guiana* (Berkeley: University of California Press, 2000).

the Limited Test Ban Treaty pushed testing underground. Larger than nine US states, the territory was carved out of a World War II–era air bombing and gunnery training range, and the installation remains surrounded on three sides by what is now Nellis Air Force Range (which includes the famed Area 51, whatever its contents). Among the widespread spaces made virtually uninhabitable for humans by military firing ranges, test sites, factories, arsenals, uranium mining, and other military-industrial metabolisms, the Nevada Test Site is located on contested federally managed lands which are claimed under treaty rights by the Western Shoshone people.[9] Military and Atomic Energy Commission (AEC) planners had been drawn to the desert by many of the same qualities that attracted astronomers, including aridity and the promise of clear flying and atomic blasting days, as well as the (relatively) sparse human population and agricultural activities. Early estimates of radioactive hazards associated with this site selection, the AEC's ability to control them downwind, and the nature of the risks posed by fallout all proved seriously inadequate, however.[10] In this sense, to call the Nevada Test Site a laboratory, in conventional terms of a dedicated and controlled experimental setting wherein knowledge of the material world can be constructed, free of "external" influence, might seem a stretch. But if we take as a laboratory, interpreted more broadly, an "enhanced environment" for the production of new scientific-technical objects and knowledges, we gain a richer—and more historically accurate—sense of the generative work of laboratories in the world and a practical view of working laboratories that also encompasses scientific and medical manufacturing, processing, testing, and training, and the scaling up of methods worked out at the laboratory bench to the site of the factory, test site, and countless "paper studies."[11] We also become attuned to the diffusion of laboratory practices—not only into "the field" (i.e., as an extension of laboratory methods into the field-based environmental sciences)[12] but, more promiscuously, among a hybrid suite of military, scientific, geopolitical, land management, engineering, public safety, and public information discourses and material practices through which, in Nevada (as in Bikini, Enewetak, and Semipalatinsk), nuclear explosives could be set off as if it *were* a laboratory, albeit one constructed to satisfy the logics and demands of a technologically dynamic nuclear arms race. In addition to atmospheric explosions set off in towers or by airdrop, the rampant experimentalism of the early Cold War US nuclear technocracy was also reflected in "blast effects" experiments conducted at the Nevada Test Site in coordination with test explosions, featuring artificial "doom towns" that included faux groceries, street signs, electrical systems, and mannequin families arranged ghoulishly at leisure in model suburban "homes," set at varied distances from ground zero, and in military training exercises involving soldiers awaiting the blast in trenches and rushing over ground zero shortly after the explosion, their individual radiation exposures recorded with film badges.

While the 1963 Limited Test Ban Treaty (among the USA, UK, and USSR) responded to the international political and scientific uproar over radiation fallout from atmospheric testing, the shift to a fully underground regime also permitted the acceleration of nuclear testing in Nevada and the diffusion of additional social and environmental costs across the geographical networks of nuclear weapons production.[13] Hence, when the Apollo astronauts visited the test site during the 1960s and 1970s, its functions as a nuclear explosives field laboratory were by no means mothballed. A full-time workforce of perhaps 10,000 government workers and subcontractors would have been engaged in tunneling beneath the desert floor (and sometimes into the sides of mountains) and constructing shafts for the placement of explosives, laying the miles of pipes, cables, and wiring that constituted the site's subsurface sensory infrastructure, and keeping the cafeteria open at the on-site "town" of Mercury, Nevada. Commonly, the underground blasts produced "subsidence craters" on the surface above ground zero, and it is these numerous, unstable

9
Valerie L. Kuletz, *The Tainted Desert: Environmental and Social Ruin in the American West* (New York: Routledge, 1998); see also David G. Havlick, *Bombs Away: Militarization, Conservation, and Ecological Restoration* (Chicago: University of Chicago Press, 2018).

10
See Scott Kirsch, *Proving Grounds: Project Plowshare and the Unrealized Dream of Nuclear Earthmoving* (New Brunswick: Rutgers University Press, 2005), 27–36.

11
Knorr-Cetina, "The Couch, the Cathedral, and the Laboratory"; Scott Kirsch, "Laboratory/Observatory" in *The Sage Handbook of Geographical Knowledge*, ed. J. Agnew and D. Livingstone (Thousand Oaks, CA: Sage Publications, 2011), 76–87.

12
Cf. Robert E. Kohler, *Landscapes and Labscapes: Exploring the Lab-Field Border in Biology* (Chicago: University of Chicago Press, 2002).

13
Scott Kirsch, "Watching the Bombs Go Off: Photography, Nuclear Landscapes, and Spectator Democracy," *Antipode* 29 (1997): 227–255.

radioactive sinkholes, the unintended consequences of more than 800 underground nuclear tests carried out at the site before the 1992 moratorium (and 1996 Comprehensive Nuclear-Test-Ban Treaty), that are most responsible for the landscape's quasi-lunar appearance, especially when viewed from above (see Figure 2), though they were not deemed safe, as the Plowshare craters had been, for lunar simulation.

Figure 2.
Nevada National Security Site,
with Sedan Crater in the foreground.
Courtesy of NNSA
[National Nuclear Security Administration].

How did the *human* figure in these cratered landscapes? For Cosgrove, in reflecting on the visual record of the Apollo astronauts padding over the talcy lunar surface in the bulky space suits that made the environment habitable for them, "we share the astronaut's own disorientation. No Vitruvian grandeur or dignity is apparent here. Despite their every second being controlled, directed and costed (at over $3300 each second) from Earth, the men on the Moon seem displaced, directionless, aimless. . . . In these grey landscapes the humans appear as melancholic, almost tragic figures, icons of loneliness rather than triumphant bearers of exploratory achievement."[14] We do not have a record of the astronauts' experience trekking any nuclear-excavated craters in Nevada, but we do have that of Lloyd Marshall, an Australian journalist who visited the test site in 1966 to descend Sedan Crater—the signature product of the Plowshare program, a 1,200-foot-wide, 320-foot-deep crater produced by a 104-kiloton 1962 nuclear excavation experiment. While the dimensions of the crater had been close to project scientists' predictions, fallout from the earthmoving blast, which by definition broke the earth's surface and vented radioactivity, had been dramatically underpredicted, resulting in five times more radioactivity than anticipated in the local fallout pattern and a dust cloud, 50 percent larger than predicted, that could be tracked all the way to the Atlantic Ocean.[15] According to Marshall's reporting, he and AEC public information officer Dave Miller were just the third and fourth people to make this expedition down Sedan Crater, following the earlier effort of two unnamed astronauts. Marshall's purpose in making the expedition was seemingly quite different, however, reflecting a campaign both to minimize the perception of risk from radioactive fallout and to promote a potential nuclear-blasted harbor project in western Australia. Fitted with a film badge to measure external radiation exposure and sporting what looks to be an Australian army beret, Marshall would back down the 40- to 45-degree slope of the crater with Miller, using a thick rope attached above them to steady the descent, eat lunch at the bottom, then haul themselves back up to the top. As Marshall described for readers of the Australian *Weekend News*, "I would see some of the scenes of the Plowshare experiments. I was determined to debunk once and for all the nonsense about 'dirty bombs'. I would go right into the very nuclear-blasted craters which had dropped down into the earth. I would eat there, drink there, get myself covered with dust, and show how the one-time horror of fall-out has been combated and defeated."[16] While Marshall assigns a dubious epistemological weight to his journey as a test of radiation safety and at times parrots or even exceeds the claims of questionable AEC talking points, his account, which is framed as both political argument and laboratory procedural, stands as a compelling record of bodily encounter with Sedan Crater.

Relating the experience descending from the lip of Sedan Crater, Marshall emphasizes the corporeal dimensions of the excursion: "As you slide down, your ankles sink deep into the dust, which wells up around your legs, your shoes are full of it, it seeps through your socks until your shoes feel too full of feet. You can feel it rasping against your skin. You breathe it. Chew it. It's all over you."[17] Photographs of astronauts in Nevada appear to show greater precaution with radioactivity hazards, including pant legs taped above boots. It is unlikely the Apollo astronauts had a picnic at the bottom of Sedan Crater, but for Marshall, the picnic was the

14 Cosgrove, "Anti-Ecumene," 109.

15 Kirsch, *Proving Grounds*, 119–134.

16 Lloyd Marshall, "Operation Plowshare: The Safe A-Bomb," *Weekend Magazine*, supplement of *Weekend News* (West Australian Newspapers Ltd.), April 30, 1966, 16–20, 18.

17 Ibid., 19–20.

point. “Between my teeth I have clamped a paper bag carrying my lunch,” he noted, having evidently forgotten a backpack (or perhaps having been told to clench his teeth to avoid dust intake). “Dave is carrying his, and I’ve got two cans of beer in an airline bag hanging round my neck.” Sliding most of the way down in the fine desert alluvium, the trip to the bottom of the crater is a quick one, even fun, and completed in just five minutes. Marshall is reassured by the presence of both tumbleweeds and beetles in the crater, adding smugly that both life forms had “not heard the stories about the ‘dirty bomb’.” The reporter had “supervised the making of [his lunch] at a Las Vegas drugstore. It is a club sandwich of toast, roast beef, tomato, lettuce and coleslaw,” to go with an orange to share with Miller, and on reaching the bottom he reports that the two “sit down . . . smothered with dust to enjoy our lunch.” His companion, whose voice otherwise surfaces only indirectly in the story, is decidedly less upbeat: “Dave commented: Well, if we never get out of here, at least our folks will know we are the first people to have walked down the side of a nuclear-blasted crater, sat in the dirt at the bottom, and solemnly had lunch.”

Marshall and Miller’s trip down Sedan Crater definitely seems a lot sadder than what the two astronauts likely experienced, whatever sense of desolation awaited them on the Moon. Despite their apparent differences, though, these journeys into the inhospitable environments of Nevada and the Moon had not been entirely dissimilar, for both cratered landscapes were “anti-ecumenes,” as Cosgrove understood the impoverished place of the human in the Apollo photographs, in which mere exposure constituted, potentially, an existential threat. Positioned as training grounds for extraterrestrial futures, the cratered landscapes of the Nevada nuclear test site were already, in a sense, the real thing. But not on this day. Scaling back up the crater was, as expected, more challenging for Marshall and Miller, requiring 53 minutes and four rest stops, but the pair reached the lip of the crater triumphant, and . . . after a reading of their film badges, “uncontaminated—cleanskins.”[18] Excelsior!

18
Ibid., 20.

Fake Earths
NEYRAN TURAN

Earthlike

In 2018, an article in the Chinese state newspaper *People's Daily* announced plans for a private aerospace institute in Chengdu to launch a "fake moon" into outer space in 2020.[1] Designed as an artificial satellite, this faux moon is proposed to orbit at near the same height as the International Space Station while emitting light eight times that of the real moon in order to replace a reliance on streetlights for the city. As a techno-optimistic geoengineering proposal situated between the preposterous and the fantastical, the fake moon prompts many questions regarding its feasibility, relevance, and ethics. What is most striking, however, is the question of the artificial satellite's appearance, and how it will replicate the moon itself. What does a fake moon's form, for that matter, tell about ourselves and our place on earth? Considering recent scholarship that calls for an archeological study of habitat in outer space, what would a fake moon used for city lighting and later destined to be space junk convey to future outer space archaeologies?[2] If the replicas, facsimiles, and imposters of fake cities—such as Potemkin villages, vehicle testing areas, military training sites, and so on, all of which imitate particular settings—always convey something about specific cultural and political constructions or imaginaries, what kind of planetary imaginations would a fake moon stand for?

Attentive analysts and scholars of copies would have a rather simple answer to this question, that "copying makes us what we are . . . and make[s] the known world our own."[3] In other words, to copy, as a way of knowing and making sense, tells us more about ourselves and our sense of belonging in the world than anything else.

1
"Chendgu to Launch 'Artificial Moon' in 2020," *People's Daily Online*, October 16, 2018, http://en.people.cn/n3/2018/1016/c90000-9508748.html. Also see "Fake Moon: Could China Really Light Up the Night Sky?," *BBC News*, October 20, 2018, https://www.bbc.com/news/world-asia-china-45910479.

2
For archeological questions in relation to outer space, see Alice Gorman, "The Cultural Landscape of Interplanetary Space," *Journal of Social Archeology* 5, no. 1 (2005): 85–107.

3
Hillel Schwartz, *The Culture of the Copy: Striking Likenesses, Unreasonable Facsimiles* (New York: Zone Books, 1996), 211.

And, in the case of the fake moon, the copy tells us a lot about specific imaginaries of place-making in relation to Earth itself. First, a fake planetary resemblance talks to the anthropocentric earth-mastering tendencies of geoengineering and the reception of mimicry as a humanist (and thus a positive) attribute. Second, and more broadly, a replica within outer space hints at the inevitable juxtaposition of the planetary and the familiar. For that, Lisa Messeri provides an excellent theoretical framework, especially in relation to the place-making practices within planetary science, by pointing to the dilemma of conceptualizing outer *space* as an outer *place* instead. For Messeri, in the extraterrestrial place-making practices of scientists and their planetary imagination—as in the case of the Mars Desert Research Station in Utah or in the imagining and visualizing of exoplanets—resemblance to Earth not only plays an important role in altering "the geographically alien into the familiar," but also "suggest[s] an intimacy that can scale down the cosmos to the level of human experience."[4] Messeri writes, "Planets are both quotidian and scientific. . . . In connecting the mundane and the extraordinary, extraterrestrial place-making grounds knowledge of other planets in familiar contexts. Scientific practices of place-making turn the infinite geography of the cosmos into a theater dotted with potentially meaningful places that are stages for imaginations and aspirations."[5]

Considered from an architectural perspective, Messeri's refreshing provocations contain the potential for alternative planetary imaginations beyond science fiction and the fantastical. Recent developments in the NewSpace industries (a neologism for a group of private enterprises that aims to commercialize outer space through services such as space launches, energy harnessing, space tourism and real estate, moon settlement, asteroid mining, and even funeral services) have relied on a mix of techno-optimist metaphors, mythologies of the American frontier, and European colonialism. Messeri's theoretical framework, however, provides an alternative to limiting the question of the cosmos for architecture to techno-optimist visualizations of earthlike urbanisms (or their satirical versions) in outer space.[6] Consider, for instance, proposals such as those of renowned physicist and space activist Gerard Kitchen O'Neill in the 1970s to colonize space with settlements that would replicate "archetypical" parts of Earth.[7] In contrast, Messeri introduces a different planetary imagination that considers a collapse of the extreme and the familiar by understanding the planetary as it is negotiated, imagined, and replicated in relation to the real sites of research stations on Earth.[8] In this way, outer space becomes both a limit and a horizon for understanding—and potentially demystifying—the very norms and assumptions of life on Earth.

4
Lisa Messeri, *Placing Outer Space: An Earthly Ethnography of Other Worlds* (Durham, NC: Duke University Press, 2016), 2–3.

5
Ibid.

6
For an excellent critical essay on recent developments within the NewSpace industries, see David Valentine, "Exit Strategy: Profit, Cosmology, and the Future of Humans in Space," *Anthropological Quarterly* 85, no. 4 (Fall 2012): 1045–1068.

7
For more on the work of O'Neill and discussions of outer space colonies, see De Witt Douglas Kilgore, *Astrofuturism: Science, Race, and Visions of Utopia in Space* (Philadelphia: University of Pennsylvania Press, 2003).

8
For more on the idea of the extreme in relation to outer space discussions, see David Valentine, Valerie Olson, and Debbora Battaglia, "Extreme: Limits and Horizons in the Once and Future Cosmos," *Anthropological Quarterly* 85, no. 4 (Fall 2012): 1007–1022. For the role of the extraterrestrial in the Anthropocene, see Lisa Messeri and Valerie Olson, "Beyond the Anthropocene: Un-Earthing an Epoch," *Environment and Society: Advances in Research* 6, no. 1 (2015): 28–47.

As also argued by anthropologist Stefan Helmreich, scientific investigations of the extreme and the extraterrestrial always come "with an attitude toward the terrestrial." This is by no means to suggest a human-centric perspective to outer space. On the contrary, Helmreich introduces the idea of an "extraterrestrial relativism," a kind of nonhuman or posthuman relativism that might prompt a more expansive repositioning of life and care on Earth.[9] While Helmreich arrives at this provocation through his case study of "alien microbes" in the deep oceans and their capacity to enliven to the idea of life on other planets in the solar system, he proposes to look at extreme and extraterrestrial sites through their potential to replicate the multispecies sensibility of Earth. Similar to the collapse of the planetary and the familiar that Messeri points to in the spatial resemblance between landscapes in Utah and on Mars, for instance, the species resemblance of deep ocean and outer space collapses notions of the extraterrestrial and the terrestrial. In the context of anthropogenic discussions, these overlaps are useful in the way they destabilize the humanist ideals of "Man" as a universalizing category and the human itself as a neutral classification, as both concepts create species hierarchy and exceptionalism while negating political questions of power, privilege, and violence. This sensibility toward the more-than-human is arguably a form of "queering" by various scholars due to its potential for "undoing normal categories," as Donna Haraway puts it, and the "unhinging of certainties and the systemic disturbing of the familiar . . . [with] uncanny—disillusioning, demystifying—effects" as elaborated by others.[10] How, then, do we imagine the more-than-human and the extraterrestrial in the context of climate change while demystifying various assumptions about the planetary and the quotidian?

Theater as a Mundane Instrument

Consider Bruno Latour's phrase "natures-cultures" referring to the relations between humans and nonhuman entities. Latour suggests that we come to know the world collectively and individually as the result of relationships forged between humans and the animate and inanimate qualities of the environment.[11] These entities range from "mundane artifacts" (instruments such as doors, door locks, speed bumps), "immutable mobiles" (representations or inscriptions, such as photographs, maps, drawings, models of buildings and cities, genetic codes, legal reports, double-entry bookkeeping, statistics, and bureaucratic paperwork), and other species, such as microbes.[12] Emphasizing

9
Stefan Helmreich, "Extraterrestrial Relativism," *Anthropological Quarterly* 85, no. 4 (Fall 2012): 1125–1139.

10
Donna J. Haraway, "Companion Species, Mis-recognition, and Queer Worlding," in *Queering the Non/Human*, ed. Noreen Giffney and Myra J. Hird (Hampshire: Ashgate Publishing, 2008), xxiv. The second quotation is from Giffney and Hird, introduction to *Queering the Non/Human*, 4. Also see Mel Y. Chen, *Animacies: Biopolitics, Racial Mattering, and Queer Affect* (Durham, NC: Duke University Press, 2012).

11
For the idea of natures-cultures, see Bruno Latour, *We Have Never Been Modern*, trans. C. Porter (Cambridge, MA: Harvard University Press, 1993). A related concept, "naturecultures," was developed by Donna Haraway to describe feminist and anti-racist scholarship within technoscience and everyday life. See Haraway, *The Companion Species Manifesto: Dogs, People, and Significant Others* (Chicago: Prickly Paradigm Press, 2003).

12
For more on "mundane artifacts," see Bruno Latour, "Where Are the Missing Masses?: The Sociology of a Few Mundane Artifacts," in *Shaping Technology / Building Society: Studies in Sociotechnical Change*, ed. Wiebe E. Bijker and John Law (Cambridge, MA: MIT Press, 1992), 225–258. For more on "immutable mobiles," see Latour, "Visualisation and Cognition: Thinking with Eyes and Hands," *Knowledge and Society* 6 (1986): 1–40. For more on microbes, see Latour, *The Pasteurization of France*, trans. A. Sheridan and J. Law (Cambridge, MA: Harvard University Press, 1993).

the power of mundane material practices along with their craftwork of representation, Latour writes, "I was struck, in a study of a biology laboratory, by the way in which many aspects of laboratory practice could be ordered by looking not at the scientists' brains, . . . at the cognitive structures . . . nor at the paradigms . . . , but at the transformation of rats and chemicals into paper."[13]

For some, Latour's network-based approach risks being too flattening, "too distributive, [and] too promiscuous in attributing cause and agency, . . . making all actions and agents seem equally empowered, or disempowered, and therefore equally responsible, or irresponsible, for the networks within which they function."[14] These criticisms point to the lack of emphasis in Latour's theories in relation to the politics of cultural imagination, power relations, and inequality embedded in these mundane measures of the familiar and the quotidian. However, if we consider the epistemology of concepts such as facts, objectivity, data, and efficiency as already constructed units of knowledge themselves—according to which paperwork, doors, and microbes are culturally imagined—we can think of Latour's emphasis on the quotidian practices and their representational forms as effective instruments in themselves, which can reveal, unhinge, and reconstitute those larger questions of imagination and power politics. Writing about one such epistemological unit, the history of the modern fact, for instance, historian Mary Poovey tackles this dilemma head-on through an emphasis on the role of representation:

> [A] history of the modern fact begins to reveal the organizational principles inherent in the kinds of knowledge by which subjects of the modern world manage our relationships with each other and with society. If one assumes, as I do, that modes of representation inform what we can know, and if one also assumes, as I do, that modes of representation embody or articulate available ways of organizing and making sense of the world, then to understand the potential and limitations of what we know, we need tools to investigate the conditions that make knowledge possible.[15]

If the process of knowledge production both affects and is affected by our everyday practices and their modes of representation, can we position the theatrical stage as one such representational mode and artifact of knowing? In its capacity to relate stories to scenography and imagination, theater architecture, in the words of historian William Alexander McClung, "ultimately affirms the world of the set as reality, or the theatre as the world."[16] On the one hand, the set can be thought of in representational terms, in its capacity to trigger relations between imagining and knowing, or as a three-dimensional replica of a setting that exists elsewhere or has never existed. On the other hand, the set

13
Bruno Latour, "Visualisation and Cognition," 3–4.

14
Sheila Jasanoff, "Future Imperfect: Science, Technology, and the Imaginations of Modernity," in *Dreamscapes of Modernity: Sociotechnical Imaginaries and the Fabrication of Power*, ed. Jasanoff and S. Kim (Chicago: University of Chicago Press, 2015), 16–17.

15
Mary Poovey, *A History of the Modern Fact: Problems of Knowledge in the Sciences of Wealth and Society* (Chicago: University of Chicago Press, 1998), xv.

16
William Alexander McClung, "A Place for a Time: The Architecture of Festivals and Theaters," in *Architecture and Its Image: Four Centuries of Architectural Representation*, ed. E. Blau and Kaufman (Montreal: Canadian Centre for Architecture, distributed by MIT Press, 1989), 86–108.

is a live scene itself, occurring between actors and an audience, thus creating a dilemma between performance and life.

Considered this way, one can think of interesting conceptual links between a theater set and a setting, such as the extraterrestrial test sites of the Mars Desert Research Station in Utah. Since the set (a Martian landscape perhaps) and the setting (Utah) are already collapsed onto one another in these landscapes, their productive confusion is at once between the original and the fake. Perhaps more important, this collapse occurs between acts of (quotidian) knowing and (planetary) imagining, an act between performance and life.

A Planetary Theater Play

Fake Earths: A Planetary Theater Play (2018) deploys the theater set as a quotidian instrument to talk about the posthuman and the extraterrestrial. Through a series of digitally rendered scenes, the project portrays a theater play that is taking place in a post-anthropocenic era, in which the earthlike replica becomes a dominant practice on and beyond Earth for depicting various forms of resource extraction, waste, and animal extinction in the form of fake mountains, fake planets, or fake cities. The theater play is about five specific sites on Earth, whose purpose and imagery are decoupled because of the various activities that they contain.

The first scene of the play takes place at the Potemkin Village, an infamous data center and e-waste dump site in Ghana. The site was designed to read as a city from above for a particular machine-oriented vision, yet its oblique reading is fake as it mischievously hides its architectural content. It looks like a city in oblique view from above, but it is in reality a waste dump (Figure 1). Fake aerial machine vision is also the theme of the second scene of the play, which takes place in the planning room of the geoengineers and designers for the Pacific Ocean Trash Mountains, a series of fake mountains that contain large-scale artificial interiors of Plasticarrium (preserved plastic trash specimens and data collection) and various other collections of the *plastisphere*: the plastic-related Fungarium (fungi collection), Herbarium (plant collection), and Bacterium (bacteria collection) (Figure 2).[17]

The scene depicts the work space where technical aspects and conceptual references relate to the construction of large-scale artifacts. The mountain studies of geographer Alexander von Humboldt and architect Eugène Emmanuel Viollet-le-Duc are negotiated and enacted through various design drawings, models, and other related everyday objects. These drawings and models of fake mountains are scattered around the work space depicted in the scene. The scene not only disassembles and disarranges discrete parts of the pictorial content of the mountains but also reassembles them as

17
Plastisphere is a neologism that refers to the microscopic ecosystem that has evolved to reside within marine plastics. See Erik R. Zettler, Tracy Mincer, and Linda Amaral-Zettler, “Life in the ‘Plastisphere’: Microbial Communities on Plastic Marine Debris,” *Environmental Science and Technology* 47, no. 13 (2013): 7137–46.

the precious miscellanies of the workplace. It decomposes the scenographic image of each setting through various props but reassembles them through the stage set. The idea of recomposition through disassembly is expanded in the project where each scene is shown either as a different type of theater—ranging from black box, outdoor stage, opera house, arena, to studio theater—or shown from different vantage points, such as the backstage area and the stage storage. In this way, the drawings of *Fake Earths* recompose the assembly of each scene in distinct ways.

The third scene of the play stages one of the asteroid mining test sites in Wyoming and is staged as an outdoor play (Figure 3). The outdoor setting and the clearing site for asteroid mining in this scene have a close resemblance to the clearings that were made shortly after the formation of European colonial settlements in the Americas and the East Indies, and particularly to the infamous image of a clearing in Savannah, Georgia, in 1734 as a mysterious wilderness hinterland.[18] In addition, since the clearing test site depicted in the scene also closely resembles the outdoor setting itself, this collapse of the setting and the set provokes necessary conflations between the familiar stories on Earth and the extraterrestrial.

This juxtaposition of the set and the setting takes another form in the fourth scene (Figure 4). This scene depicts the Spoil Tips Grand Tour, which was an important theme park site in Rome that was constructed by gathering the most celebrated spoil tips from different parts of Earth. (Spoil tips are piles of accumulated overburden or waste rock from mining.) Since the "angle of repose," the slope at which the loose material piles at the spoil tip, is different for different kinds of waste material, the spoil tips created spectacular mountain ranges. Similar to the 19th-century natural history encyclopedias such as Simeon Shaw's *Nature Displayed in the Heavens and on the Earth* (1823), in which celebrated mountains of the world were collected together to create an imaginary geologic landscape, the Spoil Tips Grand Tour was a geologic wonder and one of the most important pastoral landscapes of its time. It was also one of the earthlike "ideal sites" to be replicated in new extraterrestrial colonies as an outer space tourist destination. The fourth scene depicts the planning of that outpost process; thus, the third and fourth scenes could be considered in relation to one another. While the Asteroid Mining Test Site of the third scene is an actual site on Earth that fakes the extraterrestrial landscape of the asteroid, the Spoil Tips Grand Tour is a site on Earth waiting to be faked in outer space.

The final scene of the play takes place in the Wonder Zoo, which contains a checkerboard megastructure of simulated environments for the endangered species on Earth (Figure 5). Similar to the Spoil Tips Grand Tour of the fourth scene, the Wonder Zoo is a prototype to be replicated by humans in extraterrestrial colonies. The scene shows a film adaptation of the play, which is depicted in the studio set (Figure 6).

The main ambition of *Fake Earths* is to provoke an environmental imagination that sees the categories of the quotidian and the planetary in conversation with one another through the restaging of the posthuman and the extraterrestrial at the theater set. By revealing the politics of the making of the set itself (set presented in various types of theater as well as in construction, in storage, or in backstage areas, etc.), the correlation between the representational and the material is problematized or slowed down. In this way, the activities taking place both inside and around the stage destabilize the idealistic conception of the terrestrial and its restaging as a three-dimensional image. In that way, both the idea of the terrestrial and the image are deemed to be vulnerable.

For some, climate change is a cultural and political problem precisely because it is devoid of a deeper visual discourse.[19] There are valid reasons for this assessment. For one, despite the obvious anthropomorphism that exists in the term "Anthropocene," the expanded spatial and temporal scales of geology are beyond human comprehension. The impenetrability of the nonhuman large-scale nature of climate change is also aggravated by the abstractness and political opacity of scientific data as represented in statistics, simulations, and the infographics of data mapping. It is clear, then, that grasping climate change is complicated by the predicament of making visible its invisibilities. At this juncture, considering architecture's inherent capacity to illustrate narratives and provide spatial consciousness, it is tempting to think about the discipline's contribution to this discussion with a discourse on the problem of visualization. However, for architecture, the planetary imagination should not simply mean how to best visualize the planet. Instead of turning architecture's agency to a visualization project for a planet damaged by climate change, a much broader question might be at stake: How does one talk about, communicate, and practice an architectural aesthetics of planetary imagination? Posing the question this way would not only enable a more ambitious discourse that can provoke original relationships between the politics of content and the politics of appearance, but also it would allow us to build more meaningful interactions between what is considered to be the unhomely and the familiar.

Figure 1 The Potemkin Village scene on stage.

ANDES
141°W
142°W
143°W
144°W
39°N
38°N
37°N
150°W

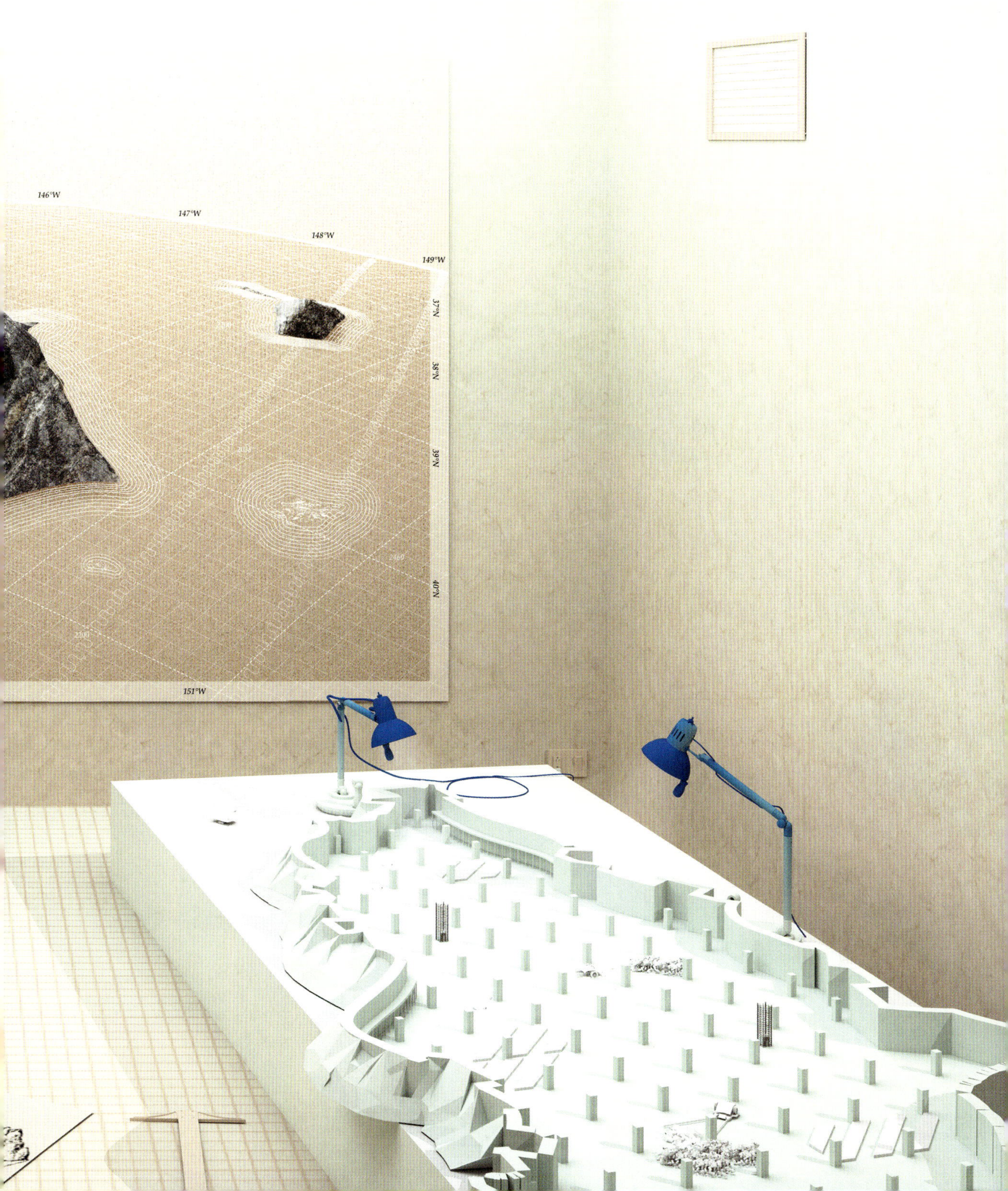
146°W
147°W
148°W
149°W
37°N
38°N
39°N
40°N
151°W

Figure 3 The Asteroid Mining Test Site scene as an outdoor theater play.

Bota-yama
Iizuka City
Japan
slag heap
141 meters
Monte Kali
Heringen
Germany
sodium chloride
250 meters
11/19
Loos-en-
Gohelle
slag heap
186 meters

Figure 4 Backstage area of the Spoil Tips Grand Tour scene at the opera house

Figure 5 The Wonder Zoo scene at the studio set.

Figure 6 *Fake Earths* stage storage.

A Long Time Ago in a City Far, Far Away
NICHOLAS DE MONCHAUX

The Mojave Desert is a frequent stand-in for distant planets and galaxies. And it was there that Reyner Banham observed, "In a landscape where nothing officially exists . . . absolutely anything becomes thinkable, and may consequently happen."[1] Here, too, is the root of the idea of capital-s Space itself, first coined by Milton as the "Space between worlds" occupied by an imagined God and the angels, including Lucifer before his demise.[2] When you add emptiness' role as vessel for imagination to space's literal definition—for a diversity of technical fields, the altitude above which we need technology to survive—we encounter the pitch-dark surface onto which we perennially project our hopes and fears for our technological future.

Yet if space is so often where we place our dreams, it turns out to be equally important to consider precisely how those dreams are built and projected there. At a time when the line between simulation and reality, and indeed between information and amusement, has become irretrievably obscured, tracing this history, and in particular its trajectory through the intersection of architecture, territory, and outer space, may not itself be just entertaining, but essential.

Pneumatic Reality

These ideas were enmeshed from the first simulations above Earth. In 1930, Edwin Albert Link patented the first airplane simulator, built with his own hands using parts and expertise from his family's pipe-organ business in Binghamton, New York. But his uncertainty as to its actual use was unmistakable. "An efficient aeronautical training aid—a novel, profitable amusement device," the patent hedged.[3] An open-bodied model aircraft, complete with wings and a stubby tail, mounted on a wheezing, pneumatic podium, the first Link simulator was marketed equally to both amusement parks and flight schools. It sold poorly to each.[4]

In 1934, Franklin D. Roosevelt's second New Deal budget stripped the nation's nascent air carriers of their lucrative monopoly on airmail and enlisted the Army Air Forces instead. Within a few months, more than a dozen military pilots were dead. To save money during the lean interwar years, it transpired, flight training had been limited to daylight flights during good weather. Here Link spotted an opportunity. While his simulator had difficulty conveying the complex experience of real flight, it could be tuned to convey a realistic experience of flight through the narrow bandwidth of the airplane's cockpit instruments. The Link trainer shrunk the wings and tail on

1
P. Reyner Banham, *Scenes in America Deserta* (Salt Lake City, UT: Gibbs M. Smith, 1982), 44.

2
See John Milton, *Paradise Lost*, Book I, line 650, Book II, lines 1052 and 1045.

3
US Patent US1825462A.

4
J. M. Rolfe and K. J. Staples, *Flight Simulation* (Cambridge: Cambridge University Press, 1986), 19.

its model fuselage and put a tightly fitting square roof over its pilot's head. The only view was of a row of indicators—compass, airspeed, altitude, an artificial horizon—all painstakingly tuned to the performance of a specific airplane. By navigating simulated routes through instrument-only flying, pilots could prepare themselves for low-visibility conditions. By 1941, 10,000 Army-Navy Trainer model 18, or "Link" trainers, were in service; the trainee pilot was ensconced in an instrumented, airplane-shaped cave, a teacher/operator watching an electro-mechanical "crab" crawl across a paper aeronautical chart, leaving a trail of ink across a virtual flight path.

As Branden Hookway has observed, the reduction of interaction with the world to the "bottleneck" of an interface carries with it, already, the ideas of simulation and mediation.[5] The systems perspective, as well as electromechanical complexity involved in such early simulators, is shown by a contemporaneous illustration of a competing German simulation system; the aircraft controls—elevator, rudder, aileron—at the center, aircraft motions and indicators spreading outward in a cascading web of cause-and-effect, with instruments and interface at the summit.

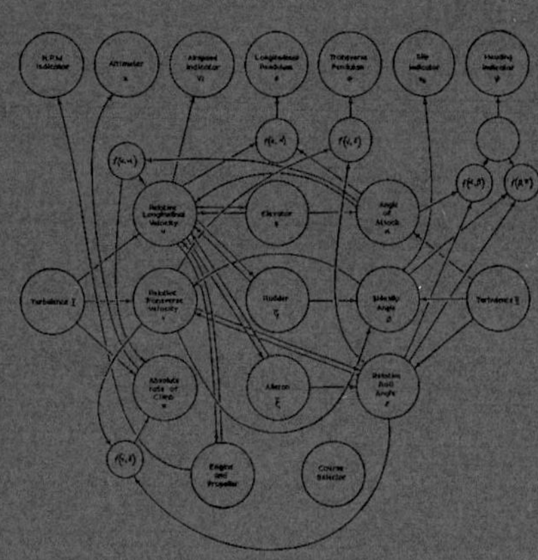

Simulation diagram by H.A. Roeder, 1929.
From Rolfe, J. M., and K. J. Staples. *Flight Simulation*. (Cambridge [Cambridgeshire]: Cambridge University Press, 1986.)

The Cybernetic Lens

The systems, simulation, and interface-led model of human experience implicit in such a diagram was not, therefore, forged from scratch during the Second World War.[6] But it was annealed, and incalculably advanced, by the conflict's vast furnace. A central role was taken by Dr. Warren Weaver, from 1943 director of applied mathematics for the wartime United States Office of Scientific Research and Development, from which post he supervised both Claude Shannon's pioneering work on information theory and Norbert Wiener's revolutionary ideas of cybernetics.[7] Prior to 1943, Weaver had served as director of fire control for the same military research bureau ("This not relating to the dangers of forestry but to the aiming and controlling of guns.").[8] In that role, he had integrated the radar targeting systems being produced by MIT with the servo-controlled anti-artillery gun being produced by his own division: "Your output . . . is our input," he explained to the radar chief.[9] In 1943, Weaver gave the mathematics of targeting systems to self-described "ex-prodigy" and MIT mathematics professor Norbert Weiner as a research task.[10] Typical of Wiener's genius, the result was a comprehensive mathematical theory of communication and control between human and machine—what Wiener termed *cybernetics*, from the Greek for oarsman—that could incidentally treat the targeting problem as a special case. "He wrote a book for us," Weaver explained, "a report which was bound in yellow covers and which was promptly dubbed the 'Yellow Peril' . . . so abstruse and difficult that practically nobody could understand any of it." Yet, published in 1948 as *Cybernetics: Or Control and Communication in the Animal and the Machine*, the book would become a bestseller, influential far beyond the military-industrial milieu—though hugely influential there as well.[11]

5
"An airplane is not directly flown, but rather at a proximity defined by cockpit instrumentation. It is the distance of this proximity that determines the abstraction of [the pilot's] activity into tasks, and so the extent to which these tasks may be transferable, to be reconstituted in other contexts—from flight to simulated flight." Branden Hookway, *The Interface* (Cambridge, MA: MIT Press, 2014), 37.

6
For an essential reading of cybernetics' prehistory, see in particular David A. Mindell, *Between Human and Machine: Feedback, Control, and Computing before Cybernetics* (Baltimore, MD: Johns Hopkins University Press, 2002).

7
Weaver wrote the popularizing introductory chapter to Claude Shannon's 1949 *A Mathematical Theory of Communication* (Champaign-Urbana, University of Illinois Press, 1949).

8
Warren Weaver, interview by Barbara Land, "The Reminiscences of Warren Weaver," *New York Times* Oral History Program and Columbia University Oral History Collection 4, no. 210 (New York: Columbia University Oral History Collection, 1962), 583.

9
Warren Weaver, diary, meeting with Loomis, December 5, 1940; Warren Weaver to Loomis, December 10, 1940; Warren Weaver, diary, December 14, 1940, ORSD7 general project files, box 70, collected diaries, vol. 1, quoted in David Mindell, "Automation's Finest Hour," in Agatha C. Hughes and Thomas Parke Hughes, *Systems, Experts, and Computers: The Systems Approach in Management and Engineering, World War II and After* (Cambridge, MA: MIT Press, 2000), 33.

Across the MIT campus, in December 1944, work began on a new, more sophisticated aircraft simulator—Project Whirlwind—that would be able to simulate more than one aircraft, and even, it was hoped, those yet to be built, informed by the advances in computing that had accompanied the wartime work of Weaver, Shannon, and Wiener. The director of the project, Jay Forrester, came to dispense with complex, analog controls (the more they were interconnected, the more inaccurate they became), instead building the first general-purpose, real-time digital computer.

By the mid-1950s, the cockpit procured for the effort lay in a Cambridge junkyard, in favor of a new, more complex mission: coordinating America's air defenseagainst Soviet bomber attack.[12] Each installation of the resulting Semi-Automatic Ground Environment, or SAGE, combined a massive IBM-built computer with new magnetic-core memory to allow it to respond in real-time, with rafts of smaller MIT-built computers, or "consoles," on which Air Force cadets viewed potential Soviet invaders as digital signals, helping the computer identify friend or foe with a light gun. Along this particularly horrifying bottleneck-of-an-interface, constant simulations of nuclear attack were par for the course. (And of course for training purposes the SAGE operators were never informed whether they were real.) The SAGE console operators left their feelings evident in graffiti; "Don't you feel useless?" reads one; another concludes, "I can't stand it any longer."[13]

Network Networks

After the unexpected success of Wiener's *Cybernetics* in 1948, the field of communication and control theory emerged not just as its own discipline, but also as a perspective on many other disciplines, reconceived as inputs, outputs, and architectures of information spanning human and technological realms. As Mark Wigley has recounted of the cybernetic discussions that connected figures as diverse as Marshall McLuhan, Margaret Mead, Buckminster Fuller, and Constantinos Doxiadis, the same networks of information that cybernetics described were also the means of the theory's rapid transmission as an intellectual scaffold through psychology, media theory, medicine, and also, of course, architecture itself.[14]

Norbert Wiener's home of MIT, itself a mile-square architectural network of interconnected buildings and hallways, proved a particularly efficient medium for cybernetic transmission and reception. Exemplary was architect and planner Kevin Lynch's *The Image of the City* (1960) and *The View from the Road* (1964), the latter written with Lynch's former students Donald Appleyard and John R. Myer.[15,16] Lynch's proposal for the books to the Rockefeller Foundation in 1953 had been made with the artist and visual theorist György Kepes, on "the relation of the individual to the urban physical environment as directly perceived by the various senses." As Reinhold Martin has observed, Kepes, at MIT since 1946, was "coiled around" the connections between visual perception and the control theories of cybernetics.[17] "We ourselves are self-regulating systems," Kepes observed. "Similarly to the guided missile, we continuously correct for error as we seek our destination."[18]

The Image of the City (at the time of its publication, Kepes was listed as an "inspiration" but not as a coauthor) dealt almost exclusively with the visual and cognitive signals that guide the pedestrian. A parallel strand of work concerned more technologically mediated travel; or, as a later manuscript by Lynch and Donald Appleyard put it, "Highways . . . judged for the effects on the driver and his passengers."[19] This became the sequel, *The View from the Road*.

10
"It seemed to me that one of the things that I could do, as a service during the war," Weaver later reflected, "was to maintain my temper and patience and keep Norbert [Wiener] working." Weaver, "Reminiscences," 627.

11
Norbert Weiner, *Cybernetics: Or Control and Communication in the Animal and the Machine* (New York: Wiley, 1948).

12
Kent C. Redmond and Thomas M. Smith, *Project Whirlwind: The History of a Pioneer Computer* (Bedford, MA: Digital Equipment Corporation, 1980), 60.

13
Graffiti recorded and displayed at the Computer History Museum, Mountain View, CA.

14
Mark Wigley, "Network Fever," *Grey Room* 1, no. 4 (2001): 82–122.

15
Kevin Lynch, *The Image of the City* (Cambridge, MA: MIT Press, 1960).

16
Donald Appleyard, Kevin Lynch, and John Randolph Myer, *The View from the Road* (Cambridge, MA: MIT Press, 1966).

17
See Reinhold Martin, *The Organizational Complex: Architecture, Media, and Corporate Space* (Cambridge, MA: MIT Press, 2003), in particular Chapter 2, "The Organizational Complex."

18
György Kepes, *The New Landscape in Art and Science* (Chicago: P. Theobald, 1956), 328.

19
Donald Appleyard and Kevin Lynch, "Sensuous Criteria for Highway Design," 1966 manuscript, Donald Appleyard Papers, Bancroft Library (DAP).

Appleyard on the Road

Beetle-browed and casually dapper, Donald Appleyard would continue his journey west: from his native England to MIT and in 1967 to the Landscape and City Planning faculty at UC Berkeley. There, he sought to build on Lynch's theories to create and validate a scientific system for simulating human experience of the built environment according to scientific and cybernetic principles, focused on automotive travel. The goal was not just to catalog but also to render the vast input of the senses that *The Image of the City* and *The View from the Road* had begun to chart.

At MIT in 1966, Appleyard had already hooked up an Optec "modelscope" to a 16 mm Bolex camera and run it by hand on a miniature wheel down a 1" = 12'0" model of Boston's Storrow Drive; the models that resulted, however, were simultaneously jerky (even a microscopic wobble became preposterously magnified across a 16 mm frame) and confounded by bridges and overpasses (which the bulky camera could hardly sneak under). In 1967 Appleyard recorded his larger ambitions at Berkeley: "Our aim is to develop a way of simulating extensive urban areas on small-scale models and recording journeys through them, first on movies and video recorders (more flexible) and ultimately on computers."[20]

Aerospace modeling and simulation were already directly influencing urban policy and planning. At MIT in 1969, SAGE architect Jay Forrester would publish *Urban Dynamics*, applying the lessons of control systems to "urban problems."[21] Closer to Berkeley, UCLA's Peter Kamnitzer was already using the world's first real-time 3-D display, developed for the Apollo Lunar Landing simulator, to chart and depict movement through a modernist proposal for downtown Los Angeles, in US Department of Transportation research on "the visual subsystem" of the highway landscape.[22] By 1971, the Department of Labor and HUD funded intensive summer schools at UC Berkeley and MIT to retrain aerospace employees in techniques of urban management and simulation, or "how to apply systems thinking in a new milieu."[23,24]

Donald Appleyard's interest in urban simulation was part of this same context, but also conceptually distinct from it. In the lineage of Kepes and Lynch, Appleyard's particular obsession was in simulating the urban image as a complete psychological, cognitive, and perceptual artifact. In this interest, Appleyard became increasingly engaged with the new field of environmental psychology. Appleyard would explain the field as an attempt to move beyond "view[ing] the world of cities as physical, functional, objective worlds to be manipulated" and toward a scientific understanding of "environment-behavior" relations.[25] One of environmental psychology's founding figures, the bearded and generous UC Berkeley psychology professor Kenneth H. Craik became Appleyard's collaborator.

Together, Appleyard and Craik sought to simulate not just the appearance of the built environment but the particular dynamics of vision we undertake in it—such as the drifting and turning motion of our cone of view as we orient ourselves while driving at speed. Such a standard—of fidelity to perception as much as objects—was necessary, it was believed, to produce the same emotional, physiological, and psychological responses to simulated environments as to their corresponding scenes in reality. As with Link's first instrument trainers of the 1930s, simulation was enabled by the understanding of an interface—but the interface of our own eyes and mind—a simulation that targeted not the surface of a screen or readout, but the surface of our pupils and the architecture of perception itself.

The ability to evoke such responses to as-yet-unbuilt environments, especially when combined with nascent technologies like two-way cable television, would allow what Appleyard describes as a "communications model of community participation"—superseding the often inaccurate, not to mention imperious, declarations of architects and

20
Donald Appleyard, letter to Alberto S. Trevino Jr., November 7, 1967 (DAP).

21
Jay W. Forrester, *Urban Dynamics* (Cambridge, MA: MIT Press, 1969).

22
Frank Hulbert Slade and Peter Kamnitzer, *Highway Transportation System Simulation: The Visual Subsystem by Means of Computer-Generated Images*. Prepared for the United States Department of Transportation, National Highway Safety Bureau (Los Angeles: Reports Group, School of Engineering and Applied Science, University of California, 1969), I-4.

23
Arthur Naftalin and Richard W. Gable, "Adapting Professional Manpower from Aerospace to Urban Government: Project Syllabus," Aerospace Orientation Program, University of California, Berkeley, CA, August 6–September 3, 1971.

24
For a concise and well-researched history of this larger intellectual moment, see in particular Jennifer S. Light, *From Warfare to Welfare: Defense Intellectuals and Urban Problems in Cold War America* (Baltimore, MD: Johns Hopkins University Press, 2003).

25
Donald Appleyard, "A Planner's Guide to Environmental Psychology: Review Essay," *Journal of the American Institute of Planners* 43 (April 1977): 184.

developers in analyzing, debating, and shaping the physical realities of cities.[26]

In the fall of 1973, Appleyard and Craik received a grant from the National Science Foundation, in the eventual amount of $348,300, for the proposal "Environmental Dispositions and the Simulation of Environments." The proposal was not just for the creation of new techniques of simulation but also their validation with psychological research. "Research participants," their proposal imagined, "drawn from a broad range of class and age groups" would be brought to a research station and randomly assigned to real or simulated experiences of the surrounding site. Thus, the psychological effect of reality and simulation could be compared: "Extensive debriefing sessions," Craik and Appleyard explained, "will examine how the travelers describe the environment they pass through, what they notice in it, what they recall of it, how they feel about it, how they evaluate elements in it, and how they mentally organize its subareas and features."[27]

Cities in Space

Particularly against this landscape, it is easy to see why Donald Appleyard was deeply moved by the graceful, gliding model photography of Stanley Kubrick's *2001: A Space Odyssey* (1968).

Most obviously, the film set about deconstructing and reconstructing the architecture of perception itself through its climactic Star Gate sequence, evoking the contemporaneous origins of psychedelic science at Harvard and Stanford in cybernetically inflected studies of the brain. More practically, and to Appleyard's own specific goals, the film contained model-driven simulations of extraterrestrial environments that were startling in their fidelity, especially (as Appleyard would have experienced it) across an enormous, curved Cinerama screen. Appleyard began to seek out those involved in the film's production—and so, it turned out, ventured into another essential intersection of aerospace military-industrial technique and experience with the production of space and culture on the surface of the earth.[28]

As with the close relationship between NASA and urban programs, this transfer had its origin as much in the Space Race's end as in its beginning. The prospects of those engaged in R&D at NASA and its web of contractors were already slipping with the rise in military spending in Vietnam after 1963; they slipped further after the construction of Apollo's vast physical architecture was completed in 1966. As well as by other branches of government, a small but essential harvest was reaped by the painstaking imagination of Stanley Kubrick.

The film's flagship, Discovery, is exemplary of this crowded midcentury circuit. The spacecraft was based directly on a 1961 nuclear-propelled design developed by engineer Howard Finger in collaboration with Wernher von Braun's Future Projects division. Versions had been rendered by the graphic artist Harry Lange and presented and promoted by Von Braun's spokesman, Frederick Ordway III. By 1966 Lange and Ordway were working directly under Stanley Kubrick on *2001*, and by the end of the decade, Finger would be reporting to the secretary of housing and urban development George Romney as HUD's first director of research and technology. Further down Kubrick's hierarchy were effects artists Con Pederson (also a former Von Braun collaborator) and Douglas Trumbull, both recently employees of Graphic Films, in Long Beach. Graphic Films' primary production had been concept films for the air force and NASA, but a film for the 1964 World's Fair, *To the Moon and Beyond*, had caught Kubrick's eye and led to early concept work for *2001*.[29] After this work ended, and with aerospace visualizations disappearing, Trumbull was fired; the expansive, wispy-haired Californian cadged Kubrick's number from Pederson, by then a newly minted Kubrick employee, and showed up in London in 1966. "I was twenty-three at the time and didn't know anything, really," Trumbull would later reflect.[30]

26
Donald Appleyard, "Understanding Professional Media: Issues, Theory, and a Research Agenda," in Irwin Altman and Joachim F. Wohlwill, *Human Behavior and Environment: Advances in Theory and Research* (New York: Plenum Press, 1977), 43-88.

27
Donald Appleyard, Kenneth H. Craik, Merrie Klapp, and Alicira Kreimer, "The Berkeley Environmental Simulation Laboratory: Its Use in Environmental Impact Assessment," UC Berkeley, Institute for Urban and Regional Development, IURD Working Paper no. 206 (February 1973), 2.

28
Since arriving at Berkeley, Appleyard had supplemented his first experiments with the purchase of a used driving simulator from Yale and the Connecticut Department of Transportation. Yet, once more, the magnification of minute instabilities in the filmed results made convincing results all but impossible. In a 1970 contract to simulate an automated highway, Appleyard managed only one slightly wobbly ground-level view; for the remaining footage, the simulator imitated a helicopter swooping around the scene. Institute for Urban and Regional Development, "The Berkeley Environmental Simulation Laboratory, Technical Report: Preliminary Report," May 1975 (DAP).

29
Michael Benson, *Space Odyssey: Stanley Kubrick, Arthur C. Clarke, and the Making of a Masterpiece* (New York: Simon & Schuster, 2018), 47.

As a physical artifact, the Discovery lay over 54 feet long on one of MGM's Borehamwood soundstages, its crew quarters a six-foot-diameter hardwood sphere. The ship did not move—in fact, the floor to the soundstage was demolished to send concrete pilings deep into bedrock to ensure the ship's otherworldly stillness. It was designed by a former architectural draftsman, *2001*'s production designer Tony Masters; to add the level of detail necessary for Kubrick's photography, Masters was successful in poaching several staff members from Gerry and Sylvia Anderson's "supermarionation" sci-fi television series, *Thunderbirds* (1965). There, the show's puppet-modelmakers had developed techniques of "kitbashing"—using parts of newly popular, mass-market polystyrene airplane and military models—to quickly add granular detail to larger set pieces, giving the eye what it needed to imagine complexity across the vast surface.[31]

To give life to the vast assembly, it was the cameras that moved around the model. But, given the need for multiple exposures at different apertures (to allow, for example, for the projection of interior action in the windows of spacecraft like the Discovery and lunar shuttle Aries), they needed to do so in a way that could be repeated accurately and consistently. The solution was ingeniously crafted by Trumbull using self-synchronizing, or "selsyn," motors. First developed in the early 20th century for lock controls for the Panama Canal, the self-synchronizing motor was improved and extensively deployed in Warren Weaver's automated targeting systems during the Second World War, where it allowed the movement of one part of a mechanical system needed to be accurately dependent on another. As encountered by Jay Forrester in his early work on the Whirlwind simulator, however, the accuracy of such analog control systems decreases exponentially with the number of synchronizing systems that are tied to each other. The pathbreaking motion-control shots in *2001* were therefore limited to long, linear trajectories—as along the vast body of the Discovery—with cameras driven along enormous, machined worm gears whose delivery to Borehamwood Trumbull arranged from a machine shop in Detroit.

Kubrick's demand for deep focus meant exposure times a second or more for each single frame of film before the camera crept another fraction of an inch on its worm-geared track and paused again, with "all the excitement of watching a minute hand creep across the face of a clock."[32] Beyond the very stately speed that became *2001*'s signature, the star-specked backgrounds would strobe, double, and even triple as they moved between each 1/48-second flash of the Cinerama projector, giving what Trumbull described as the film's "speed limit."[33]

The techniques developed for *2001* were refined by Douglas Trumbull's first ventures for his own special-effects firm, established on his return to Los Angeles: the arrival and departure from Earth of the alien heroine of the ribald 1968 comedy *Candy* and the multiplying crystalline alien microbes in 1971's *Andromeda Strain*. Starting with the latter film and continuing to Trumbull's directorial debut with *Silent Running* (1972), Trumbull was assisted by an industrious young dropout from Long Beach State's Industrial Design Department, John Dykstra. Chewbacca-tall, with a ponytail, beard, and piercing eyes, Dystra had generosity and charm that would evoke a passionate loyalty in those who worked with and for him. For *Silent Running*—an ecologically inflected fable about a lone astronaut caring for Earth's remaining supply of plants beyond the rings

30
Ibid., 130.

31
The plastic-parted models had replaced so-called solids—carved wooden kits—in the UK before the Second World War, but the durable polystyrene injection molding that made kitbashing possible was itself a product of World War II innovations. The models were made popular in the UK initially by the Airfix corporation, with which they were at one point synonymous. Jonathan Mock, *The Airfix Book of Scale Modeling* (London: Conway, 2011), 12–13.

32
Benson, *Space Odyssey*, 326.

33
Ibid., 351. The apex of the motion-control work on *2001* occupied the same position in the film itself—the aforementioned Star Gate sequence, which combined three different kinds of special-effects footage. First was the very first footage shot by Kubrick for the film, macro-lens experiments shooting colored oils in tanks of ink in a deserted brassiere factory on the Upper West Side in 1965. Second were brightly discolored airborne shots of landscapes, including Scotland's Ben Nevis and Utah's Monument Valley; the discovery of the color process, which the effects crew called "Purple Haze," resulted from randomly recombining the separate cyan, yellow, and magenta film separations that were used by the production to keep fidelity as shots throughout the film were combined and re-reprinted in the masking process. The third technique was the first encountered by Keir Dullea's Dave Bowman on his entry into the Star Gate, and it was developed by Trumbull using selsyn-coordinated motion control. As the regular movement of large, transparent photographic prints produced with the "Purple Haze" process was moved by one worm gear behind an illuminated slit, another gear at 90 degrees moved a camera, aperture open, away from the slit, while a final motor maintained a constant focus on the slit opening. Here, the motion-control process was used not for a completely focused image, but its reverse—a deliberate, screen-spanning blur. When the resulting images were doubled across the frame, a sense of vertiginous motion was created between the two virtual surfaces. As a copywriter for the film's 1974 rerelease termed it, "the ultimate trip."

of Saturn—Dykstra, as effects director, developed more sophisticated motor-control systems based on stepping motors and transistor-based circuits; this brought the reliability of digital circuits to the system, although the simple transistor-based controls still allowed only linear camera motion.

While technically remarkable—especially given its one-million-dollar budget—and now a cult favorite, *Silent Running* was a commercial failure. As a result, when Donald Appleyard contacted Douglas Trumbull on receipt of his NSF funds seeking assistance with model photography, Trumbull demurred on his own part but was happy to pass Appleyard on to the newly-out-of-work Dykstra.

Before Dykstra's arrival in Berkeley, the model-building company Scale Models Unlimited of Palo Alto had been contracted to produce a model of two square miles of Marin County, "similar in many respects to conventional architectural models . . . the differences in the emphasis on the foreground detail." Resembling a model train set more than the common, abstracted language of architectural presentation, the elaborate Marin County model incorporated accurate signage, building facades reproduced through photography onto Plexiglas, and hillsides made of sawdust, velvet, and fine foam and painted a golden color to match the dry summer surroundings of a "control" film journey through the site captured in July 1972.[34]

Yet while the scale architecture of the Marin hillsides was complete when Dykstra arrived in 1973, the architecture of the simulator was barely begun. After initially considering several locations and orientations for model photography—including suspending the hillsides vertically in the belfry of an abandoned Baptist seminary—the team secured a storage room underneath the Wurster Hall library. More than a year was spent designing and building a gantry system to sit over the model, suspending a camera and long, thin, prism-tipped "probe" that could explore every cranny of an architectural model and was designed to magnify a model-surface view to the lens of both video and 16 mm film cameras. When it finally began working over the model in 1974, the system consisted of a 26-foot gantry running on 2½-inch bearings along a 56-foot rail, with camera gondola suspended below. The probe tip, by consequence, could "explore any point with a 24 × 44 × 3 foot volume."

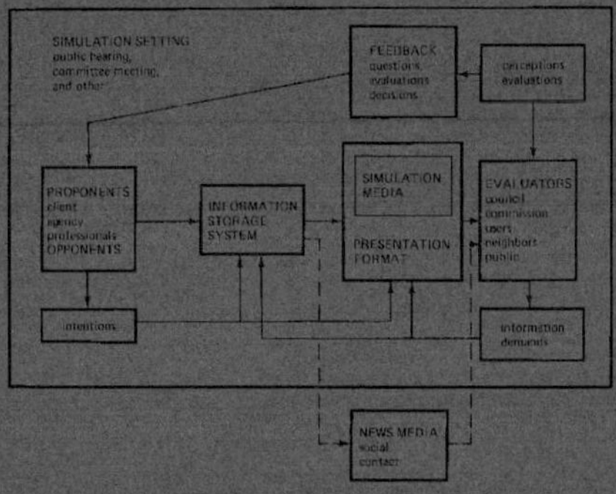

"A Communications Model of Community Participation" from Appleyard, Donald "Understanding Professional Media: Issues, Theory, and a Research Agenda" in Altman, Irwin, and Joachim F. Wohlwill. *Human Behavior and Environment: Advances in Theory and Research, Volume 2.* New York: Plenum Press, 1977. P. 49

Far more complex even than the structural design of the gantry, however, were the electronic systems that controlled its movement. While initially an analog control system was contemplated—and significant resources expended to undertake its development alongside alternate systems—the great innovation of the Wurster simulator ended up being its digital approach, driven by a new Digital Equipment Corporation (DEC) PDP-11 minicomputer. This machine was the descendant not of the massive, midcentury mainframe, but rather very specifically of the SAGE consoles that interpreted and directed its operations. Ken Olsen and Harlan Anderson from MIT's Lincoln Labs, two engineers of the SAGE consoles, had decamped a few towns over to Maynard, Massachusetts, to launch DEC in 1957, with an emphasis on consoles providing real-time computing to universities and smaller businesses.

Crucial assistance in the design and operation of the gantry and its complex control systems came from a trapezoidal, fog-filled building at Berkeley's Richmond Field Station. Beginning in 1961 under an FAA grant, the massive building was crafted to contain a 1/10 scale model of an airport runway and an airplane's descent trajectory above it, which could be filled with mist and used to simulate low-visibility landings. A cockpit ran on rails hung from the long, wedge-shaped roofline, allowing repeated, safe observation of lit-and-unlit runway markings at precise speeds. All needed to be controlled very precisely. The system's principal electronic technician, Karl Mellander, was an early consultant to Appleyard on his simulator proposal;

34 IURD, BESL *Technical Report*, 73.

35 Ibid.

Dykstra would work even more closely with two more of its designers and operators, Jerry Jeffress and Alvah Miller.[36]

When operational in 1974, the Berkeley Environmental Simulation Laboratory (BESL) would first allow the user to employ a downward-facing TV, complete with a military-style crosshair, to drive a two-dimensional "rail" along one of the model's roads. Then, via a second series of controls, the speed and orientation of the camera would be added, including its vertical position, rotation, and angle of the view, all centered on the "pupil"—the technical term for the very center—of a tiny lens sitting just 1/10" above the model's surface. This approach allowed not just the linear, cinematic gaze of Kubrick and Trumbull's earlier efforts, but a much closer simulation of actual human views of the environment—not just along our axis of view but all around it, like gazing around a corner before turning into it as we anticipate a new world about to appear.

Once the complex view trajectory was set, the PDP-11 would calculate the position and orientation of the camera for every frame of a 16 mm film of up to several minutes, recording the result to disk. Like *2001*'s model-photography rigs, the BESL was designed to produce what were essentially stop-motion films. To dispense with the vibration that had plagued Appleyard's previous efforts, the film would be exposed, one frame at a time, along the predetermined driving route, with the camera and probe pausing for several seconds between moves to damp vibration, and then exposing a single frame of film for up to 1½ seconds through a narrow-stopped lens to ensure a deep depth of field.

As the most valuable and sensitive member of the team, the PDP-11 was contained within an air-conditioned control room in the simulator space. Other team members were not so fortunate. Given the need for not only a deep depth of field but also the complex optics and tiny opening of the miniature prism at the probe's tip, over 100,000 watts of lighting had to be delivered to the model's surface. This was accomplished by blanketing the ceiling of the space with fluorescent tubes (with every third bulb on the same AC phase to minimize flickering). Between the ceiling fluorescents and strong floor-standing halogen lights to simulate the sun's shadows, temperatures would approach 100 degrees during the many hours of filming.[37]

The first version of the BESL probe camera exploring the Marin County Model, 1974. Donald Appleyard Papers, Bancroft Archives, University of California, Berkeley.

By the summer of 1974, the BESL's first films were complete. Appleyard and Craik's elaborate experiments to "validate" the model through psychological testing would continue for several years. Five years before his untimely death in 1982, Appleyard published his proposal for the simulator's role in a "Communications Model of the Planning Process," an explicitly cybernetic network enabled by simulation, connecting "proponents," "opponents," and "evaluators" by "simulation media" in a feedback loop of "questions, evaluations, decisions, perceptions and evaluations." For Appleyard, the effective simulation of the dynamic human gaze was a scientific instrument to cut through a fog of power, aspiration, and assumptions in the creation of cities and landscapes. Writing to the Link Foundation in 1974, Appleyard outlined his ambitions to grow the project into a "real-time interactive simulator" to communicate with "citizenry on a day to day basis."[38] Here was the cybernetic lens, but with a view also through the optics of 1960s Berkeley. Along with his colleague Sim Van der Ryn, Donald Appleyard had brought his students to the front lines of experiments in participative design like Berkeley's People's Park; at the time, he wrote of a larger "revolutionary change in the context of professional life . . . forcing professionals to reevaluate their roles and their products."[39]

36
IURD, *BESL Technical Report*; John Dykstra, Interview with Nicholas de Monchaux, April 4, 2018, audio recording.

37
Ibid.

38
Donald Appleyard, letter to Marilyn C. Link, Link Foundation, February 12, 1974 (DAP).

39
Donald Appleyard, "Professional Priorities for Environmental Psychology" (paper delivered at the second International Psychology Conference, University of Lund, Sweden, June 26–29, 1973).

The BESL, 1974, showing the modular 1"=30' Marin County Model. Notice tightly packed flourescent lighting and spot halogens. Donald Appleyard Papers, Bancroft Archives, University of California, Berkeley.

The Berkeley simulator would indeed be world-changing. But not as a precise instrument of truth; rather as a sledgehammer of fiction.

The Star Wars

"Every time there was a war movie on television, like *The Bridges at Toko-Ri*, I would watch it—and if there was a dogfight sequence, I would videotape it."[40] George Lucas recalls of his efforts to build the visual language of *Star Wars*' (1977) space battles, which continued throughout his two years of scriptwriting between 1973 and 1975: "I had twenty to twenty-five hours' worth of videotape. . . . I condensed that down . . . [and] transferred about an hour to 16 mm film, and then I cut that down to about eight minutes. I would have the plane going from right to left, and a plane coming toward us and flying away from us, to see if the movement would generate excitement."[41]

Seeking a collaborator for what was then called *The Star Wars*, Lucas and his producer, Gary Kurtz, showed the footage to a series of special-effects experts throughout 1975, including Douglas Trumbull. No technology existed, they were told, to combine effects photography with the vintage, first-person aerial views Lucas had collected. Trumbull, though, recommended that Lucas talk to Dykstra, who was again without work.

"It had never been done before," Dykstra recalls of his initial discussion with Lucas. "He wanted to be able to create the illusion of photographing spaceships, flying like WW2 fighters, from a handheld camera; not just showing what it looked like, but what it felt like."[42] Dykstra immediately saw the connection to Lucas's ambitions and his computer-driven motion-control work in Berkeley; within a few weeks he agreed to join the production, supervising the startup of what would become Industrial Light & Magic (ILM). "I said I could do it, but only because I knew it could be done."[43]

Among the first calls Dykstra made were to Alvah Miller and Jerry Jeffress, his colleagues from the BESL's control systems. Only Miller would move full-time to Dykstra's new domain, a warehouse in Van Nuys; Jeffress would join ILM full-time when it moved to the Bay Area in 1978. The three together, however, would share a Scientific and Engineering Award at the 1978 Oscars for the development of the resulting "Dykstraflex camera and Electronic Motion Control System." While the system added many new features—shooting in 35 mm VistaVision instead of 16 mm to aid in optical printing, 12 channels as motion control, and the ability to move models as well as the camera in concert—it was credited from the outset as a direct evolution of the system developed for Appleyard and Craik.

Motion blur—essential for *Star Wars*' high-speed feel—was in many ways the simplest addition, accomplished by leaving the camera shutter open for a fraction of its movement between frames. But the particular, astonishing realism of the shots comes not from the detail of the models or the speed of filming, but from the painstaking reproduction our own pupils' mobile gaze; pivoting and moving around the center of the frame, placing us into space, and Space, as never before.[44] The so-called Dykstraflex system—its name a pun on proprietary camera nomenclature—produced more than 350 effects-laden shots for *Star Wars*' 1977 premiere.

40
George Lucas, interview at https://www.starwars.com/news/from-world-war-to-star-wars-dogfights, April 20, 2018. Permalink at https://web.archive.org/web/20190606182227/https://www.starwars.com/news/from-world-war-to-star-wars-dogfights.

41
J. W. Rinzler and Charles Lippincott, *The Making of Star Wars: The Definitive Story behind the Original Film: Based on the Lost Interviews from the Official Lucasfilm Archives* (New York: Ballantine Books, 2007), 50.

42
Dykstra, interview by Nicholas de Monchaux.

43
Ibid.

44
As well as the camera systems, even more ambient structures of the Berkeley simulation process—like the massive, three-phase banks of fluorescent lighting developed at Wurster Hall, used at night for filming to spare electrical load—would move directly to the new ILM warehouse in Van Nuys. Dykstra, interview by Nicholas de Monchaux.

More than character, plot, or dialogue,[45] the effects sequences would become the emotional core of the film, garnering the only spontaneous applause at the movie's 1977 premiere.[46]

The Explosion at the End of the World

Even more than its hero's mythical progression, *Star Wars* hit on a fundamental truth of storytelling as it relates to outer space in particular, and its relationship to our hopes and dreams on earth. Among the Mojave Desert's many star turns in science fiction is a series of scenes in *Star Wars*; along with the desert sands of Tunisia, it is the first world we encounter in Lucas's universe. Like those deserts, outer space's most essential quality is that there is nothing there. And so, as Banham aptly observed, we read our imagination into it far more clearly than the complex realities of earth.

But what a reality we are living in. The Internet excels in two-way connectivity far beyond the wildest dreams of the civic networks imagined by Donald Appleyard in 1977. As in the world of *Star Wars* we can indeed summon the power of massive connectedness from small devices cradled in our hands. Yet from the endless images of Instagram culture to the unregulated fake news of Facebook, neither the profound connectedness of contemporary culture nor for that matter the sophistication of simulations present in it has led on its own to a legible improvement in social or civic life. In fact, often the reverse. In the culture of architecture and the built environment, small square images, beautiful but rarely true, have come to matter much more than measurement—or public participation. Recalling Edwin Link's patent confusion of 1930, the line between simulation and reality has become as hopelessly confused as that between amusement and training.

This history of picturing *Star Wars* emphasizes one of the central themes of its world, and our own: that the transition between upstart and empire is constant, fluid, and ever unexpected. As simulated by John Dykstra with a 120-frame-a-second combination of propane, fireworks, and welding oxygen in a Van Nuys warehouse, filmed from below against a black ceiling, the explosion of the Death Star that brings *Star Wars* to its close is but one such essential marker—of technology and of society's predictably unpredictable outcomes.

45
"You can type this shit, George, but you sure can't say it," Harrison Ford would famously exclaim. Peter Biskind, *Easy Riders, Raging Bulls: How the Sex-Drugs-and-Rock-'n'-Roll Generation Saved Hollywood* (New York: Simon & Schuster, 1999), 329.

46
Nicholas de Monchaux, interview with Patricia Rose Duignan, May 3, 2019.

The Second Copernican Revolution

NEIL LEACH

The movie *Blade Runner* (1982) depicts a dystopian future world involving "replicants"—bioengineered robots—manufactured by the Tyrell Corporation to have superhuman abilities so they can survive in hostile conditions of off-world colonies.[1] The replicants are potentially dangerous and as a safety measure are given a limited life span of four years. In the movie a group of replicants return to Earth in a bid to extend their lives. Rick Deckard, played by Harrison Ford, is a "blade runner," a kind of policeman/bounty hunter charged with hunting down and "retiring" (killing) these replicants. The problem, however, is that replicants look almost identical to human beings and can be distinguished only by using the so-called Voight-Kampff test to examine their emotional responses and eye reflexes. The movie is all about the difference between human beings and robots. Replicants become a mirror to understand what it is to be human. As Rutger Hauer, who plays the lead replicant, Roy Batty, comments, "In many ways, *Blade Runner* wasn't about the replicants. It was about what does it mean to be human. It's like *E.T.*"[2]

Fast-forward to 2019, the year in which *Blade Runner* is set. It is worth reflecting on how prescient the movie has proved to be. We don't have replicants, but we do find ourselves in a world where AI personal assistants Siri, Alexa, and Google Assistant have infiltrated our everyday lives, and where AI filters spam messages, sorts out Instagram images, and identifies Facebook friends. We don't have flying cars, but we do have drones and self-driving cars. Although we don't have the Tyrell Corporation, corporate life is dominated by high-tech companies, such as Google, Amazon, Apple, and Microsoft. And, as predicted in *Blade Runner*, we do talk to our computers and have LED advertising all over our buildings.

Artificial Intelligence

Although it is unclear whether replicants are controlled by AI, 1. they are clearly robots and offer a productive vehicle by which to introduce the subject of AI. With regard to AI, there are three important distinctions to be made.

First, we should distinguish AI from the intelligence of human beings and describe it as the "intelligence" of machines. Although the same term, "intelligence," is used for both human beings and machines, the concept is not the same. AI merely mimics or simulates human intelligence. Second, we should also distinguish between artificial general intelligence—also known as superintelligence, strong AI, and general AI—and weak AI or narrow AI. At present, artificial general intelligence is well beyond the range of our technical capabilities and

1
Blade Runner, directed by Ridley Scott, 1982.

2
Scott Roxborough, "Rutger Hauer on 'Blade Runner 2049' and Why Films Today 'Lack Balls,'" February 18, 2018, https://www.hollywoodreporter.com/heat-vision/rutger-hauer-blade-runner-2049-why-films-today-lack-balls-1085827.

appears only in the world of fiction, as in the case of Skynet in the Terminator franchise. In fact, we are still limited to a relatively modest realm of narrow AI, although the general public tends to fetishize it and exaggerate its potential. Third, we should also distinguish between the broader category of AI itself, machine learning, and deep learning.

These can be seen as nested within each other—somewhat like Russian dolls or layers of an onion—in that deep learning is part of machine learning that is itself part of AI. Deep learning is the most advanced form of AI, whereby the machine is not programmed in any way but teaches itself about a particular subject based on a form of "neural network" that mimics the human brain. The recent success of deep learning has been facilitated by the vast quantities of data available, the introduction of cloud-based computing, and greatly improved algorithms. The achievements of AI, especially deep learning, are indeed impressive. In 1997 the IBM supercomputer Deep Blue beat world chess champion Garry Kasparov at chess.[3] In 2011 IBM's Watson computer beat two of the world's best players at the general-knowledge quiz show *Jeopardy!*[4] In 2016 Google's AlphaGo beat the world's leading Go expert, Lee Sedol.[5] And in 2019 DeepMind thrashed the top human players at the video game StarCraft II.[6]

AI is already impacting the areas of labor and employment. For example, IBM's Watson has been deployed in the field of medicine and used for diagnosing illnesses. This has led to the replacement of doctors.[7] In the context of architecture, there are a number of noteworthy achievements. Autodesk is developing a range of AI-based applications, such as Fusion 360, for automating various aspects of design. Likewise, Xkool, a start-up in Shenzhen, China, set up by former OMA architect Wanyu He, is developing a smartphone app to make the design process more efficient by using deep learning not only to search through a vast range of possibilities but also to automate designs based on trained models. Those models then evaluate and produce outcomes from various evaluation models. From this perspective, the potential of AI is quite alarming. Indeed, it has been predicted AI will soon replace many white-collar jobs and lead to the demise of all professions, including architecture.[8] As Richard and Daniel Susskind predict: "We are on the brink of a period of fundamental and irreversible change. . . . Technology will be the main driver of this change. And, in the long run, we will neither need nor want professionals to work in the way that they did in the twentieth century and before."[9]

Consciousness

It is clear AI will match and eventually surpass human intelligence. Ray Kurzweil defines this as "the Singularity," a moment of technological change so rapid it amounts to a "rupture in the fabric of human history" with enormous consequences for the future of the human race. "The implications include the merger of biological and nonbiological intelligence, immortal software-based humans, and ultra-high levels of intelligence that expand outward in the universe at the speed of light."[10] The important question, however, is whether AI will ever achieve consciousness. In other words, might computers move beyond narrow AI to achieve artificial general intelligence?

In *How to Create a Mind* (2012), Kurzweil argues that it is entirely possible to achieve artificial general intelligence and to produce an artificial brain with consciousness by replicating the behavioral processes of the human brain.[11] American philosopher John Searle, however, argues that simulating

3
Steven Levy, "What Deep Blue Tells Us about AI in 2017," May 23, 2017, www.wired.com/2017/05/what-deep-blue-tells-us-about-ai-in-2017.

4
John Markoff, "Computer Wins on 'Jeopardy!': Trivial, It's Not," February 16, 2011, www.nytimes.com/2011/02/17/science/17jeopardy-watson.html.

5
Cade Metz, "In Two Moves, AlphaGo and Lee Sedol Redefined the Future," March 16, 2016, www.wired.com/2016/03/two-moves-alphago-lee-sedol-redefined-future/

6
Chris Stokel-Walker, "DeepMind AI Thrashes Human Professionals at Video Game StarCraft II," January 24, 2019, https://www.newscientist.com/article/2191910-deepmind-ai-thrashes-human-professionals-at-video-game-starcraft-ii/.

7
Richard Susskind and Daniel Susskind, *The Future of the Professions: How Technology Will Transform the Work of Human Experts* (Oxford: Oxford University Press, 2015), 48.

8
Susskind and Susskind, *The Future of the Professions*; Martin Ford, *The Rise of the Robots: Technology and the Threat of a Jobless Future* (New York: Basic Books, 2015); Darrell M. West, *The Future of Work: Robots, AI and Automation* (Washington, DC: Brookings Institution Press, 2017).

9
Susskind and Susskind, *The Future of the Professions*, 1.

10
Ray Kurzweil, "The Law of Accelerating Returns," March 7, 2001, http://www.kurzweilai.net/the-law-of-accelerating-returns.

something is not the same as replicating it.[12] Searle critiques Kurzweil's argument using a reworking of his famous Chinese Room thought experiment.[13] Imagine a computer program that seems capable of understanding Chinese. The program is able to take Chinese characters as input and can output Chinese characters so convincingly that it passes the Turing test, persuading everyone that a human is producing the responses. Imagine that a human being who does not understand Chinese is positioned in a closed room equipped with an English print version of the computer program. Here English words are input into the room and as with the original test, Chinese words are output. Given the right instructions in the print version of the computer program, that person would be able to process the material in a similar way, but manually, and would pass the Turing test. The problem is, the person in the room does not understand Chinese. By extension, Searle claims, the computer program likewise does not understand Chinese. Whereas artificial general intelligence could *actually* understand Chinese, narrow AI could only *simulate* an understanding of Chinese.

Deep Blue, according to Searle, might have "won" the game of chess against Kasparov but cannot be aware that it is even playing chess, because it does not possess consciousness. As such, Deep Blue might be good at processing symbols, but it has no idea what they mean. Hence, for Searle, it is clearly absurd to imagine that a computer would one day achieve consciousness. Although philosophers such as David Chalmers argue that computers might achieve consciousness, it would seem AI is incapable of acquiring consciousness.[14]

Simulation versus Reality

The underlying assumption behind the quest for artificial general intelligence is the supposed superiority of human intelligence. It subscribes to the same logic as the Turing test and follows the same logic as realistic humanoid robots, such as Sophia, that can almost pass themselves off as humans.[15] In each case, the ultimate goal is to simulate human intelligence, as "real" human intelligence represents the very pinnacle of intelligence.

What if this approach is wrong? And what if our perception of the world is itself a simulation? Slavoj Zizek argues that we never have unmediated access to reality. What we take for the real is in fact the imaginary, and we only ever access reality in the bittersweet experience of *jouissance*, such as in the moment of aesthetic contemplation, and what comes to us from the external world is filtered through the maze of the imagination, such that fantasy becomes constitutive of what we call reality: "Far from being a kind of fragment of our dreams that prevents us from 'seeing reality as it effectively is,' fantasy is constitutive of what we call reality: the most common bodily 'reality' is constituted via a detour through the maze of imagination."[16] As such, the lesson of virtual reality is not that virtual reality is a form of fake reality, but rather that our engagement with reality is always virtualized: "The ultimate lesson of virtual reality is the virtualization of the very true reality."[17]

Zizek goes on to engage with AI, regarding the computer as "a thinking object" that has begun to infiltrate the imagination and to be embraced by human thought. As such, the computer also becomes a medium through which we might challenge existing assumptions about simulation itself and the nature of "reality," assumptions that always threaten to become inverted:

> The computer works most effectively of course as an "evocatory object" in the

11
Ray Kurzweil, *How to Create a Mind: The Secret of Human Thought Revealed* (New York: Penguin, 2012).

12
John Searle, "I Married a Computer," review of Ray Kurzweil, *The Age of Spiritual Machines: When Computers Exceed Human Intelligence*, *New York Review of Books*, April 8, 1999.

13
John Searle, "Minds, Brains and Programs," *Behavioral and Brain Sciences*, 3, no. 3 (1980): 417–457.

14
Max Tegmark, *Life 3.0: Being Human in the Age of Artificial Intelligence* (New York: Vintage, 2017); David Chalmers, "The Singularity: A Philosophical Analysis," http://consc.net/papers/singularity.pdf.

15
Sophia has been decried by many leading roboticists, such as Rodney Brooks, as being a total sham. As Benedict Evans puts it, "It's a tape recorder with a rubber head on top," "Sophia the Robot, More Marketing Machine Than AI Marvel," Skynet Today, November 20, 2018, https://www.skynettoday.com/briefs/sophia.

16
Slavoj Zizek, "From Virtual Reality to the Virtualization of Reality," in *Designing for a Digital World*, ed. Neil Leach (London: Wiley, 2002), 122.

17
Zizek, "From Virtual Reality to the Virtualization of Reality," 125.

> question of "artificial intelligence"—here, an inversion has already taken place which is the fate of every successful metaphor: one first tries to simulate human thought as far as possible with the computer, bringing the model as close as possible to the human "original," until at a certain point matters reverse and it raises the questions: *what if this "model" is already a model of the "original" itself, what if human intelligence itself operates like a computer, is "programmed,"* etc.? The computer raises in pure form the question of semblance, a discourse which would not be a simulacrum: it is clear that the computer in some sense only "simulates" thought; *yet how does the total simulation of thought differ from "real" thought?*[18]

The premise behind Zizek's argument is that human beings tend to think not in reality itself but in models of reality. In other words, the human brain operates through cognitive symbols that *represent* external reality, and any representation of reality is only a *model* of reality. Thus we find ourselves in a situation where the distinction between a simulated representation of reality (as in the computer) and a reality that is already representational (as in the mind) becomes so blurred that we might easily invert one into the other. This applies especially to the standard critique of the computer—that it only simulates the thought process: "Instead of the computer as a model for the human brain, we conceive of the brain itself as a 'computer made of flesh and blood'; where instead of defining the robot as the artificial man, we conceive of man 'proper' as a 'natural robot.'"[19] The lesson of AI is not that AI is a form of simulated intelligence. Instead, our own intelligence is always simulated. The ultimate lesson of AI is the artificiality of our very own intelligence. AI becomes a mirror in which to understand our own intelligence, no less than replicants become a mirror in which to understand what it means to be human.

Vision beyond Anthropocentrism

Anthropomorphism, it would seem, is a natural tendency in all human beings. As Lacan notes, there is a "primordial anthropomorphism" behind all knowledge.[20] Lacan therefore questions "whether all knowledge is not originally *knowledge of a person* before being *knowledge of an object*, and even whether the knowledge of an object is not, for humanity, a secondary acquisition."[21] Anthropomorphism applies equally to anthropocentrism. To view the world in human terms is effectively the same as putting human beings at the center of that world.

What if we were to judge AI not in terms of human intelligence but on its own terms? As such, the question of consciousness becomes irrelevant. The issue becomes what tasks AI can perform, not whether AI can replicate human achievements. As Yuval Noah Harari notes, "There might be several alternative ways leading to superintelligence, only some of which pass through the straits of consciousness."[22] This leads Harari to pose the important question, "Which of the two is really important, intelligence or consciousness?"[23] As far as corporations and armies are concerned, the answer is clear: "Intelligence is mandatory, but consciousness is optional."[24] Harari goes on to give the example of a taxi driver: "The conscious experiences of a flesh-and-blood taxi driver are infinitely richer than a self-driving car, which feels absolutely nothing."[25] But as far as the passenger is concerned, the consciousness of the taxi driver is irrelevant. Harari proposes, we will have autonomous taxis that are far more reliable than taxis driven by conscious drivers. "Taxis," he comments, "are highly likely to go the way of horses."[26] In fact, Harrari notes that a Google self-driving car was once involved in an accident when hit from behind by a sedan "whose careless human driver was perhaps contemplating

18
Ibid., 123.

19
Ibid., 125.

20
Mikkel Borch-Jacobsen, *Lacan: The Absolute Master*, trans. Douglas Brick (Stanford, CA: Stanford University Press, 1991), 57.

21
Jacques Lacan, *De la psychose paranoïague dans ses rapports avec la personnalité*, followed by *Premiers écrits sur la paranoia* (Paris: Éditions du Seuil, 1975), 326, as quoted in Borch-Jacobsen, *Lacan: The Absolute Master*, 57.

22
Yuval Noah Harari, *Homo Deus: A Brief History of Tomorrow* (New York: Harper-Collins, 2017), 314.

23
Ibid.

24
Ibid.

25
Ibid.

26
Harari, *Homo Deus*, 315.

the mysteries of the universe, instead of concentrating on the road."[27] Consciousness, in other words, is not only optional, it also becomes a liability.

Here I want to introduce the notion of "the Second Copernican Revolution."[28] I use the term in a loose way to describe a strategy of moving beyond the anthropocentric approach outlined above, where AI is presumed to be inferior to human intelligence, because robots lack consciousness. In simple terms, then, if in the "first" Copernican Revolution Copernicus argued that we need move beyond the perception of the Earth as being at the center of the universe, then the Second Copernican Revolution is the moment when we move beyond the perception of human beings as being the center of intelligent life.[29]

I would argue that we need to embrace AI as a radically "other" form of alien intelligence. It is not simply that AI becomes a mirror in which to understand human intelligence, much as replicants in *Blade Runner* become a mirror in which to understand what it means to be human. As Zizek argues, we can begin to understand human intelligence as a form of simulation, no less than AI. Nor is it that arguments about the importance of consciousness are appearing increasingly irrelevant. Rather, if we keep clinging to our mistaken belief in the superiority of human intelligence, we human beings risk becoming utterly irrelevant. We will simply be left behind, much as in the past horses were abandoned for cars, and in the future cars driven by drivers are likely to be abandoned for self-driving cars. The future of the universe does not depend on human intelligence.

27
Ibid.

28
I am grateful to Jared Grogan who introduced me to the notion of "the Second Copernican Revolution."

29
There is, however, a counterargument to be made here. Increasingly calls are being made not for AI, but for Intelligence Augmentation [IA]. Under the logic of IA, AI becomes a prosthetic extension to the human imagination. But if so, does human intelligence not remain at the center? Neil Leach, "We Have Never Been Digital," in Phillip Anzalone, Marcella del Signore, Andrew Wit, *ACADIA 2018: Recalibration: On Imprecision and Infidelity, Proceedings of the 38th Annual Conference of the Association for Computer Aided Design in Architecture*, Universidad Iberoamericana, Mexico City, 2018.

Metabolism as Technology: Toward an Ecological Era of Terrestrial Inhabitation

RACHEL ARMSTRONG

Konstantin Tsiolkovsky observed that the "problem" of biology, rather than engineering challenges, would be key to settling spaces beyond the Earth.[1] Drawing on Bruno Latour's notions of Earthbound[2] and geostory,[3,4] I investigate the potential for terrestrial life on alien worlds and the planetary-scale forces that travelers, settlers, and colonists will need to overcome to achieve this aim. Providing an alternative reading of life in space than the present inescapably anthropocentric and terrestrial view of reality, alternative scenarios—such as directed panspermia and the Living Architecture project, which involve spatially and temporally "programming" the metabolism of microbes using a range of technological apparatuses from bioreactors to space probes—are proposed that engage with the physics, chemistry, and potential life-forms that may render space a fertile terrain for alternative kinds of life and modes of inhabitation.

To begin at the end, our Sun, which nurtures life on Earth, runs out of nuclear fuel within the next five billion years—but long before this, our world will be uninhabitable. Stephen Hawking predicted that, given the substantial increase in frequency and intensity of various climate extremes in recent decades due to global warming, our world is unlikely to sustain us for longer than one thousand years. Even if we are able to turn around the malignant forms of industrialization and natural-resource consumption that stoke our present ecological crisis, the Laboratory for Dynamic Meteorology in Paris suggests that we have around a billion years before our world is no longer viable. The critical question here is not simply the fate of humanity but the deep future of terrestrial life. At some point—in the near or longer term—we will have to find another habitable planet if we value life on this world enough to find a way to survive,[5] but in settling extraterrestrial realms, Konstantin Tsiolkovsky's observation needs to be heeded—that the "problem" of biology must be "overcome."[6] In so doing, it is pertinent to consider the present state of the art in off-world

1
Freeman Dyson, "The Green Universe: A Vision," *New York Review of Books*, October 13, 2016, https://www.nybooks.com/articles/2016/10/13/green-universe-a-vision/.

2
Earthbound highlights our attachment to the Earth beyond the terrestrial soils, which give rise to the words "humus" and "human."

3
Geostory offers a nonhuman narrative of the fabrics of our planet.

4
Bruno Latour, "Once out of Nature: Natural Religion as a Pleonasm," Gifford Lecture, University of Edinburgh, 2013, http://www.youtube.com/watch?v=MC3E6vdQEzk.

5
Our present search for exoplanets aims to characterize planetary systems and Earth-like planets around nearby stars. As we move from an era of detecting exoplanets to one of characterizing them, we are looking for signs of possible extant life, as well as identifying worlds that are similar to ours. Specifically, we are looking for an "Earth 2.0," where future terrestrial settlements may be established. These habitable zones are defined according to our understanding of biological terrestrial life and do not include unusual or alien life-forms, as these are not known to us. Therefore, we do not consider habitable zones in interstellar clouds or the vacuum of space, as this does not help us narrow down our search for life elsewhere, within what is already an effectively infinite terrain.

6
Dyson, "The Green Universe: A Vision."

life support. The International Space Station is a "machine" that, since 2000, has enabled a varying community of people to live and conduct experiments in low Earth orbit, 400 km above the surface of the planet. Despite providing protection from the vacuum of space, it requires a constant supply of terrestrial resources and cannot fully preserve human biology owing to environmental perturbations such as microgravity, altered circadian rhythms, and radiation, which produce measurable, cumulative effects on the human body like changes in bone density, visual impairment, neurological syndromes, and alterations in gene expression.[7] While the human inhabitation of space is a very different kind of challenge than dwelling on Earth, we nevertheless transpose our known principles of terrestrial settlement and geostory, "as if" we were inhabiting a life-bearing planet, because this is what we understand works.

The most fundamental challenge faced by all human space explorers, however, is that the assumptions that support life on Earth do not apply beyond it. Far more concerning than being unable to preserve our personal biology in hostile environments is our overall inability to recognize and support the ecosystems that make the world livable. As beings on a planet that supports life, these unique processes are mostly invisible to us and their strangeness assumed to be "constants."[8] Regardless of "sustainable" intentions, the net effect of our constructed habitats—which include an entire assembly of atmospheric, ecological, and biological systems—and the way we occupy them significantly contributes to the widespread collapse that presently characterizes the third millennium.[9] This is further undermined by our general tendency to simultaneously undervalue and overconsume the smallest, weakest units of the global fabric that make life possible—from ecosystems to civilizations, modern progress is an irrefutable process of ecocide.

> All this mirrors the collapse of food chains, glaciers, and oceans, too, in a way that's impossible to unsee once you've seen it. Collapse from the bottom up. The insects die off first. The glaciers melt from the bottom. The oceans warm fastest. In society, the poor die off first. The most vulnerable are hit the hardest and impoverished the fastest. The inner mechanism of bottom-up collapse is this: the most defenseless things—whether they're animals, people, rivers, or rocks—are torn apart fastest and most ruthlessly. But the result is not prosperity and triumph. It is depletion. Ruin. Implosion.[10]

Through site-specific, life-promoting practices, however, we can work alongside and value the weakest agents that constitute the very fabric of our ecosystems and societies by building livability into habitats from the bottom up—not as a practice of designing and engineering individual buildings or structures, but through a holistic process of world-making, or worlding,[11] which marks an Ecological Era of human development.[12]

While we presently choreograph elements within an already life-bearing world within which humanity is a single constituent species, it does not follow that terrestrial ecosystem ingredients such as plants, soils, water, and organisms can be seamlessly transplanted into alien sites and inevitably knit themselves together to become an "ecology." Although

7
Nadia Drake, "No, Scott Kelly's Year in Space Didn't Mutate His DNA," *National Geographic*, March 15, 2018, https://news.nationalgeographic.com/2018/03/scott-kelly-astronaut-space-station-dna-health-science/.

8
Here, the term "constant" is used in its scientific context, where the effects of these variables do not change during an experiment.

9
Naser Odeh, Nikolas Hill, and Daniel Forster, "Current and Future Lifecycle Emissions of Key 'Low Carbon' Technologies and Alternatives," *Committee on Climate Change*, April 17, 2013, https://www.theccc.org.uk/wp-content/uploads/2013/04/Ricardo-AEA-lifecycle-emissions-low-carbon-technologies-April-2013.pdf.

10
Umair Haque, "The Age of Collapse: Why Everything's Collapsing and What to Do about It," *Eudaimonia*, January 24, 2019, https://eand.co/the-age-of-collapse-e606bfc1b46d.

11
The term "worlding" originates from Heidegger's notion of being-in-the-world, which involves both the process of experiencing reality (inhabiting) and making reality (constructing), thereby setting in motion a global-scale choreography of lively, material events that provide alternative trajectories for human development (Michael Wheeler, "Martin Heidegger. 2.2.3, Being-in-the-World," *Stanford Encyclopedia of Philosophy*, October 12, 2011, https://plato.stanford.edu/entries/heidegger/). In this context, worlding is used to denote an entanglement of processes that are orchestrated through the process of inhabitation, or "dwelling." Going beyond the simplistic perspectives of top-down or bottom-up notions of design and control by introducing the properties of matter, contingent events, and context, "worlding" does not de-problematize the complex relationships between possibility, intent, and desire.

12
Rachel Armstrong, *Star Ark: A Living, Self-Sustaining Space Ship* (Chichester, UK: Springer/Praxis, 2015).

terrestrial terrariums,[13] which are colonized by autotrophic organisms like plants or algae, can make their own food from sunlight and survive effectively untended for decades, this does not apply to larger or significantly more diverse ecosystems, where the myriad interactions between the co-constitutive bodies generate outcomes that are almost impossible to predict, fathom, or replicate.[14]

Such gaps in our understanding of ecosystem design were underscored during the Biosphere 2 experiment in Arizona during the early 1990s. This self-sustaining replica of Earth's ecosystem hosted two crewed human missions to investigate how long they could be sustained in a "closed-loop" environment. In the first mission, which took place between 1991 and 1993, a crew of eight biospherians were sealed off from the rest of the world, practicing advanced sustainable lifestyles that were scientifically monitored. Nonetheless, tipping points in atmospheric carbon dioxide concentration were reached, so composting was stopped to preserve oxygen levels. Consequently, the soils collapsed, resulting in a catastrophic loss of biodiversity. Eighteen months into the project, the system was uninhabitable.[15]

Recapitulating the established hierarchies of specific "biological objects" alone does not make an ecosystem. Something "else" is needed to facilitate the persistent "global" material dynamics that characterize our biosphere. These principles fall beyond the dominant narratives about how life "works," narratives framed by the "central dogma" of biology. Here, DNA is cast as playing a "strong" role in providing instructions to RNA molecules, which pass them on to proteins in a sole unidirectional flow of information and command—from the strongest to the weakest. DNA is responsible for coordinating all the functions of life and making sense of the organization of organic molecules, within its specific boundaries of influence, prioritizing the biological "object" over the soft forces that shape the metabolic exchanges that make matter lively.[16] In practice, life is permeable to its surroundings, being neither entirely determined nor wholly at the whim of random processes; rather, it is constantly negotiated—or "worlded"—within its specific context.[17]

After many years of trying to genetically reprogram environmental bacteria for release as agents of *in situ* bioremediation of toxic pollutants, Victor de Lorenzo decided that the interplay between genetics and metabolism is like that of politics and economy. Proposing that metabolism is the economy of living systems, which comprises all the networks of chemical transactions that are essential for life, he suggests this enabling milieu ultimately decides whether or not a given genetic program, or political decision, can be deployed. Metabolism therefore establishes which molecules can be exchanged to carry out the specific "motives" of the organism encoded in its DNA.[18] This is so important to bacteria that their evolutionary "drive" is enabled through the expansion of their metabolic networks toward new chemical landscapes, rather than by spreading their DNA sequences.[19] From a microbial perspective, the propagation of metabolism may be considered a technological infrastructure that enables its highly plastic genetic sequences to be effectively deployed across varying sites in response to changing contexts. While microbes are not usually imagined as world-building agencies, they formed the first communities that collectively generated the conditions that made early Earth livable. We will turn to their ability to manipulate the world through their metabolism, as a means of enlivening places.

When developing a test for NASA that could establish whether a planet was life-bearing, James Lovelock compared both the Martian and Venusian atmospheres to that of Earth. While our planet's nearest neighbors were in chemical equilibrium, Earth's atmospheres were characterized by

13
A terrarium is sometimes called an "ecosystem in a bottle."

14
Jeffrey P. Cohn, "Biosphere 2: Turning an Experiment into a Research Station," *BioScience* 52, no. 3 (2002): 218–223, https://doi.org/10.1641/0006-3568(2002)052[0218:BTAEIA]2.0.CO;2.

15
Jayne Poynter, *The Human Experiment: Two Years and Twenty Minutes inside Biosphere 2* (New York: Thunder's Mouth Press, 2006).

16
Victor de Lorenzo, "It's the Metabolism, Stupid!" *Environmental Microbiology Reports* 7, no. 1 (2015): 18–19, https://doi.org/10.1111/1758-2229.12223.

17
Ben McFarland, *A World from Dust: How the Periodic Table Shaped Life* (New York: Oxford University Press, 2016).

18
De Lorenzo, "It's the Metabolism, Stupid!"

19
Victor de Lorenzo, "From the Selfish Gene to Selfish Metabolism: Revisiting the Central Dogma," *Bioessays* 36, no. 3 (2014): 226, doi:10.1002/bies.201300153.

20
Diane R. Hitchcock and James E. Lovelock, "Life Detection by Atmospheric Analysis," *Icarus* 7, nos. 1–3 (1966):149–159, https://doi.org/10.1016/0019-1035(67)90059-0.

the presence of two types of gases that theoretically should neutralize each other—namely, reducing gases, such as methane, coexisting alongside free oxygen—yet they did not.[20] Lynn Margulis proposed an "active" organic cause for these findings, where microbes were capable of atmosphere-making, since ancient cyanobacteria in massive formations were known to be responsible for changing the early Earth's reducing atmosphere to an oxidizing one through the process of photosynthesis.[21] Chemical disequilibrium in an atmosphere was therefore indicative of life. Today, the descendants of early microbes comprise a heterogeneous "fabric" that is made up of more than 1030 cells, which span a trillion species,[22] possess a biomass of roughly 1017g,[23] and constitute an active terrestrial-scale metabolic platform.[24]

The ability of microbes to transform inert worlds into life-bearing systems was also noted by Iosif Shklovsky and Carl Sagan in 1996, as well as by Francis Crick and Leslie Orgel in 1973; they suggested that terrestrial organisms were catalyzed by the arrival of alien "seeds" that landed on the surface of early Earth—a process called panspermia. Turning these principles toward a technological goal, Crick and Orgel proposed that directed panspermia could, through human design, deliberately disseminate life throughout the universe.[25] While the approach is somewhat hit-or-miss and chances of success are low, any successful payloads would enable humankind to increase the spread of organic life by altering the composition of habitable planets so they are compatible with Earth's DNA/protein organisms. Michael Mautner and Gregory Matloff characterized the necessary "seeds" as diverse microbial payloads with various environmental tolerances, proposing that they could be sent in robotic capsules toward new solar systems, solar nebulae, and star-forming interstellar clouds.[26] On landing, the microbes would be released and their metabolisms would transform potentially viable alien landscapes into fertile planets, capable of hosting advanced terrestrial life-forms.[27]

Microbial metabolisms need not be deployed in a scattergun way but can be curated to address specific aspects of how we live and work.[28] Such possibilities are explored in the Living Architecture project, which reduces the uncertainty deployed in directed panspermia by choreographing a specific metabolic sequence of microbial events. Specifically, it aims to generate a domestic "economy" from liquid waste—namely, urine and gray water as the currency recognized by its constituent microorganisms.[29] Taking the form of a modular "wall" system, which is about the size of a large bookcase, it is suitable for installation in a bathroom, kitchen, or spacecraft. Each of its stacking "brick-like" components houses a specific colony of microbes that produce desirable metabolites. Two basic metabolic types of microorganism are employed. One is anaerobic, which constitutes a composting process that

21
James E. Lovelock and Lynn Margulis, "Atmospheric Homeostasis by and for the Biosphere: The Gaia Hypothesis," *Tellus* 26 (1974): 1–10, https://doi.org/10.1111/j.2153-3490.1974.tb01946.x; Lynn Margulis and James E. Lovelock, "Biological Modulation of the Earth's Atmosphere," *Icarus* 21 (1974): 471–489, https://doi.org/10.1016/0019-1035(74)90150-X; John F. Stolz, "Gaia and Her Microbes," *FEMS Microbial Ecology* 93, no. 2 (2016): 1–13, doi:10.1093/femsec/fiw247.

22
Kenneth J. Locey and Jay T. Lennon, "Scaling Laws Predict Global Microbial Diversity," *Proceedings of the National Academy of Sciences of the United States of America* 11, no.3 (2016): 5970–5975, https://doi.org/10.1073/pnas.1521291113.

23
William B. Whitman, David C. Coleman, and William J. Wiebe, "Prokayrotes: The Unseen Majority," *Proceedings of the National Academy of Sciences of the United States of America* 95 (1998): 6578–6583, https://doi.org/10.1073/pnas.95.12.6578; Sean McMahon and John Parnell, "Weighing the Deep Continental Biosphere," *FEMS Microbiology Ecology* 87 (2014): 113–120, https://doi.org/10.1111/1574-6941.12196.

24
This was "a complex entity involving the Earth's biosphere, atmosphere, oceans, and soil . . . constituting a feedback or cybernetic system which seeks an optimal physical and chemical environment for life" (Lovelock and Margulis, "Atmospheric Homeostasis by and for the Biosphere: The Gaia Hypothesis").

25
Christian Orlic, "The Origins of Directed Panspermia" (guest blog), *Scientific American*, January 9, 2013, https://blogs.scientificamerican.com/guest-blog/the-origins-of-directed-panspermia/.

26
Michael Noah Mautner and Gregory L. Matloff, "Directed Panspermia: A Technical and Ethical Evaluation of Seeding Nearby Solar Systems," *Journal of the British Interplanetary Society* 32 (1979): 419–423.

27
Lisa Zyga, "Professor: We Have a 'Moral Obligation' to Seed Universe with Life," *Phys.Org*, February 9, 2010, https://phys.org/news/2010-02-professor-moral-obligation-seed-universe.html#jCp.

28
This curation is not without rebellion, as Victor de Lorenzo noted, and refers to an ongoing negotiation between willful bodies, which may be human or not. For a specific outcome to be achieved, this negotiation is ongoing, never final, and may be understood as a "lived" engagement between participants who have a specific stake in the outcome.

29
The Living Architecture project is funded by the Horizon 2020 Research and Innovation Programme under EU Grant Agreement no. 686585. It brings together experts from the universities of Newcastle, UK; the west of England (UWE Bristol); Trento, Italy; the Spanish National Research Council in Madrid; LIQUIFER Systems Group, Vienna, Austria; and Explora, Venice, Italy.

can be harvested for electricity, water, and oxygen. When stand-alone, it is known as a microbial fuel cell—a kind of battery that is powered by organic matter.[30] The other is a photo-bioreactor, an autotrophic system that uses the photosynthetic power of tiny green organisms (algae) to trap sunlight and carbon dioxide to produce solid biomass.

The main challenge of the project is how these systems are brought together so that their products mutually support each other through various transactions. Modules can be spatially sequenced, stacked together, and biochemically "programmed" to form metabolic "apps" that comprise a variety of desired domestic products—specifically, electricity, inorganic phosphate, polished water, oxygen, heat, and biomass, which can be used as compost. This metabolic integration of microbes changes the very notion of "waste" because the outputs of one system can be used directly by another, generating a "cyclical economy" of matter by linking the cycles of life and death. The iterations of these processes are not entirely "circular" but receive light from an external source, which enables them to respond to input variations in different ways.[31] Marking a step change in technological robustness in integrating household resource and waste streams, Living Architecture addresses fluctuations through its programmability, responds to the specific needs of inhabitants,[32] and transforms our living spaces from sites that exclusively consume resources to regenerative sites. Within the context of a spacecraft or within a closed-system off-world biosphere, such an apparatus could provide the kind of resource recycling and regeneration functions that are presently performed by terrestrial soils. Specific metabolic "apps" could also be deployed to increase the chance of preferred biochemical reactions taking place through technologically mediated processes, rather than submitting to the laws of chance. In this way, space habitats could potentially evade specific resource shortages even with scant supplies or prevent ecosystems from reaching disastrous tipping points. By working with the smallest aspects of livability, their collective outputs summate to refresh the atmosphere, reduce the circulation of toxic compounds, such as nitrogen oxides, or make forms of edible biomass.

Reminiscent of those exchanges that took place between the first protolife, the biochemical webs of metabolic technologies, such as Living Architecture, increase the overall livability of a space through the genesis of myriads of "weak" transactions and processes. By recognising and identifying with the bacterial "bodies" with which we are deeply entangled,[33] an implicit relationship is struck between us and our intimate nonhuman communities within a new "economy of life," which we will come to regard and value as natural extensions of our own existence. As the range of tools for "conversing" with microbes is expanded,[34] increasingly more creative and diplomatic approaches will unfurl the diverse potential of those "living" metabolisms in which we are immersed, which perform equivalent roles to our terrestrial soils. In this way, the very process of human development is entangled with "metabolic" worlding, using the "language" of (bio)chemistry to establish the principles for an Ecological Era that equally applies to activities on Earth and in alien environments. Since life is continually testing the limits of its existence, such processes are likely to be exploratory endeavors—including difficult negotiations with existing alien ecosystems. Success will not be defined by the triumph of an individual's fitness, or selfishness, but through the creativity of mutual exchanges between organisms that enable each other to thrive. These first outposts will not be achieved by one dominant

30
Ioannis A. Ieropoulos, Andrew Stinchcombe, Iwona Gajda, Samuel Forbes, Irene Merino-Jimenez, Grzegorz Pasternak, Daniel Sanchez-Herranz, and John Greenman, "Pee Power Urinal: Microbial Fuel Cell Technology Field Trials in the Context of Sanitation," *Environmental Science: Water Research and Technology* 2 (2016): 336–343, doi:10.1039/C5EW00270B.

31
The long-term implication of open iterations, as opposed to a closed-loop system, is that they have the potential to evolve.

32
Sylvia Thompson, "Living Architecture: Investigating the Interface between Biology and Architecture: A New Vision for Homes and Cities," *Irish Times*, December 27, 2018, https://www.irishtimes.com/news/science/living-architecture-investigating-the-interface-between-biology-and-architecture-a-new-vision-for-homes-and-cities-1.3733994.

33
These include the internal microbiome as well as microbial metabolic technologies.

34
Stephen C. Winans and Bonnie L. Bassler, *Chemical Communication among Bacteria* (Washington, DC: ASM Press, 2008).

35
Our biological identity is problematic when it comes to embracing nonbiological life-forms, as they do not meet our present criteria for being truly "alive" and therefore raise problematic ethics with regard to how we should care for, relate to, and cherish them—particularly if their presence is contrary, or toxic, to our own. For example, in 2010 an organism GFAJ-1 was reported as having rewritten the recipe for DNA using arsenic, which disrupts the energy-producing molecule ATP, which is essential to biological life. These findings were later debunked but serve as an example to consider questions regarding our encounters with creatures whose existence and proximity may be lethal.

species or another but through establishing entire, initially fragile ecosystems. Such alliances will define the character of the new Earthbound, strengthened by enabling metabolic networks that generate the necessary resilience to support communities of many species of terrestrial settlers (e.g., people, microbes, trees, pollinators) in new worlds. Over time and with technological assistance, metabolic economies and landscapes will diversify to increase their resilience and generate the nature of organisms in relationship to the terrains they inhabit. These reinforcements will include: linking the cycles of life and death; reformulating definitions of alien/immigrant/settler/colonist to celebrate diversity rather than establish hierarchies of order; developing an ethics concerned with the propagation of terrestrial life and its appropriate relationship with alien life-forms; raising the status of a spectrum of "living" agents compared with biological systems that are typical of Earth, which may not meet the full terrestrial criteria for being "alive" but are essential to the community of "life" in alien environments[35]; paying due care and attention to soft and weak worlding forces; engaging the technology of metabolism to perform life-promoting "useful" work; developing appropriate, evolvable forms of diplomacy through which the terms of mutual co-inhabitation are established, where metabolism becomes a "universal" language that diversifies relationships rather than homogenizes them. By establishing a platform for evolving modes of meaningful exchange capable of drawing together different kinds of worlds, metabolic technologies will play a critical role in establishing empathy with nonhuman agents; learning nonhuman languages; accommodating the risk associated with probabilistic operations; appreciating the appropriate limits of material performance; anticipating tipping points of order; designing for change; dealing with unexpected transformation within systems; and evolving habitable spaces within specific locales, rather than installing universalized, ready-made objects-for-living-in. This necessary era of human development will not take place all at once, but its radical impacts will be effected and evolve through many persistent acts of settlement.[36] In these ventures and explorations, the technology (and chemical "language") of metabolism will play a critical role in establishing the infrastructure for life, with impacts on how we design, inhabit, and reimagine how diverse life-forms can live meaningfully together in alien spaces. Many, like Biosphere 2, will not prove successful, but collectively they will both provide insights regarding the (re)settlement of the terrestrial sphere at a time of ecocide and open up new modes of exploration that engage humanity's irreducibly problematic imperative[37]—to thrive beyond our home planet[38] and disseminate terrestrial life throughout the cosmos.

36
There is no one approach or "solution" to settlement. This term applies equally to how we inhabit Earth during an age of widespread collapse, as much as it indicates our desire to inhabit other worlds and spaces beyond our own.

37
The ethical implications of the colonial terrestrial imperative must not be overlooked. While advocates like Michael Mautner suggest an ethics for the community of life where the presence of "life" is *good* and its absence *bad* (Michael Noah Mautner, *Seeding the Universe with Life* [Christchurch, NZ: Legacy Books, 2004]), the nuances of our inescapably anthropocentric perspective must be appropriately critiqued. Even deeper ongoing questions about the nature of the question must be raised. Importantly, the nature of life itself must not be assumed, and we must consider, What does *matter* want? These discussions exceed the scope of this present essay.

38
Russian cosmist Nikolai Fyodorovich Fyodorov refused to accept the physical constraints of our planet as the limits to humanity and proposed that, through our reason and technology, we could "storm the heavens and conquer death" (Benedict Singleton, "Maximum Jailbreak," *Journal of the British Interplanetary Society* 67 [2014]: 266–271). Attributing these constraints to the unruly forces of nature, he suggested its unpredictable character could be controlled by introducing will and reason into the natural realm, which would grant knowledge and control over all atoms and molecules of the world, which would in turn carve out a greater space for life.

Afterworld: The Cosmic Ecology of Reenchantment

DANIEL DAOU

For through astonishment men have begun to philosophize both in our times and in the beginning.
—Aristotle, *Metaphysics*, A2, 982b, 13–16

1972: Modern, Postmodern, and Cosmodern Ecologies

Do we witness a new cultural sensibility? Consider three images, all appearing in the same year, and the things we can surmise upon a quick comparative analysis.

First, the *Blue Marble* (1972) photograph shot by the crew of the Apollo 17 mission. It was released in the same year as the all-time best-selling environmental publication *The Limits to Growth* (1972) and the celebration of the first World Conference on the Human Environment in Stockholm. Together with these events, the photograph helped usher environmentalism into its "planetary" stage. The technology that made shooting *Blue Marble* possible from outer space was the same that was used to model the environmental predictions in the *Limits to Growth* report. The cybernetic model known as World3 modelled both the crew's life support systems that enabled this seemingly impossible photograph and the future prospects of "Spaceship Earth" itself. Apollo's eye was a Hasselblad 500 EL camera, and it showed us Earth as a singular, lone island suspended in a fathomless abyss.

Next, consider the painting titled *The City of the Captive Globe* (1972) by artist Madeleine Vriesendorp. It depicts the Earth in a pit at the center of an urban grid bringing to mind a quote by philosopher Jacques Derrida: "There is no world, only islands." Instead of the lone oasis, an archipelago. Instead of outer space, the isomorphic grid of an ideal where every block represents an ideology. Together, they participate in the pluralistic "incubation of the world."[1] Produced the same year as the demolition of the high-rise public housing project known as Pruitt-Igoe (which marked the symbolic death of modernism, according to historian Charles Jencks) and as the publication of *Learning from Las Vegas* (1972)—a postmodern manifesto in its own right—*The City of the Captive Globe* illustrates the postmodern take on ecology as a social construct.

Lastly, think of the Pioneer plaque designed by Linda Salzman, Carl Sagan, and Frank Drake in 1972—later included in the Golden Record onboard the 1977 Voyager probes missions. The plaque depicts the human figures next to a schematic drawing of the probe itself, the position of the sun with respect to other celestial bodies, and the cosmic address of the Earth within a diagram of the solar system. With a hydrogen atom as a unit, the plaque bootstraps an entire code system so its message can be deciphered if ever found by others. The plaque's

1
Terence Riley, "Drawn into a Collection: A Context of Practices" in *Envisioning Architecture: Drawings from The Museum of Modern Art*, ed. Matilda McQuaid (New York: The Museum of Modern Art, 2002), 172.

diagrams constitute an earnest effort in a cosmopolitan universalism.

If the *Blue Marble* photo's rendering of ecology represents the modern view of ecology (detached, dualist, positivist) and *The City of the Captive Globe* painting represents the postmodern (hybrid, pluralist, and contingent), then the diagram featured on the Pioneer plaque (along with a plethora of media, from whale songs to the brainwaves of a woman thinking about falling in love, included in the Golden Record) could stand for a view of ecology we could call "cosmodern," borrowing the term from physicist and philosopher of science Basarab Nicolescu.[2]

This essay recovers and expands the notion of cosmodernism by incorporating three seemingly disconnected subjects—cosmopolitics, cosmology, and cosmism. But like stars, to see them aligned in a constellation, these three topics need to be regarded from a specific angle.

Reenchantment

Political ecology argues solutions to our environmental problems aren't exclusively techno-managerial. Today's "singular, but manifold" crisis calls for an urgent reorientation of our political affects.[3] Defining the grounds on which such a reorientation ought to take place amounts to nothing less than a reenvisioning of our conception of the world. As philosopher Bruno Latour points out, "Despite appearances, what counts in politics are not *attitudes*, but the form and the weight of the *world* to which these attitudes have the function of *reacting*. . . . This is the decisive discovery of political ecology."[4] The project of reenchantment is the reconstitution of the world. Cosmopolitics, cosmology, and cosmism come together in it: cosmopolitics, as a timely political sensibility (a remedy not only to xenophobia but to anthropocentrism), cosmology as the stage where natural philosophy's speculations on the unknown are grounded in material scientific practice, and cosmism as an example of the political horizons such reorientation would make accessible.[5]

Our political imagination is depleted.[6] Philosopher Jean-Jacques Rousseau's "noble savage" or philosopher Thomas Hobbes's "Leviathan" illustrate how political imaginaries are founded on myths. There's no more primordial myth than nature

2
See Basarab Nicolescu, *Théorèmes poétiques* (Monaco: Éditions du Rocher, 1994). See also Christian Moraru, *Cosmodernism* (Ann Arbor: University of Michigan Press, 2011) and Basarab Nicolescu, *From Modernity to Cosmodernity* (Albany: SUNY Press, 2015).

3
I don't feel the need to elaborate on how (1) the environmental, financial, social, and political crises are all facets of a "singular, but manifold crisis" with its root in the totalizing algorithm of capitalist neoliberalism, and (2) how, out of these, the environmental crisis imposes the greatest objective urgency. Enough critical debate has taken place around the proper calibration of scientific affects leading to a tacit consensus around "climate realism" (borrowing the term from scholar Andreas Malm). For converging critical views on this matter, see, for instance, Jason W. Moore, *Capitalism in the Web of Life* (New York: Verso, 2015); Andreas Malm, *The Progress of This Storm* (London: Verso, 2018), and Bruno Latour, *Down to Earth*, 1st ed. (Cambridge, UK: Polity Press, 2018).

4
Bruno Latour, *Down to Earth*, 52.

5
Cosmopolitanism for the Greek cynics revolved around a sense of belonging—not to a state, but to the world. For Kant, it was a matter of hospitality, a condition necessary for "perpetual peace." For Latour and philosopher Isabelle Stengers, cosmopolitics is a matter of inclusion, of which modes of knowing can assert their claim to truth and how political assemblages are constituted beyond the human. In this manner, both cosmopolitanism and cosmopolitics are related through the notion of belonging.

"Cosmopolitics" was developed by Stengers in her eponymous series, *Cosmopolitics* (2003). Characteristic of postmodern critiques of "scientism," the term challenges the hegemony of science in modern societies. She proposes taking competing worldviews seriously rather than condescendingly tolerating them in a manner that levels the field between the modern and the premodern. This formulation was welcomed in a postcolonial context that tried to bring back the voices of those historically excluded (women, lgbt+, minorities, animals, etc.). It was also welcomed in the context of the so-called science wars of the 1990s—a reaction against techno-managerialism (erroneously perceived as apolitical). However, as some critics note, Stengers's formulation leaves the question of pluralism and inclusivity unresolved. For instance, philosopher Steven Shaviro's has asked, "Where do Stengers' and Latour's anti-modernist imperatives leave us when it comes to dealing with the fundamentalist, evangelical Christians in the United States today?" The postmodern affect not only failed to produce an agreeable, progressive alternative to capitalism, but its analytical arsenal is now weaponized by movements such as climate change denialism.

On the potential for reenchantment found in cosmology, geographer Denis Cosgrove writes in reference to Humboldt's *Kosmos*: "But if Humboldt embraced a characteristic Enlightenment belief in positive scientific progress moving from myth to enlightenment by way of empirical observation within a disenchanted physical universe, he shared with Ruskin and other nineteenth-century students of nature the fascination with natural form and phenomenological apperception articulated by Johann Wolfgang Goethe. Humboldt acknowledged the enduring power of human imagination and speculation in making and framing science." See Denis Cosgrove, *Geography and Vision* (London: I. B. Tauris, 2008).

and its corollary, human nature. In "Nature at the Millennium: Production and Re-enchantment" (1999), geographer Neil Smith observed that for all its analytical antisepticism, the Left has failed in formulating a powerful anti-ideology of nature that takes seriously the realities of the production of nature but is simultaneously capable of appealing to a deeper layer of emotional significance.[7] As to where such a project could begin, inadvertently paraphrasing poet Stéphane Mallarmé, he hints: "the desolate junction of poetics and political economy." But he also warns, "Access to poetic nature is thoroughly policed by politico-economic power."[8]

Sociologist Max Weber lamented the fate of our times as being characterized by "rationalization and intellectualization and, above all, the 'disenchantment of the world.'" If disenchantment translates into a strictly materialist naturalism, then it was biologist Charles Darwin's evolution theory that delivered the death blow to supernatural accounts in nature. Before him, Western enlightened thought remained teleological: philosopher Georg W. F. Hegel's notion of evolution was orthogenetic, philosopher Immanuel Kant thought the ultimate station of human societies was eternal peace, and, in philosopher Karl Marx's politico-economic vision, capitalism necessarily led to communism.[9] Evolution demoted progress (unavoidable and irreversible) to mere change (random and contingent); it turned the arrow of time into spaghetti. Cognitive scientist and philosopher Daniel Dennett calls Darwinism a "universal solvent" that removes any "trace of purpose or meaning in either nature or life." Evolution is a process with no ulterior goal other than conjugating creatures with their environment strictly in the present tense. In other words, evolution, unlike progress, is blind to the future.[10]

Given the nearly full scientific consensus around the neo-Darwinian materialist conception of the physical universe, a project for the reenchantment of nature entails a great deal of diplomacy. Many, including Smith, warn about the dangers of falling for the naivete of Romantic, premodern, and magical worldviews or the corrupting mysticism of the so-called dark enlightenment. To avoid these dangers, we ought to recognize that our understanding of nature is always technologically mediated, as philosopher Yuk Hui suggests through the concept of cosmotechnics.[11] A quote mistakenly attributed to the poet William Butler Yeats goes: "The universe is full of magical things patiently waiting for our wits to grow sharper." In the original passage, writer Eden Phillpots, who describes the beauty of a flower under a magnifying glass, refers to the development of sufficient technology to reveal the splendor of the cosmos. Today, nothing embodies this better than the gold-coated beryllium mirrors of the James Webb space telescope—an instrument many hope will allow the detection of life biosignatures in exoplanetary atmospheres.

6
The 2007–2009 recession exposed the neoliberal farce. Trump's election, the Brexit vote, and the general regression of democracy worldwide are symptomatic of societies fed up with a political economy indefensible by its beneficiaries and unsustainable for the affected. The recent trends show political change is possible, but in the absence of an agreeable, progressive alternative, the world is retrenching into ethno-nationalism, xenophobia, and unilateralism.

In "To Modernize or to Ecologize" (2004), Latour suggests, "The present historical condition is defined by a complete disconnect between two alternative narratives—one of emancipation, detachment, modernization, progress, and mastery, and the other, completely different, of precaution, attachment, entanglement, dependence, and care." His is the outline of the age-old tension at the heart of every narrative of progress. Just a few years after the perfecting of the steam engine set off the Industrial Revolution, economist Robert Malthus wrote: "It has been said that the great question is now at issue, whether man shall henceforth start forward with accelerated velocity toward illimitable, and hitherto unconceived improvement; or be condemned to a perpetual oscillation between happiness and misery, and after every effort remains still at an immeasurable distance from the so-wished goal." The greatest promise of reenchantment is to ignite a narrative to expand our political horizons beyond these poles.

7
See Roland Barthes, *Mythologies* (Paris: Éditions du Seuil, 1957).

8
Here, following philosopher Roland Barthes's elucidations on myths and power, it's useful to remember that one function of myth is naturalizing certain worldviews. Paraphrasing writer Anaïs Nin, we should remain alert, for "we see nature not as it is, but as we are." On the relationship between myths and cosmology, see Stephen Toulmin, *The Return to Cosmology* (Berkeley: University of California Press, 1985). "If we do think ourselves myth free, when we are not, that is (I am suggesting) largely because the material from which we construct our myths is taken from the sciences themselves," 24.

9
See Hui Yuk, "Cosmotechnics as Cosmopolitics," *e-flux* 86 (November 2017). "Kant maintains that this relation between nature and cosmopolitics is necessary. If Kant sees the republican constitution and perpetual peace as political forms that may be able to bring forward a universal history of the human species, it is because he understands that such progress is also a progress of reason, the telos of nature. This progress toward an end goal . . . is the 'completion of a hidden plan of nature.' What does it mean for nature to have a hidden plan? And why is the realization of cosmopolitics the teleology of nature?"

10
See Brian Snyder, "The Darwinian Nihilist Critique of Environmental Ethics," *Ethics & the Environment* 22, no. 2 (2017): 59–78.

Cosmic Imaginaries

Our imagination for the extraterrestrial is more relevant than ever. We witness a burgeoning new space race and accelerated progress in cosmological discoveries.[12] Beyond science and technology, even culture and politics are developing new cosmic sensibilities with the discovery of the radical altermodern project of Russian cosmism by the West and reinvigorated debates around cosmopolitanism and cosmopolitics. At the historical junction where we find ourselves, perhaps a "cosmodern" sensibility can serve as a "soft heuristic" to reorient our questions not as independent political, ecological, or aesthetic matters, but rather as a matter of "civilization itself."[13]

In "Back to Sublunar Earth" (2010), Latour presents the setbacks in space exploration since the end of the Apollo program to illustrate that technological progress is not inevitable and irreversible, as thinkers of the Enlightenment believed. The timing of his conclusion—unavoidable under the "hermeneutics of suspicion" characteristic of postmodern critique—couldn't be more off. At the time of his writing, a fledging new space race unfolded. Starting in the late 1990s, a new generation of billionaires embarked on a new privately funded space race.

In a lecture at Harvard almost ten years later, Latour again casts outer space negatively. He sees capitalism's endgame in the renewed interest in space: an escapist fantasy that negates the limits of our "climate regime."[14] He calls this the "out-of-this-world attractor," characterizing it as a utopia for the few. Ironically, on the very same day, Jeff Bezos, world's richest man and CEO of Amazon and aeronautics company Blue Origin, expressed his goal of seeing "a trillion humans inhabiting the solar system."[15] These contrasting takes around space fantasy illustrate that, more than "socialism for the rich and capitalism for the poor," what we experience is manifest destiny for the billionaires and existentialism for the rest. But instead of condemning the extraterrestrial imagination, the Left ought to reclaim it.

Latour proposes the "terrestrial" not only to counter the "out-of-this-world" attractor, but to counter the long-standing dichotomy between the local and the global. For him, the view from "the Great Outside" that characterizes the "out-of-this-world" attractor is simply too abstract—a dangerous illusion. The local and the global have redeeming moments but also pitfalls. The terrestrial aims to refine a delicate balancing act: "The soil allows us to attach ourselves; the world allows detachment. Attachment allows us to get away from the illusion of a Great Outside; detachment allows us to escape the illusion of borders."[16] In this regard, Latour's "terrestrial" shares a goal not too dissimilar from scholar Christian Moraru's "planetary," which tries to reclaim the space of the world from the totalizing paradigm of globalization. Both concepts plot different paths toward a process of "worlding" that doesn't relinquish the space of possibility of the largest of scales—that of the planet, the world, the globe, or Gaia—to the suffocating singularity of globalization.[17] To paraphrase Robert Venturi, both

11
The invention of the telescope and the microscope in the 1600s revealed hidden magnitudes resulting in a new relation with the cosmos. On one hand, nature ceased to be anthropomorphic with humans at the center. On the other, vast vistas opened, ready to be explored. It's a dual moment of enchantment and disenchantment.

12
At the time of writing, Vice President Michael Pence announced plans to send humans back to the Moon by 2024. See, among others, Christian Davenport, *The Space Barons* (New York: Public Affairs, 2019).

13
On cosmism's rediscovery, the first Western publication was historian George Young's *Russian Cosmists, The Esoteric Futurism of Nikolai Fedorov and His Followers* (London: Oxford University, 2012). Alex Williams and Nick Srnicek, authors of "#Accelerate: Manifesto for an Accelerationist Politics" (2013), reference cosmism as a source for political ambition. Writings by Fyodorov and Tsiolkovsky are included in *#Accelerate: The Accelerationist Reader* (Edited by Robin Mackay and Armen Avanessian, published by MIT Press, 2014.), and *e-flux journal* dedicated its February 2018 volume to cosmism. Princeton's School of Architecture held the "Cosmism-Superhumanity" symposium in 2017, and theorist Boris Groys edited an anthology, *Russian Cosmism* (Cambridge, MA: MIT Press, 2018).

On cosmodernism, "Moraru has observed that the post-1989 historical intermezzo of 'cosmodernism' translates . . . primarily into an imaginary, a way of picturing the world." See Christian Moraru and Amy J. Elias, *The Planetary Turn: Relationality and Geoaesthetics in the Twenty-First Century* (Evanston, Illinois: Northwestern University Press, 2015), xxv.

On the notion of totality or society-as-a-whole, Latour writes: "The current situation . . . is not simply a contradiction, . . . a matter of economics, but rather of civilization itself." See Bruno Latour, *Down to Earth*, 89 and also György Lukács, *History and Class Consciousness* (Cambridge, MA: MIT Press, 1968).

14
Bruno Latour, "A Tale of Seven Planets—An Exercise in Gaiapolitics" (lecture, Harvard University, Cambridge, MA, October 16, 2018).

15
Jeff Bezos, remarks delivered at the 25th anniversary event for *Wired* magazine (San Francisco, October 15, 2018).

16
Bruno Latour, *Down to Earth: Politics in the New Climatic Regime*, 1st ed. (Cambridge, UK: Polity Press, 2018), 41.

17
See also Jean-Luc Nancy, *La création du monde ou la mondialisation* (Paris: Galilée, 2002).

the terrestrial and the planetary look for a process of worlding that embodies the difficult unity of inclusion rather than the easy unity of exclusion.[18]

The "planetary" and the "terrestrial" are associated with the "geo-" prefix (as in geosocial, geophilosophical, geohistory, or geopolitical). A "cosmodern" affect would take them a step further, substituting the "geo-" with the "cosmo-." Otherwise, any new geo-affects risk having the same failings as previous "ecological movements."

Geographer Alexander von Humboldt, in his magnum opus *Kosmos* (1845–1862), used the term "cosmos" to refer to heaven and the heavens *together*. It's not an opposition, but an extension—vis-à-vis the cosmic, the terrestrial seems parochial. For all the importance Latour gives to ecology, there's a frustrating inwardness in his narrative, especially considering the speculative nature of his call to imagining new modes of existing in the world. Ecology released from its terrestrial horizon to include the entirety of the universe governed by the laws of physics reveals itself as cosmology. Why the obsession with "sublunar Earth" when what is required is nothing less than a "moon shot" effort? To quote geographer Denis Cosgrove, "To lose the sense of heavens is to risk losing also that of Earth."[19]

Ecological movements are suffused with a scarcity worldview. This is best illustrated by the commonsensical argument of the limits-to-growth apologists: in a finite world, growth cannot be limitless. Few would dare challenge this self-evident statement.[20] Yet economists do, and, for that, they get criticized for not grounding their doctrine in material reality. In response, the so-called ecological economists have fashioned an economic theory from the ground up based on their understanding of the laws of physics.[21] It is ironic, then, that the second group that goes against the limits-to-growth argument is composed of physicists. The argument is summed up by physicist Frank Tipler: "Being too frugal with our resources today in the mistaken belief that they are forever finite may prevent us from developing the unlimited resources permitted by the laws of physics."[22]

Examples of "nonscarcity" or "open" worldviews (sometimes also called "postscarcity" or "cornucopian") that lie beyond the Manichean space of the limits-to-growth framework are rare.[23] All the more reason to turn our attention to the recent discovery of Russian cosmism by the West. Cosmism is the name given to a set of ideas put forth by a group of Soviet philosophers, artists, and scientists in the late 19th and early 20th centuries. The head figure of the movement was philosopher Nikolai Fyodorov. His writings were collected posthumously by his followers in *The Philosophy of the Common Task* (1916). Fyodorov's Common Task can be summarized as the abolition of death and the resurrection of the dead. It ought to be understood not as a theological eschatology but as the radical conclusion of a rational emancipatory project—one that wasn't encumbered by the normative definitions of the terrestrial while still being grounded in science and technology.

Immortality for all is the concrete result of the collectivization of time. For Fyodorov, private property (of space) could not be abolished unless it also involved private property of time. Truly emancipated individuals experience themselves as the ones to be preserved. Progress is the tyranny of future generations over the present. Therefore, the only true technology is the technology of sustainability: mastery over time is the artificial production of eternity. For the cosmists, death is always artificial since it can be technologically prevented.

Another central cosmist figure was Konstantin Tsiolkovsky. Though he is known as the father of the Soviet space program, he saw his technical writings on rocketry only as a supplement to his

18
Robert Venturi, *Complexity and Contradiction in Architecture* (New York: The Museum of Modern Art, 1966), 88.

19
Denis Cosgrove, *Geography and Vision: Seeing, Imagining and Representing the World* (London: I.B. Tauris, 2008), 48.

20
See Leigh Phillips, *Austerity Ecology: A Defence of Growth and Progress* (Winchester, UK: Zero Books, 2015).

21
Historical accounts on the "underground" school of economics are rare. See Luis Fernández-Galiano, *Fire and Memory* (Cambridge, MA.: MIT Press, 2000) and Jeremy L. Caradonna, *Sustainability* (New York: Oxford University Press, 2014).

22
See Frank Tipler, "There Are No Limits to the Open Society," *Critical Rationalist* 3, no. 2 (September 23, 1998).

23
See Alf Hornborg, "Cornucopia or Zero-Sum Game? The Epistemology of Sustainability," *Journal of World-Systems Research* 9, no. 2 (2003): 205–216. See also Karl R. Popper, "Natural Selection and the Emergence of Mind" (lecture, Darwin College, Cambridge, November 8, 1977). "Although science has nothing to say about the personal creator, the fact of the emergence of novelty and of creativity can hardly be denied. I think that Darwin . . . himself would have agreed that though natural selection was an idea which opened up a new world for science, it did not remove from the picture of the universe that science paints the marvel of creativity, nor did it remove the marvel of freedom to create and the freedom of choosing our own ends and our own purposes."

Besides Russian cosmism, the only example that comes to mind is Bataille's notion of a "universal economy." See Georges Bataille, *La Part Maudite* (Paris: Éditions de Minuit, 1949).

philosophy of space exploration. Tsiolkovsky's *Will of the Cosmos: The Unknown Intelligence* (1928) is a rare illustration of the biopolitics of panpsychism.[24] For him, the brain is only a material part of the universe. All its processes originate in the cosmos. Therefore, the will of the mind is the same as the will of the universe. If the human brain is part of the cosmos and transmits its cosmic energy, then the human being is itself cosmic.

These ideas are further developed in philosopher Evald Ilyenkov's *Cosmology of the Spirit* (ca. 1950). Ilyenkov tried to answer an ambitious question at the intersection of evolutionary biology and philosophy: What is the function of life at the scale of the universe? "Matter constantly possesses thought, constantly thinks itself," he writes. "Since the universe is infinite, probabilistically, there will always be another instance of matter that develops thought in some other time and space. Thus, the 'thinking brain' always emerges and reproduces somewhere in the cosmos. It is in this specific sense that 'matter constantly thinks itself.'"[25]

In Ilyenkov's view, as in Tsiolkovsky's, mind emerges from matter. But, in a dialectical moment, a subtler materialism, as philosopher Alexei Penzin explains, would also have it the other way: mind is necessary for matter. Indeed, Ilyenkov writes, "Matter cannot exist without thought." Using philosopher Baruch Spinoza's language, what Ilyenkov says could be stated thus: if mind (the highest form of matter) were only accidental, it would be merely a "mode" and not an "attribute." The radical proposition of cosmopsychism is reconciling Spinoza with Darwin in a cosmos where the ultimate goal of mind is not self-perfection or absolute knowledge, as suggested by idealistic or religious teleologies, but something "endlessly greater"—a vision of cosmology where the destinies of mind and matter are inexorably intertwined. To the "the great question of whether man is of nature or above her" once formulated by conservationist George Perkins Marsh, cosmism answers: we are of nature, except nature isn't what we think it is.

Cosmology is the study of the universe, its origin and its evolution. As physicist Freeman Dyson recounts, up until the 1940s, "the early universe was not a fit subject for experimental or theoretical effort" (before the inflationary theory, the prevalent view was that the universe had no beginning).[26] The beginning of the universe became a respectable field of scientific inquiry thanks to the courageous speculations of a few scientists. Similarly, Dyson argued in the 1970s, the turn should come for the end of the universe. The physical eschatology Dyson outlines is remarkable for the role he believes life could play in the evolution of the universe.[27] After all, if the universe has existed for some 13 billion years—of which Earth has been around for 4.5 billion—and the current stelliferous era is supposed to last for 100 *trillion*, who is to say the milestone of the emergence of intelligent life couldn't mark another era, a "cosmic Anthropocene" of sorts?

Indeed, the realization that we live at the very beginning of time in an embryo universe raises the question of whether life could play a role in its future evolution. One of the earliest modern figures to ponder this question formally was astrophysicist Iosif Shklovsky in his *Universe, Life, Intelligence* (1962). Chapter 34 of the English version—coauthored by cosmologist Carl Sagan—is titled "Intelligent Life as a Factor of the Cosmic Scale." It presents these questions: "Are any of the phenomena which we observe in the universe inexplicable in terms of the physics of non-living matter? Can some phenomena be understood only if we invoke the intervention of living organisms in technical civilizations? We cannot yet answer this question." Project Cyclops (1971), a preliminary study for a SETI project coauthored by NASA and Stanford University, states under the header "Biocosmology": "So long as we are limited to physical cosmology and to geocentric biology, many enormously exciting and very fundamental questions will remain unanswered. Does life itself serve a role in the evolution of the physical universe, perhaps modifying it in some way; or does it exist completely at the mercy of the latter?"[28] Darwinian evolution theory might have disenchanted terrestrial nature, but as the "evolutionary turn" in cosmology shows, it has certainly been a great source of reenchantment for extraterrestrial nature. The question

24
On cosmopsychism in relation to the anthropic principle, see Philip Goff, *Consciousness and Fundamental Reality* (New York: Oxford University Press, 2017).

25
Alexei Penzin, "Contingency and Necessity in Evald Ilyenkov's Communist Cosmology," *e-flux* 88 (February 2018).

26
See Freeman Dyson, "Time without End: Physics and Biology in an Open Universe," *Reviews of Modern Physics* 51, no. 3 (July 1979): 447–460.

27
Physical eschatologies include the Big Rip, the Big Crunch, and, popularly, thermal death. None of these considers the role life could play in the evolution of the universe. See Milan M. Ćirković, "Resource Letter: PEs-1: Physical Eschatology," *American Journal of Physics* 71, no. 2 (February 2003): 122–133.

28
NASA, Ames Research Center, and Stanford University, "Project Cyclops," 1971, https://ntrs.nasa.gov/archive/nasa/casi.ntrs.nasa.gov/19730010095.pdf, 30.

of what the role of life could be in the evolution of the cosmos might perhaps be the purview of a speculative bio-cosmological program.[29]

Turning our attention back to the "terrestrial," a most pressing matter left unanswered by Bruno Latour is, Where does his eschatology leave us *in the end?*[30] He speaks of "destiny," but he refuses to go "faster than history." Is his hypothesis for a "political fiction" of any use if the conclusions lead us nowhere new? Is his insistence on the "new materialism" of the terrestrial a call for a "minimal bioeconomic program" like the one economist Nicholas Georgescu-Roegen once proposed? Or is his formulation open to the unaccountable, excess energy—the accursed share of writer Georges Bataille's universal economy?[31] Latour insists that the view from outside is an impossible view from nowhere. But physicist and philosopher of cosmology Milan Ćirković suggests that the view is not from, but toward, that outside functions like a "magic mirror" that forces us to see ourselves *into our future*.[32] At the end of his text, Latour writes, "The point of this essay is not to disappoint, but one cannot ask it to go faster than the history that is underway." Except that that is precisely the most urgent task at hand. If the "decisive discovery of political ecology" is that we ought to change our territories rather than our attitudes, then the popular saying "think global, act local" should be rephrased as "think cosmic, act global"—or, as Latour would have it, "terrestrial."

29
On biocosmology, see James N. Gardner, *Biocosm* (Makawao, HI: Inner Ocean, 2003). See also Dorion Sagan, *Cosmic Apprentice* (Minneapolis: University of Minnesota Press, 2013). "Understanding ourselves as exponents of a natural, rather than a special teleology is, I would argue, a scientific satori that gets to the root of the connectedness of all things. It brings together Darwin and Spinoza, Gaia and microbial ecology, phenomenology and materialism," 239.

30
Bruno Latour, *Down to Earth*, 85. "What the New Climate Regime calls into question is not the central place of the human; it is its composition, its presence, its figuration, in a word, *its destiny*." (emphasis mine)

31
Georgescu-Roegen's minimal bioeconomic program was more radical than the steady state economy of his student, Herman Daly. Georgescu-Roegen recognized mineral wealth is finite, and therefore the only way forward is minimizing its consumption to maximize its duration. For Bataille, the problem is the opposite: "The world is sick of wealth, and the apparent scarcity is only a sign of the misuse of energy." See Allan Stoekl, *Bataille's Peak* (Minneapolis: University of Minnesota Press, 2007).

32
On the philosophy of cosmology, see Milan M. Ćirković, *The Great Silence* (Oxford, UK: Oxford University Press, 2018).

Cosmorama: A Peep Show of the New Space Age

RANIA GHOSN and EL HADI JAZAIRY

In 1968 Buckminster Fuller wrote, "We are all astronauts." In his book *Operating Manual for Spaceship Earth* (1969), the planet is compared to a vessel hurtling through space, with limited provisions and humanity as its crew. For Fuller, Earth could no longer be thought of as a natural object but instead must be recognized as a huge artificial construct. Originally delivered as a lecture to the American Planners Association, Fuller's "Spaceship Earth" challenged designers and policymakers to consider our planet part of a larger universe. Fuller also experimented with storytelling to engage cosmic imagination. In his *Tetrascroll: Goldilocks and the Three Bears, A Cosmic Fairy Tale* (1982), Fuller narrates ideas and structures about the universe and man's place in it to his daughter Allegra. Gradually, the story becomes a cosmic seminar, with Goldy leading the Polar Bear family in a teach-in sky-party.

How do we narrate and tackle 21st-century tales of the New Space Age—asteroid mining, life in zero gravity, and space debris? Space, the final frontier, recently regained significance with private space initiatives speculating in off-sourced extraction for water, platinum group metals, and other resource riches. Commercial companies are increasingly invested in exploratory missions to map, visit, and return astronomical rock samples to Earth. Until recently, commercial companies' claim to business in space seemed nearly impossible. Not anymore. Companies like Planetary Resources plan to extract billions of dollars' worth of ore from near-Earth asteroids. In February 2018, Elon Musk's Tesla Roadster and its dummy driver, Starman, made headlines when the car blasted off with David Bowie's "Space Oddity" booming from its speakers. The symbolism of a dashboard screen displaying DON'T PANIC resonates with billionaire entrepreneur Elon Musk's worries about the next extinction and his thoughts that humans need to evacuate Earth and become interplanetary, with plans for the ecological colonization of Mars. In this emerging New Space Age, outer space is no longer the "common heritage of mankind," as declared by the United Nations' Outer Space Treaty (1967) but now an extension of private corporations tied to politics on Earth.

The following three geographic stories stage these concerns and invite a consideration of environmental politics in the heavens as it is on Earth.

Mining the Sky

The franchising of outer space will become reality. According to the 2015 US SPACE Act (Spurring Private Aerospace Competitiveness and Entrepreneurship Act), US citizens have the right to engage in the "exploitation of extra-planetary resources," which essentially allows them to trade in resources from other planets—a clear violation of the 1967 Outer Space Treaty that prevents any state from exercising national appropriation of sovereignty or by any other means. The privatization of outer space is expected to drive the nascent New Space entrepreneurial movement. The captured asteroids will be despun and towed to a mining depot at the Earth-Moon L1 Lagrange point—a position where the combined gravitational pulls constitute a stable equilibrium point. Robotic arms will process the asteroid in one of two ways: hollow out the core, collecting the trail of debris in the fabricated cave, or mine the surface to carve faces of the gods of the New Space Age (a cosmic Mount Rushmore). The mining station will serve the human settlements via the Interplanetary Transport Network. Objects travel through gravitational highways in the solar system, requiring minimal energy. Extraction stations will constitute the first artificial constellations visible by the human eye from Earth. A modern astronomical sense of the term "constellation" is a recognizable pattern of stars whose appearance is associated with mythological characters or creatures or with earthbound animals. The Capitalocene civilization creates its own pattern in the sky based on stories and people that are deemed important.

Planetary Ark

Planet Earth is in the midst of its sixth mass extinction of plants and animals, with as many as 30 to 50 percent of all species heading toward extinction by midcentury. Climate change and uncertain futures define a new normal on Earth. Animal species at (or past) the brink of extinction are sent out in a cubicle on a Planetary Ark. The animals march into the Empire State to embark on their journey. Scientists on board believe humans have an ethical obligation toward all life-forms: no to extermination, extinction, and genocide. The anthropocenic version of the ark includes "sacrificial" animals that were launched into space on scientific experiments to test the human body's ability to survive spaceflight. Laika, one of the first animals in space, was never expected survive and died within hours from overheating. The Planetary Ark—or "ship of fools"—is also a place of refuge for scientists and environmentalists, after denialists have dismissed global warming as "nonsense" and a "hoax" and omitted the words "climate change" altogether from all government communications. In this microcosm, travelers embrace their fellow travelers with remarkable care, so a few thousand years later their offspring form a new creature made entirely of the merger from all forms of life on the spaceship. The ark takes seriously the relations between people and other critters, animal or not. Its return to Earth appeals for a radically altered sense of subjectivity and terrestrial values.

Pacific Cemetery

Already in 1966, a *Life* magazine photo essay alerted its readers to the "growing clutter of space trash" and observed, just as cities had become clogged with animal waste and garbage, space trash could eventually become the proper concern of extraterrestrial street cleaners. Over the coming decades, thousands of satellites will be launched into space and eventually decommissioned after 15 years of operation. More than 1,400 nautical miles from the nearest land, Point Nemo is already the cemetery of deorbited spacecraft. The cemetery includes the Soviet-era MIR space station, the Jules Verne ATV, European Space Agency cargo ships, and a SpaceX rocket. The US designates Point Nemo as the Strategic Trust Territory of the Space Age, building on the precedent of the Pacific Proving Grounds. In 1947, the US secured an agreement with the UN, designating the islands of Micronesia as the Strategic Trust Territory. The US conducted nuclear testing at such sites between 1946 and 1962. Yet the directive stated that the US should "promote the economic advancement and self-sufficiency of the inhabitants, and to this end shall . . . protect the inhabitants against the loss of their lands and resources." Dubbed the "Oceanic Point of Inaccessibility," Point Nemo becomes the landfill of the Space Age. In a vortex spiral island, decommissioned satellites and other space debris are brought back from orbit. Point Nemo Pacific Cemetery doubles as a terraforming project, recycling deorbited space objects into bits of sovereignty to house climate refugees from Pacific Islands. Such low-lying coastal countries are particularly vulnerable to sea level rise, and the loss of physical territory implies they no longer meet the UN criteria for statehood. The first submerged Pacific Islands become a US Strategic Territory, not unlike the Marshall Islands, where the US buries its space trash and promotes economic advancement and right to self-determination of such planetary refugees.

Cosmopgraphy, Cosmopolitics, Cosmorama

The three geographic fictions constitute Cosmorama; they reshape the registers of humanity's relationship to the cosmos: namely, those of aesthetic knowledge, political relations, and scientific curiosity. The media devices of speculative fiction and the spectacle are tools to make explicit, as if viewed through a magnifying glass, those same politics that shape planet Earth and the extraplanetary.

First, *Cosmorama* is cosmography; it is a form of unified and aesthetic knowledge responding to the current ecological crisis as well as to the newly opened extraterrestrial spaces of human occupation. Alexander von Humboldt's influential treatise *Cosmos* had achieved such a synthesis of the geographic and the cosmographic, drawing *together* heaven and earth.[1] Humboldt's vision of the globe presents a totality of scales and sciences on Earth in an assemblage of studies in astronomy, geography, and geology. His "portrait of nature" draws together a physical geography of the Earth

1 Alexander von Humboldt, *Cosmos: A Sketch of a Physical Description of the Universe* (London: George Bell and Sons, 1883).

2 Peter Sloterdijk, "On the Emergence of the World System," *In the World Interior of Capital: Towards a Philosophical Theory of Globalization* (Cambridge, UK: Polity, 2013).

and of outer space—cosmic nebulae and planets. Humboldt reimagines the big picture by visualizing connections and dependencies across local, planetary, and cosmic scales. Humboldt did not choose Earth as the vantage point from which to look out into the expansive space. Instead, he took up a position in extraterrestrial space to approach Earth like a visitor from a foreign planet.[2] Cosmography is important because it uses visual agency to synthesize scientific knowledge into a holistic representation.

Second, *Cosmorama* is cosmopolitics; the scale of extraterrestrial geography has the power to explicate politics of the cosmos, as suggested by Isabelle Stengers. Historically, the cosmos is a premature closure of a political sphere, whereby cosmopolitanism and cosmology have sought to establish power and legitimate authority through the ever-imminent promise of equal citizenship and the ventriloquizing of the heavens. Far from understanding the cosmos as "an Earth finally united, in which everyone is a citizen,"[3] Stengers, following Latour,[4] insists that "*politics* keeps the cosmos open and ever reconciling" to reach outside the human and terrestrial realm. The cosmos becomes a critical concept because it counters both anthropocentrism and geocentrism, in the old sense of Earth being the center of the universe and of man being the highest being there is. Thus, for Stengers, to engage in cosmopolitics is to *design* simultaneously the spatial and political assemblies. Cosmopolitics is the tool to build a world from a situated location where practitioners operate—a practice without the dogma of expertise. In her "Cosmopolitical Proposal," Stengers advocates for the notion of thought experiments that "'slow down' reasoning and create an opportunity to arouse a slightly different awareness of the problems and situations mobilizing us."[5] Fictions are put forth as thought experiments for science speculation. Stengers asks, "What if they were crafting tales that disclose their epoch's capacity to feel that there are other possible ways for a world to consist?"[6] Science-fiction author Ursula Le Guin observes that the metaphors of fiction are ways of seeing reality with "spaceships faster than light, the weird worlds and alien beings, the intolerable or utopian societies, the dooms envisaged, the glories imagined. . . . They are the medium to describe what in fact is going on, what people actually do and feel, how people relate to everything else in this vast sack, this belly of the universe, this unending story."[7]

And last, *Cosmorama* is the site of spectacle. Similar to earlier image machines—panorama and diorama—the cosmorama is a form of popular entertainment, a peep box or rarity show through which the spectator views a set of scenes—of distant lands and exotic subjects. The peep box or room was often decorated to resemble theatrical scenes. It put the cosmos on stage: it materialized gods, magnified minuscule creatures, pulled faraway things and placed them near. The show was accompanied by spoken recitation that explained or dramatized what was happening inside. In the New Space Age, the cosmos is once again something that needs to be collected, put together, however provisionally, and *Cosmorama* gives form to such an ephemeral common world. *Cosmorama* is a series of scenes that might be deemed inappropriate to be discussed explicitly and on Earth: a mise-en-scène that challenges the transformation of space into grounds for private profit. *Cosmorama* hacks the popularized spectacle-machine to render sensible the uncanny underbelly of both the New Space Age and the event of the Anthropocene. In doing so, it recenters the political in technological and environmental narratives. Its most obscene tactical work might be to remind us that that terrestrial politics are also and always a politics of the cosmos.

Cosmorama was commissioned for the 2018 Venice Architecture Biennale U.S. Pavilion "Dimensions of Citizenship," curated by Niall Atkinson, Ann Lui, and Mimi Zeiger.

Design Earth Project Team
Rania Ghosn, El Hadi Jazairy, Reid Fellenbaum, Monica Hutton, Kelly Koh, Jia Weng, Shuya Xu.
With contributions from: Lex Agnew, Garine Boghossian, Rawan Al-Saffar, Ranu Singh, Sihao Xiong, Tianwei Ye

3
Isabelle Stengers, "The Cosmopolitical Proposal," *Making Things Public*, ed. B. Latour and P. Weibel (Cambridge, MA: MIT Press, 2005), 994–1003.

4
Bruno Latour, "Whose Cosmos, Which Cosmopolitics? Comments on the Peace Terms of Ulrich Beck," *Common Knowledge* 10, no.3 (2004), 450–462.

5
Isabelle Stengers, "The Cosmopolitical Proposal," *Making Things Public*, ed. B. Latour and P. Weibel (Cambridge, MA: MIT Press, 2005), 994–1003.

6
Isabelle Stengers, *Gaia, the Urgency to Think (and Feel)*, 2014, https://osmilnomesdegaia.files.wordpress.com/2014/11/isabelle-stengers.pdf.

7
Ursula K. Le Guin, *Dancing at the Edge of the World: Thoughts on Words, Women, Places* (New York: Grove Press, 1997), 170.

Mining the Sky; Cosmic Rushmore
The exploitation of raw materials from asteroids carves out a constellation of large-scale sculptures of the Gods of private interests

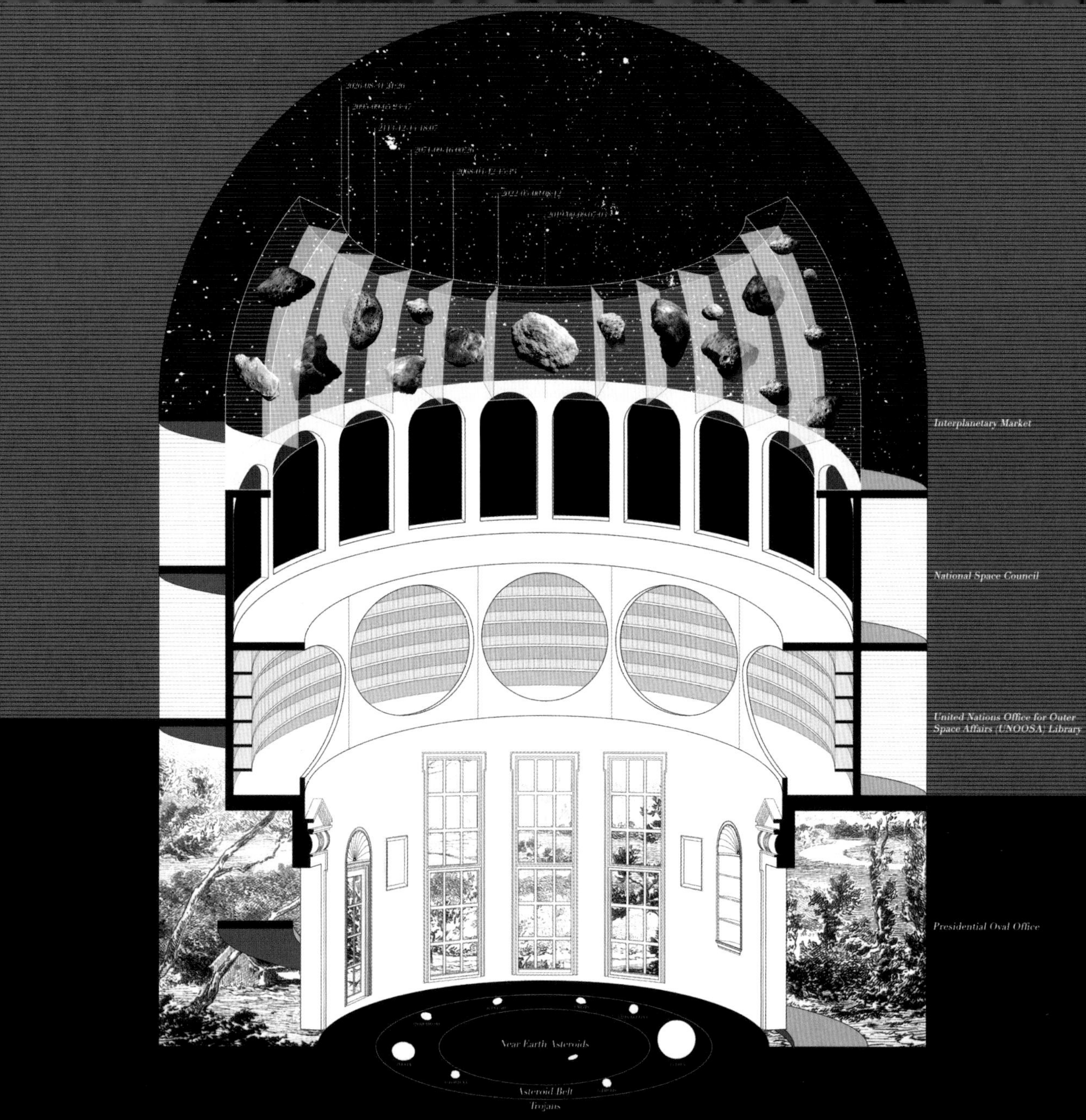

Mining the Sky; The Architecture of the New Space Age
Conceptual section of the New Space Age making visible the intertwined and conflicting interests of United States, United Nations, and space industry and investors

Mining the Sky; Lagrange Point Fortification
The mission partnership between NASA and the U.S. Air Force maintains security of rare earth storage at Lagrange points, places in space where celestial forces essentially cancel out gravity.

Planetary Ark; Empire State Ark

The animals go into the Empire State Ark. The collection of animals includes those launched into space on scientific missions and other species threatened by the sixth mass extinction in Earth's history.

Planetary Ark; (All Aboard) the Architekton
The multi-species architekton embarks on its cosmic journey.

Planetary Ark; 10000 Years Later Between Venus and Earth
The descendent of the Ark's population returns to Earth

Pacific Cemetery; Point Nemo
Decommissioned satellites and other space debris are brought back from orbit and recycled at Point Nemo, also dubbed the Oceanic Point of Inaccessibility.

Pacific Cemetery; Space Junk Island

The debris of the New Space Age at Point Nemo forms a vortex cemetery, with de-orbited spacecraft such as the Soviet-era MIR space station, the Jules Verne ATV and SpaceX rockets.

Pacific Cemetery; Pacific Refuge
The vestiges of space objects are recycled into bits of sovereignty to house climate refugees from Pacific Islands.

"Wilderness and Utopia": On Post-capitalist Urbanization and the Extraterrestrial Imaginary
Interview with KIM STANLEY ROBINSON
by DANIEL DAOU and MARIANO GOMEZ-LUQUE

As critical scholars have suggested,[1] both Science Fiction and Critical Theory constitute mirror-image projects with equal footing in utopian thinking. The following interview with science fiction author Kim Stanley Robinson suggests reading his work through the lens of urban and design studies. The shared affinities revealed in the course of the conversation make us think that there is room to extend this initial formulation into a triad that includes Science Fiction, Critical Urban Theory, and Design—a critical project yet to be systematically undertaken.

For philosopher Henri Lefebvre, the "urban" is a historical socio-spatial process that unfolds at a planetary scale, reshaping not only cities but all kinds of territories. The notion of "urbanization" is meant to capture the dynamism of this process in contrast with the formal fixity of "the city." Your novels strike us as "urban" in the Lefebvrian sense, as you meticulously describe a synthetic landscape in which buildings, cities, territories, and even planets are reshaped by human activity (and vice versa). Is the category of the "urban," understood in this dialectical way, a useful rubric to grasp the nuanced spatiality of your novels, and if so, to what extent do you think the notion of "planetary urbanization" could be a complement to the more technical concept of "terraforming" as deployed in science fiction (SF)?

Coming from science fiction as I do, the urban is my genre's home space, historically speaking. Early science fiction and "Golden Age science fiction" consisted of stories written mainly by urban men, as an expression of people in industrial cultures noticing the speed of technological change and writing that feeling into future histories. Thus the beginnings in Britain, France, and the US. In the US there were some outliers like Clifford Simak, Edgar Pangborn, and even Ray Bradbury, who celebrated the persistence of the pastoral in the face of this rapid industrialization, but they were also emphasizing thereby the main line of SF, which was very strongly urban. The spaceship itself was a symbolic image of the city, and Asimov, the epitome of this urban mentality, gave us the purest form of this impulse in his *Foundation* (1951) trilogy's Trantor, the world city that covered an entire planet and was the capital of the galaxy. This was an image of his beloved New York, which also took center stage in his city novel *Caves of Steel* (1954), also

Note
Footnotes by interviewers

1 Carl Freedman, *Critical Theory and Science Fiction* (Wesleyan University Press, 2000); see also Darko Suvin, *Metamorphoses of Science Fiction: On the Poetics and History of a Literary Genre* (Yale University Press, 1979), and Fredric Jameson, *Archaeologies of the Future: The Desire Called Utopia and Other Science Fictions* (Verso, 2007).

in its "open landscape" sequel, *The Naked Sun* (1957). As an agoraphobic he loved these all-encompassing cities, and so he stands at the center of this moment in science fiction.

I've always been interested in opposing this strand of science fiction, by emphasizing that the entire planet's biosphere, what in earlier times would have been called the natural world, or wilderness, or even Nature, would never go away. The whole planet is a necessary support system for humans, our extended body so to speak. We may entrain this body to our uses and organize much of it, but we can't do without it; it doesn't go away, and it's as interesting as the cities themselves, especially as a story space. My ability to make a contribution to the ongoing conversation that is science fiction has rested partly on my feelings about this planetary context. Wilderness and utopia: this odd combination of interests got me started and gave me my way into the long conversation of my genre.

That said, it's easy for me to transcode and comprehend your question, and its assumption that urbanization organizes the entirety of the planet. The etymology of civilization illustrates this: humanity has indeed organized life on the planet, not entirely but to a large extent. There almost seems to be a kind of gravitational pull exerted by cities on people, from the first moment of their appearance some ten to twelve thousand years ago. At first just tiny nodes in a vast natural landscape organized by the biosphere as a collective, cities eventually became the organizing principle around which people lived and dominated (partly) the rest of our biosphere. Agricultural regions created the surplus of food necessary to feed the populations of cities, so cities and farms have always been interrelated; and then beyond and outside these humanly organized areas, there were residual wild regions where a few humans lived as they had before cities came into being. But these were small populations in big regions. If you want to call this whole process urbanization, I can see the sense of it, although you could flip the valence and say it's all about agriculture and the resulting surpluses finding their places. I recognize urbanization as one aspect of this, and it seems to me to capture the historical process at that infrastructural and conceptual level.

Whether my novels are doing anything like describing this process, I think is possible, but I can't say myself with any certainty, as I'm too close to my books to see them very well from perspectives so broad and theoretical. But I do think it makes sense that when writing science fiction, which is so often about people on a planet, making history together, that these aspects will come into play. Science fiction allows and even insists on being about more than just individual human relations. The crucial addition is the planet, so that you get not just literature about people, but about people and planet. This is one of the things that gives science fiction its power.

In this context, "terraforming" is what people have done continuously on Earth, but applied in fictions to other planets. The way this is metaphorical for what we do on Earth is obvious, and again the terms can be flipped, as in any good metaphor, vehicle and tenor illuminating each other.

As a public intellectual, you have outlined a vision where cities play a fundamental role in preserving the biosphere.[2] Following biologist E. O. Wilson's "Half Earth" proposal, you have suggested humans ought to move to dense, sustainable, "neo-traditional" urban centers. Unlike Wilson, you don't characterize the

2 "A Functional Form Has Its Own Beauty: An Interview with Kim Stanley Robinson", by McKenzie Wark, *Los Angeles Review of Books*, September 1, 2013.

uninhabited remainder as "wilderness," but instead as managed landscapes. Such vision relies on a pattern of uneven spatial distribution between dense agglomerations and remote hinterlands. On the other hand, as a science fiction writer, your nuanced depictions of planetary terraforming blur the lines between the putative categories of the built and the unbuilt, cities and their extended "operational landscapes." This vision seems closer to the notion of "planetary urbanization," which entails what urban theorist Neil Brenner describes as the "disappearance of the constitutive outside." That is to say, the urban not as a bounded interiority (as traditionally represented by cities) but as a dynamic process that traverses all scales and territories. The resulting geographies are better described by the synthetic nature of their landscapes and the dissolution of the boundaries between sites of extraction, production, consumption, and dwelling.[3] How would you address the perceived tension between your position as a public intellectual, which seems to endorse a city-centric environmental vision, and the more radical view put forward in your novels, where landscapes and cities are often complexly intertwined and the boundaries between "agglomerations" and their extended and operational spatial realms seem to blur?

I would always go with my novels as being my best attempts to articulate my views. My positions as a public intellectual, such as they are, being mostly articles and talks, are greatly simplified, and consist mainly of guesses taken on the fly, in essays that are written to order, and are usually required to be too short to do justice to their topics. I try to treat them as short stories, but their form hinders me, as I can't quite get a handle on it—how to be provocative, how to capture large complex situations in a quick line of words. So for me there is no contradiction here, just different forms in which I have different commitments and competencies.

I think E. O. Wilson is a major public intellectual, a scientist/philosopher/popular writer reminiscent of people like Benjamin Franklin or William James. His "Half Earth" idea is important, and I think should be much more discussed than it has been; possibly it's too radical to be faced directly, and there might be some ageism involved as well, as he is now one of our elders. However that may be, his idea is a great one for forcing an evaluation of how we organize our activities, and how we treat our fellow creatures and the surface of the planet more generally. It's a charismatic mega-idea, both utilitarian, in that it is in our self-interest as a species to keep all our cousin species healthy and happy, and also moral, emphasizing the intrinsic value of other life-forms, which we should respect as we do any other people we know.

So I wrote about this in one essay, and I'm always happy to say more. For our discussion here, I can expand to say that I think "wilderness" is now an odd word, with a history that doesn't quite fit this "Half Earth" idea. "Wilderness" as a concept comes from a specific historical moment, which imagined that there are parts of the Earth's surface that both are and should be free of humans—"where man is a visitor only," as the US Wilderness Act of 1964 put it (approximately). Given what we know now, I think this is too pure—wrong historically, and not a helpful way to think about landscape. Humans have been on all parts of the Earth's land surface for 20,000 years now, all but

3
For instance, even *New York 2140* (2017), undoubtedly focused on the city as such, is consistent with this view of the urban as a totalizing process, as it describes an anthropocenic environment in which the skies are populated by "skyvillages," "skyscrafts," and "everything in between."

Antarctica, and we've been making changes to the landscape all along—at first perhaps minor, although fire has never been a small force. So really the whole of the Earth's surface has been, and is, a human space. So instead of calling it wilderness, which has a particular value, I think we should imagine the empty parts of Wilson's Half Earth idea as just that—empty—empty of humans, but not entirely. This is partly because I feel humans should be able to briefly visit anywhere on Earth, for the joy of it and the love of Earth itself, and partly because any ideas of purity make me unhappy and nervous. I prefer mongrelization, compromise, slippage, bricolage, "enough," and so on.

So, this is to address just one part of your question. "Wilderness" designates a kind of space where I've spent some of the happiest hours of my life, so I want space like it to survive for personal reasons. Can we rethink wilderness to be a particular kind of ethical position we have toward certain biomes, as a kind of human space that we have decided to cede largely to the other animals and plants and life-forms, partly in order to increase our own health? Here I'm trying to think the "Half Earth" idea and welcoming how much landscape might become at least "half empty."

Can we rethink agriculture also, as something more like what permaculture suggests? This is a set of problems in ecological technology that really must be solved. The permaculture perspective is similar to the urbanization concept, in that again cities are only part of a larger fabric, but not the most important part, because we can't live without food. So it's not that the planet has been or must be urbanized, but that cities have been or must be incorporated into a more biocentric total lifeway. Empty land, agriculture, and cities are all interpenetrated, but not entirely. Not agglomerations everywhere, a bit more differentiated than that; but all of these uses integrated, and crucial parts of a functioning whole.

You call Wilson's idea of concentrating human population on half the earth "radical" and suggest "centralizing" humans in cities to save the environment. But what about being radical in the opposite direction: if capitalism produces and is propelled by uneven development (both social and spatial), can we think about the opposite of Wilson's idea and imagine a radically decentralized "civilization" where population is spread in a novel form that is neither suburb nor metropolis, neither city nor hinterland, which might somehow lead to more evenly developed landscapes, both socially and environmentally?

My sense is that capital created uneven development by following the highest rate of return wherever it leads and abandoning regions once they don't give that highest rate. This is Arrighi's insight, and it seems right to me. So when you suggest a radically decentralized "civilization," neither cities nor hinterland, I have two immediate negative reactions: one, it sounds like suburbia, and I don't think that's a good use of space; and second, what about the animals? If humans are evenly distributed everywhere, I don't trust the animals will do well, and that to me is a priority. In that sense, I still believe in the empty spaces we used to call wilderness, and maybe here I can call them "animal spaces," without being too pure about it. But they should be left to live their lives autonomously, and not always by sneaking around the backs of human spaces either.

It's necessary to separate out the social and the environmental here, at least for my purposes of hoping for egalitarian cities, cities filled with public spaces, commons, cooperatives, and urban agricultural spaces. I think it should be possible to imagine cities where everyone shares the political and economic power about equally, while concentrating humans in the landscape to leave a good bit of the land surface of the Earth to our fellow creatures.

Post-capitalism

As geographers David Harvey and Neil Smith have argued, the variegated geographies of uneven development are not just an aftereffect of capitalism's own internal contradictions, but the very material configuration that enables capital's logic of surplus extraction to unfold. This suggests that any attempt to supersede capitalism must by necessity be linked to a different spatiality. In other words, the question of post-capitalism is also an urban project. For all the recent theorization on possible post-capitalist political economies and ecologies, this spatial dimension remains largely undertheorized. Yet, as Lefebvre strikingly put it: "A revolution that does not produce a new space has not realized its full potential." As you have stated, your writings have been, from the beginning, "about imagining various postcapitalisms."[4] We read your books as "spatial novels" in which the interaction between people and environments is portrayed at a high level of resolution.[5] To what extent can your work be read as a deliberate attempt to reveal the spatial dimension of post-capitalism? How instrumental is the SF novel in raising awareness about the importance of the spatial question in the articulation of alternatives to capitalism?

This idea of a post-capitalist space is really interesting to me. It makes sense, and it would come about in part as the result of a deliberate and conscious post-capitalist urban design.

I suppose I've been exploring elements of this idea in my novels, but seldom if ever with conscious intent. Some of my characters, like Arkady Bogdanov in *Red Mars* (1992), were more explicitly interested in this aspect of things than I was myself. But now that you mention it, other manifestations of this kind of thing in my work occur to me. There are the various asteroid interiors in *2312* (2012), and the old Met Life tower in *New York 2140*, and the free crater in *Red Moon*, and the town of El Modena in *Pacific Edge* (1990). No doubt other examples exist; I recall in particular having the opportunity to design city after city in my Mars trilogy and enjoying that immensely. There I was often thinking about the ancient Greeks' placement of their cities on overlooks or in other locations with a fine view. Visiting the ruins of these places in the mid-1980s, I often felt the Greeks' locations were as much aesthetic as strategically defensive. They had beautiful prospects. And as I studied the new topographic maps of Mars generated by the Viking orbiter, I saw there would be many opportunities on Mars to build in similarly dramatic places, just for the pleasure of being there and looking around.

So that was about pleasure over profit, and even over utility. But also my Martian settlements often included ideas about a more egalitarian built environment. Surely the concept of the commons must come into play when trying to imagine any post-capitalism—the commons or else other kinds of public space, meaning owned by all, or by no one.

4 "The Realism of Our Time", Interview with Kim Staley Robinson by Helena Feder, *Radical Philosophy* 2.01, February 2018.

5 Fredric Jameson, *Archaeologies of the Future* (Verso, 2007), 400.

It's notorious that the privatization of everything (except risk) has reduced public space in all the landscapes to a minimum, and most especially in cities. And the commons was a pre-capitalist dispensation, with things to teach us going forward. The commons was never unregulated or free space, rather it was regulated by norms, and it's quite possible there was an element of gangsterism in the practice of their regulation, but also, in village life, it was probably more often a matter of propriety, and getting along by way of sociability. Now, in our world, the Maine lobster fishery can be understood as a kind of commons providing a usufruct, and its regulation of that taking is legal and strict, being a matter of managing a finite resource without ownership per se. One owns tenure rights in such a system and can only take enough from the commons to make a living, not a profit over and above that living. This is suggestive for a more comprehensive approach to the world.

I'm also thinking now of the somewhat non-capitalist enclaves within the global capitalism system that I have experienced myself. One is the scientific station, which I've seen in Antarctica. McMurdo and South Pole stations are run by the National Science Foundation for the pursuit of science, and while living there one exists in a non-monetary collective situation, where housing, food, and even clothing are provided, and the scientists are doing the work that will make their careers in academia, while the support crews are making a salary banked for use back in the world. So while living there, even though there is no such thing as a pocket utopia, it feels different—at least it did to me. And I saw that people were fond of it in ways they often couldn't explain, attributing their pleasure to the landscape (which is also inexplicable in terms of how pleasing it is), or to the general feeling of companionable dedication to a shared enterprise that is created by the rules of the place. The infrastructure itself is only incidental to that experience, it's more a matter of rules of conduct; the design is no more than a kind of "adhocitecture," a ramshackle and accidental assemblage of buildings without urban design. Villages in the Arctic look much nicer and more intentional than McMurdo, and I wonder what the lived feeling in these places is like.

Also, I've lived for nearly 30 years in Village Homes, a neighborhood of Davis, California, that was designed and built in the 1970s to resemble in certain ways European village life. One owns one's house and the property under it, but the rest of the land in the village is owned in common by all its residents, and that part of things is run as a collective, with an emphasis on food production, common spaces, and shared buildings for communal activities. It's really just a tweaking of ordinary suburbia, but the small tweaks have created big effects. Having grown up in an ordinary suburbia, I feel the differences in Village Homes acutely, and it's been a great pleasure to live in this newer-based-on-older designed space.

I wonder, thinking about this, if there shouldn't be an "Institute for Post-capitalist Studies," maybe one in every university—a multidisciplinary institute like many that are springing up around one topic or another—in this case combining inputs from economics, ecology, engineering, philosophy, architecture, sociology, history, literature, materials science, design, urban planning, anthropology, and so on, all gathered to theorize this very pressing problem in human history. Since we need post-capitalism to survive, surely it should be studied and designed.

In such institutes, it would make sense to go to Mondragon, Spain, and study the place, especially by asking residents what it feels like to live there, or grow up there. Same with Kerala in India, and in any other place around the world where there seems to be some kind of emergent post-capitalism, or precursor states, already alive in the world and available as a modeling exercise to be studied.

For me, Mondragon has always stuck out as an example of an alternative way already existing. I've never been there, but I've had some extraordinary encounters with it because I've mentioned it so often in my books. In the Wikipedia article on it there is a section called "Mondragon in Fiction," which I was excited to see, until I found only my books were mentioned in it; I was hoping for more. Once I got a call from people at a radio station in Mondragon, asking what I thought of a financial crisis they were suffering and wondering if I had any advice for them, which I was not competent to give. But that event indicated that at least some people there are aware that the town has been featured in my work. Lastly, a kind professor from a nearby university sent me his book describing how Mondragon came to be, so now I know its history better. It's interesting, because its origins came out of something like Catholic liberation theology, appearing in Spain rather than Latin America. During the Franco regime, a single priest was sent to the region as part of a pacification effort of the Basques, and he talked with people there for 15 years before helping them to initiate and design their alternative system, which they all thought of as "capitalism with morals"—which is another way of saying post-capitalism.

So, how has that worked? And what does it feel like? This would be one fruitful area of study. And there would be many others.

The idea of "pocket utopia" is very interesting to us because it alludes to the problem of scale. You mention the case of the community of Mondragon in Spain. Do you think models like these can be scaled up? In your novels, you navigate between and across multiple scales: a city, a spaceship, a planet, the solar system. But how freely can we extrapolate between scales when thinking about "global" systemic change? A big critique of the notion of "carrying capacity," for instance, is that it's a concept originally linked to human-made seafaring vessels that is now being "upscaled" and applied to the whole Earth as such. Is this trans-scaling process possible, or are there thresholds where differences in degree become differences in kind that make any extrapolation impossible?

Multiple scales exist but they are not the same in terms of the scaling problems involved, some being simply bigger than others. For example, the trip to Tau Ceti is ten billion times longer than the trip to our moon. Very little scales across this huge change; we can't get to Tau Ceti just because we can cross space to our moon.

On the other hand, regional governments compared to world government; that's not such a huge shift. Could the whole world be run as a Mondragon? Could it be run as a Finland? Is the international treaty system, the loose agglomeration of treaties that runs the world now, hugely different from any nation-state governmental system? I don't think so. Here the scaling problems are not so evident to me.

Scaling is often just capitalism talking about maximizing profit; the more you can exploit with one law or one system, the more "efficient" it is, the better it "scales." But the words here are not referring to the same things, as far as I can tell. I don't trust network theory or complexity theory, or any other theoretical construct in which language is mixed with mathematics to come to something like a scientific conclusion. So often it is an ideological construct pretending to be a science like physics. And I fully believe physics is an ideological construct also, but it has reiterative and reductive aspects to it that make it easier for me to agree that what is being asserted has a real reality. For words like "scale" you might as well be using metaphors; in fact it kind of is a metaphor, right? Something from mapping, applied to economics or the like.

I think carrying capacity comes not from shipping, i.e. how much weight a ship can take, but from population biology on islands, i.e. how many animals can live on an island without destroying the plant base, and then up to predators etc. So Earth's carrying capacity for humans is a function of Erhlich's IPAT formula, and yes that makes it ridiculously problematic, as all kinds of values have to be taken into account. I've read carrying capacity estimates for humans on Earth ranging from 100 million to 12 trillion, and even when you throw these out as crazy outliers, the serious estimates range from 2 to 30 billion. Despite this wide variance it's a good way to discuss values, or maybe because of it; it's worth considering for how it focuses attention on the factors going into the judgment.

So, to the point of your question: I don't see why the world couldn't run as Mondragon runs. But this isn't to say that there aren't even better systems out there.

There are many instances of spatial invention in your work.[6] This inventiveness parallels some radical design visions from the 20th century, such as the "città nuova" of the Italian Futurists, Archizoom's "No-stop City," or so-called 'arcologies' from the 1970s. To what degree do you keep radical design projects in mind when designing your spatial universes?

I've scoured the literature looking for alternative models that already exist in the world to help me imagine my futures. I haven't found that much, but that may be my deficiency as a researcher. Still, I would wish for more in the way of models to imitate. If they are theoretical constructs only, rather than built environments already existing, they are of less help to me, because in essence they too are science fiction stories, written in a nonfiction form. That's just a genre difference, and I see the utopian elements in them quite clearly, but I would like to see more tangible demonstrations.

In general, I'm acutely aware of science fiction when I see it in its various disguises, such as declarations of human rights, financial predictions, demographic forecasts, and any kind of so-called futurisms—all these are to me science fiction stories, pretending to be something more to gain more authority. Often, they seem to be evoking status as science itself, other times as prophecy, a very ancient mystical power. I prefer to understand all of these as fictions, often utopian fictions.

Extraterrestrial

You once summarized capitalism's logic as the algorithm "More is better."[7] Today, a new breed of private space entrepreneurs seeks to extend this logic into new extraterrestrial frontiers of surplus extraction. Jeff Bezos's recent update of Gerard O'Neill's iconic space settlements from the 1970s is problematic because it reproduces two of capitalist urbanization's most distinct spatial tropes: the megalopolis and the suburb. Likewise, Elon Musk's city on Mars appears very much as an extraction camp. These are prime examples of how a naively utopian mainstream "extraterrestrial aesthetic" betrays the underlying logic of capitalism. In contrast, your work offers a nuanced spatial portrait of life in extraterrestrial

6
Many examples come to mind, from the moving city of Terminator and the hollowed asteroids ("terrariums") in *2312* to the space elevator of the *Mars* trilogy to the vertical archipelago of superscrapers in *New York 2140*.

environments.[8] Yet, despite its evocative power, the language of the SF novel resists any easy visual representation. Given the problematic nature of the mainstream "extraterrestrial aesthetic" articulated by entrepreneurs like Bezos or Musk, how could a more fruitful relationship between the utopian language of SF and the critical representational apparatus of the design disciplines be staged so as to reclaim the extraterrestrial horizon as an alternative utopian space?[9]

The highly publicized visionary statements of the space-cadet billionaires are basically celebrity hobbies. Musk has done really good work in cars and batteries and solar power and rocketry, so whatever his personal idiosyncrasies, his actual work has been innovative and positive. His Mars project looks to me like more of a hobby than a practical proposal, in effect his own version of doing science fiction.

Bezos also has a useful interest in space, and his own science fiction stories about O'Neill colonies and the like have to be taken as such and separated out from the real work of Blue Origin, which is making great progress on next-generation rocketry.

Always, in the case of these two and any other space-cadet individuals, wealthy or not, it has to be remembered that their science fiction stories may be far off the cutting edge of what the sciences are actually doing now, and where we are in human and planetary history. Their stories, expressed as plans or pronouncements, may chiefly reflect the science fiction they read when they were young. I know that feeling myself, as I often feel that the New Wave science fiction of 1965–75 was as good as the genre ever got as a literature. But this probably has something to do with me being young and the genre surprising me with new things.

Now there are ongoing new developments in all the sciences, and this means that new science fiction stories have to change with the times. This accounts for the rise of climate fiction, which is just a name for science fiction concerned with the near future, which we now know will be massively impacted by the climate change we've already initiated. Then also, materials science and ecological economics have changed what utopian fiction should read like. And so on. The danger is getting stuck in the dreams of your youth, when the situation is changing so rapidly that these dreams have become antiquated before being enacted.

This happens to science fiction all the time. Images of the future reflect psychic energies so powerful that they act like a hose on the ground, whipping side to side and shooting water out at a tangent to the eventual real course of events. It's always necessary to adjust one's science fiction imaginary to the current moment and the reality that we're inventing together. Even that imaginary will be at a tangent and later obviously wrong, but at least it's ours now.

So, given our current dilemma, your phrase "extraterrestrial utopia" now identifies what has now become a kind of fantasy space. Space settlements are going to remain at the level of scientific stations for decades to come; the crucial story for the next century is completely Earthbound. This is not a bad thing. People who are still conceptualizing space as the locale for utopia have missed the point of the Anthropocene and are mainly indulging in fantasies of escape. They're marginalizing themselves from the real problems of our time.

7
"Power and the Space of the Planet", Columbia GSAPP, April 15, 2016.

8
For instance, the *Mars* trilogy suggests a complex amalgamation between human architecture and the eeriness of the Martian landscape—a distinct "Martian urbanism" that does not resemble or mimic Earth's precisely because it results from the struggle to find alternatives to the imperative "More is better."

9
By design disciplines we mean architecture, urban design, and landscape architecture.

During the latest World Ecology Network conference, you referenced a debate taking place in the most recent volumes of *New Left Review* around the problem of economic growth.[10] In short, it's clear there's a fault line between the economy and planetary ecology, but where that fault line resides is not so clear. Some argue the problem is not so much capitalism but growth, suggesting there can be a "stationary-state" capitalism or implying that growth would be a problem even under socialism. Others suggest that growth can be decoupled from the environment. Being as it is, material economic growth seems to be intertwined with capital and fundamentally at odds with the biophysical well-being of the planet. Most environmentalists agree that, on a planet with finite resources, growth can only be finite as well. Your novels depict future scenarios where humanity has gone on to grow into other planets or the entire solar system. What, from your perspective, is the logic of the transition that would take us to such a historic stage? Is your position fundamentally different from that of "terrestrial" environmentalists? Let's say endless expansion weren't at odds with ecological viability and were technologically feasible, would it still be desirable?

I think I'm a terrestrial environmentalist. It's just that if you take the long view, if we manage to get into balance as a global civilization with the biosphere of Earth, a sustainable civilization here, then we might explore our solar system as an interesting addition to what we do; but it can't happen without the successful Terran civilization coming first. And a few space colonies wouldn't help us to create a sustainable civilization here either. So it's a matter of taking a really long and utopian view; if we succeed on Earth, we'll play around in our solar system. And not among the stars, because they are too far away. So I've come to a very particular and circumscribed vision of humanity's future, or so it seems when I answer these questions.

Growth in this context is very much a capitalist word, having to do with GDP and profit. These have to grow, or the system falls apart from internal logical contradictions of its own rules. These rules have nothing to do with biosphere health or human welfare. They are like a game we play, with high stakes because of uneven returns and simply because of the power of the few over the many, whether that can be maintained or not. But it's a very destructive game, if sustainability and justice are the goals. It's feudalism liquified.

One thing happening here, at the level of language, is a slippage between capital and capitalism. If you define capital as the useful residue of human labor, as some people do, then capital is a good thing. Then capitalism, distinct from this good capital, is a power relation, a hierarchy of few over many, as in feudalism; capitalism is clearly bad for people and the biosphere, even though the 1 percent do well, and really the top 20 percent of the economic order. But the rest of humanity suffers, and the entirety of the biosphere is strip-mined, so it's a bad system that we have to change for civilization to survive.

But still, back to capital and growth of capital: A refrigerator is a health need. Toilets are health needs. Medicine and education are human goods. If these are defined as capital, then capital has good forms. If capital on the other hand is defined as nothing more than the M prime in the M-C-M prime formula, then capital is simply profit and is no more than an index, like any other financial index, of the success of power relations

10 See Kim Stanley Robinson, "The Good Anthropocene," keynote address presented at the World Ecology Network 5th annual conference, "Planetary Utopias / Capitalist Dystopias," San Francisco, June 2, 2019; and Lola Seaton, "Green Questions," *New Left Review* 115 (January–February 2019).

and indirectly as an indicator of the destruction of the biosphere. So it's crucial to define our terms here, or we can get confused discussing these issues. It happens all the time.

So, in regard to growth, there are indexes like the Human Development Index, instead of GDP, to measure a different kind of growth—growth in human welfare, which implies biosphere welfare too. That kind of growth is good and is more likely to happen in socialism than capitalism. Growth of GDP, on the other hand, is in the end terrible for all concerned. So this all has to be destranded, and discussed one term at a time, in some detail—more than we have space for here.

But it should be said that there is a kind of continuing, never-ending work of improvement of our systems and all our efforts, socially and technologically, that could be called growth and yet would be compatible with biosphere health. In essence, the work of integrating a human population of say eight billion people into Earth's biosphere successfully—that is how civilization's project should be defined, and increasing success at that could be defined as growth if you want to, although that risks confusion with capitalism's use of the word which usually denotes GDP or profit or some other index of bad growth. Better to say that the necessary good work will never end. It's a project of integrating two different worlds (biosphere and human cultural) as intelligently and successfully as possible. This is so hard that it won't ever be solved completely, so it's an ongoing project and means that most of this debate concerning growth versus de-growth is off the mark and confusing the issue.

Future

You have often brought up the usefulness of Raymond Williams's notion of the "residual" and "emergent" cultural elements in bridging the present with fictional futures. In this regard, the historical horizon of your novels remains relatively close in time.[11] In contrast to Williams's *cultural* residual, today we face a novel *ecological* residual (anthropogenic CO2, nuclear waste, plastic pollution) whose effects will extend tens of thousands of years into the future. The Anthropocene, understood as the inscription of human action in geological time, has meant that scientific fact has begun encroaching into a temporal horizon traditionally associated with science fiction. Indeed, H. G. Wells's foundational *Time Machine* (1895) comes to mind as the most prototypical case in which the future horizon itself reaches the very limits of what can be thought. Have you ever considered writing a novel that goes that far into the future, a kind of *Time Machine* for the Anthropocene—or, to put it in terms of your own work, a sort of "inverted" *Shaman* (2013)? How do you calibrate the historical distance between your novels' future horizons and our own present?

You surprise me here, because I have indeed considered this figure you mention in the question, wondering if I could go as far into the future as I went into the past in *Shaman*. That would mean 32,000 years into the future, and so my answer was no, I couldn't do it. In fact I was so boggled at the idea that some kind of circuit breakers in my head flipped to prevent conceptual overload.

11
Red Mars begins in 2026; New York is drastically altered by anthropocenic dynamics in 2140; by 2312 the solar system is inhabited; *Aurora* (2015) is centered on an intergenerational starship launched in the 26th century, and *Galileo's Dream* (2009) catapults us into the year 3020.

For me, even thinking about the year 2312 felt like imagining a very distant far future. And the year of the future action in *Galileo's Dream*, something like 3100 CE, is mainly a way of indicating that that novel's story is some kind of Renaissance fantasia of the type seen in the fictional work of Kepler or Bruno, or the *Hypnerotomachia Poliphili* (1499) by Francesco Colonna. Putting that part of my story so far in the future gave me some cover for my time travel technology, which is so fantastical, in effect a fantasy element, that it requires some pretty vigorous hand-waving.

For me, the future quickly exceeds our ability to imagine it. Some of my fellow science fiction writers are fearless in this regard, but what they do in their far futures is really a kind of fantasy, designed to emphasize certain aspects of human existence. They are writing philosophical romances, or science fantasy, as the work of Jack Vance and Gene Wolfe is sometimes called. Iain Banks's Culture novels also come to mind. I wrote a science fantasy story myself, called *A Short, Sharp Shock* (1990), and enjoyed it very much. The far future is a great story space, but my imagination doesn't usually run in that direction. If I had an idea that seemed interesting to me, I might try it. Because ultimately it does seem like a good symmetry to do a novel that matches *Shaman* in temporal distance from us, but in the other direction. A real challenge.

We would like to conclude with a final question alluding to Asimov's quintessential "Last Question," (1956) which deftly navigates the challenges of representing an utterly unimaginable future. His story deals with the prevailing natural eschatology of thermodynamic fatalism which pervades most environmental thinking. The "last question" is in fact whether entropy can be reversed. Yet, in facing this seemingly insurmountable question, Isaac Asimov seems to be enacting what Jameson defines as the function of utopia: to think that which appears as unthinkable from our own historical vantage point. Given your championing of utopianism in SF at times when most of the field seems dystopian, what do you think is the most intractable challenge for the utopian imagination today? In other words, what is your "last question"?

For me, "the most intractable challenge for the utopian imagination today" is taking the first step to get from here to there. What policies and actions might initiate rapid change for the good? There are lots of good ideas, even entire systems that if instituted worldwide would almost certainly be hugely better for all concerned than the way we live now. Say the whole world worked like Mondragon, or Finland; things would be better, and of course there are even more radical plans that exist in theory. But how do we start that process and get it going fast enough to match the crisis?

In other words, how do we seize capital? How do we seize finance? How do we pay everyone to do the work the biosphere urgently needs? How do we make that good and necessary work earn the "highest rate of return"?

This is perhaps an amazingly literal response to something so philosophical as "the last question." Maybe I've reversed figure and ground somehow. I often do that. Or maybe I'm saying "the last question" is always the first one you can't answer, the one where you get stuck. If you can't answer it, it becomes the last question for you, in the way that the thing you find that you are searching for is always in the last place you look, because you stop looking after that.

Or maybe what I'm saying is that right now, nothing else matters but avoiding a mass extinction event. This has become my baseline definition of utopia, given where we are now. If we can avoid a mass extinction event, then all kinds of possibilities open up. Then there won't ever be a last question. . . .

International Space Station
ROLAND MILLER

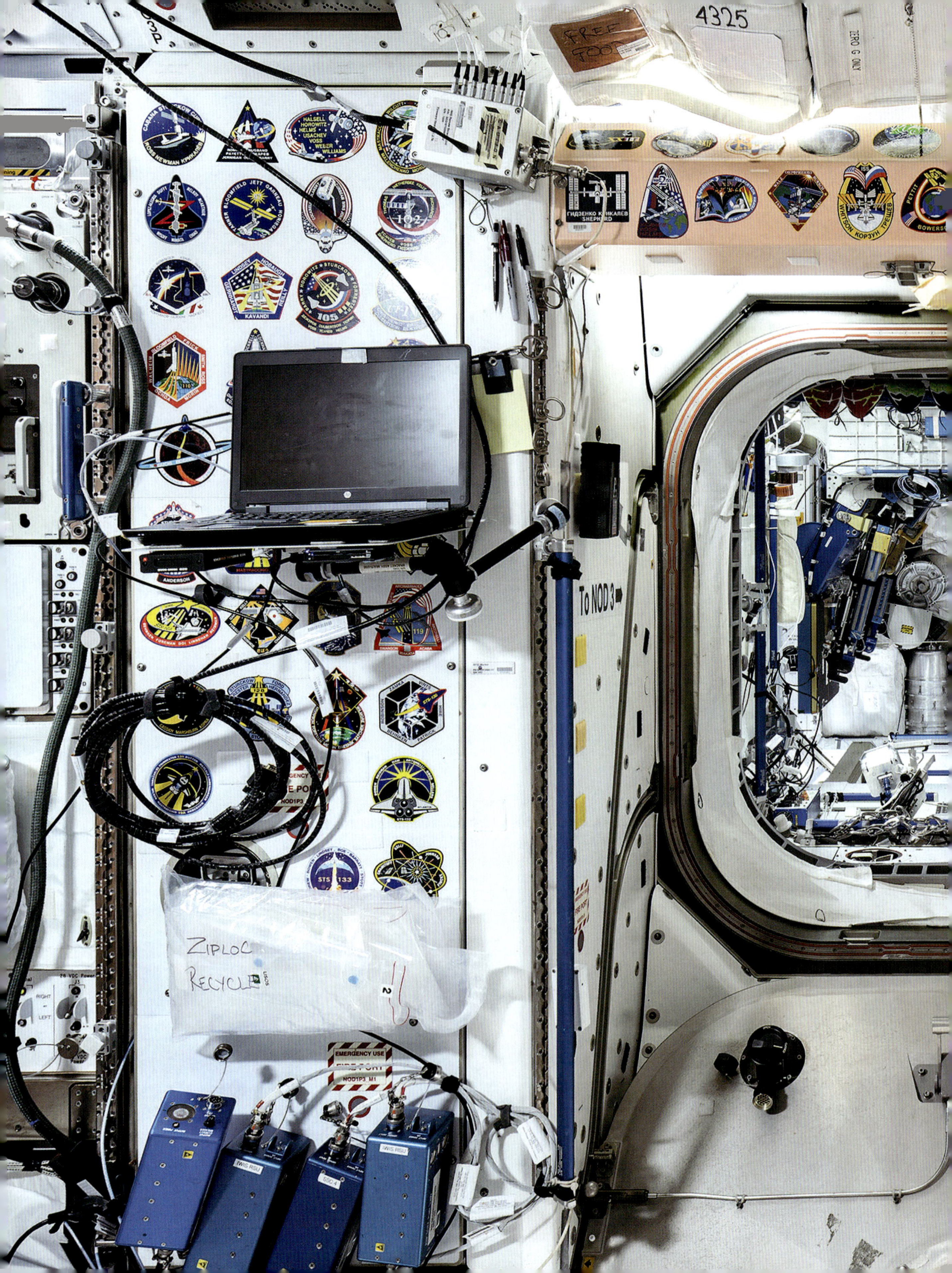
4325
FREE FOOD
ZERO G ONLY
To NOD 3
ZIPLOC
RECYCLE
EMERGENCY USE

CIDERS + Smoothies
COFFEE WITH OUT CREAM
TEA
MILK COCOA BREAKFAST DRINK
WATER
CO2 PPE
To NOD 3
NUTRITION BARS (23 days)
SABOT
ARMY OF ONE... STOMACH OF TEN
CANDY
ACABA
HARD CORPS... PEACE CORPS
Foam Food Locker
EMERGENCY USE
FIRE PORT
NOD1P1_M1
CLOSING HATCH

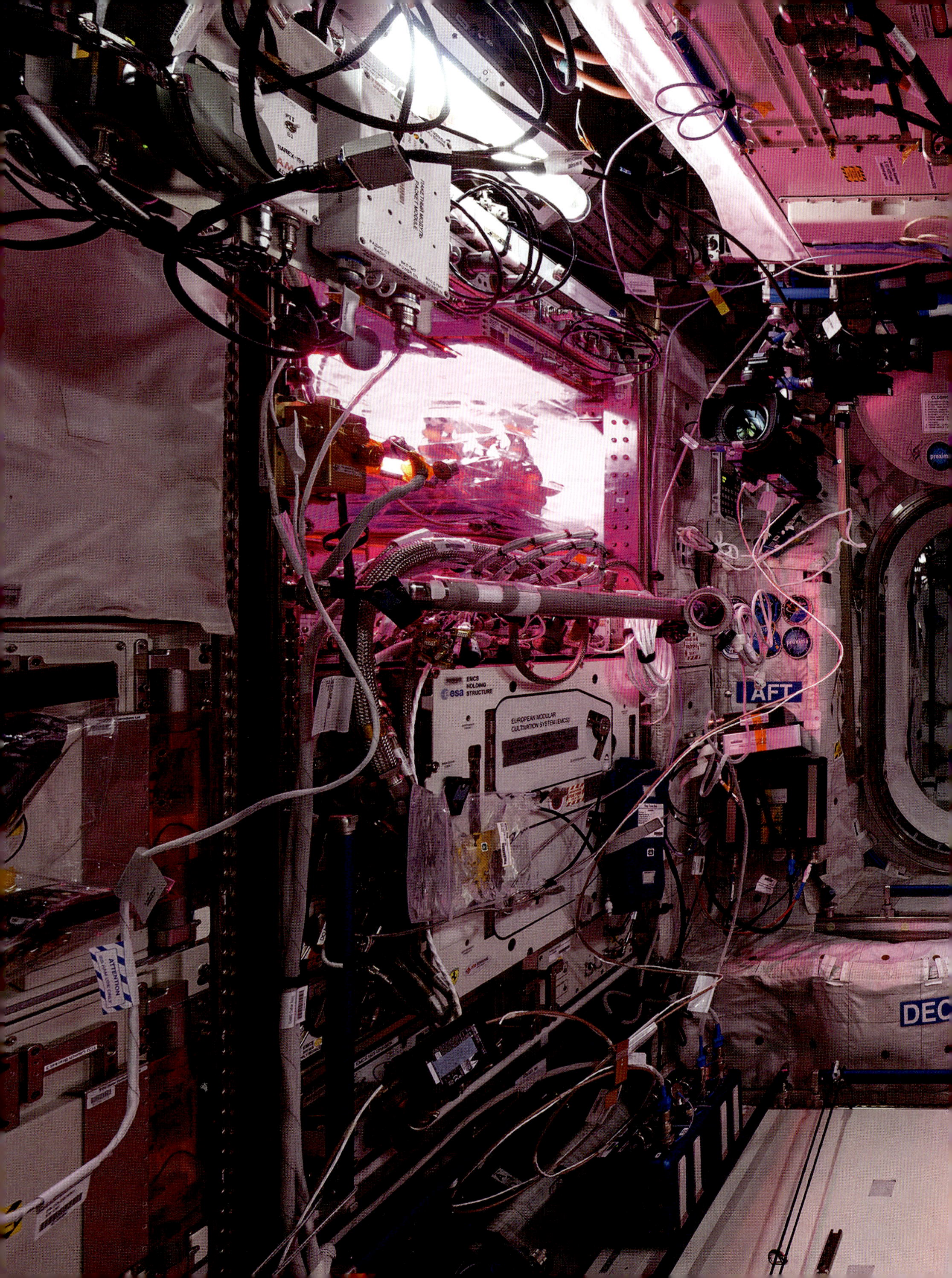
EMCS
HOLDING
STRUCTURE
esa
EUROPEAN MODULAR
CULTIVATION SYSTEM (EMCS)
AFT

HD
EXIT
FWD
MagVector
COL EDR LAPTOP
esa

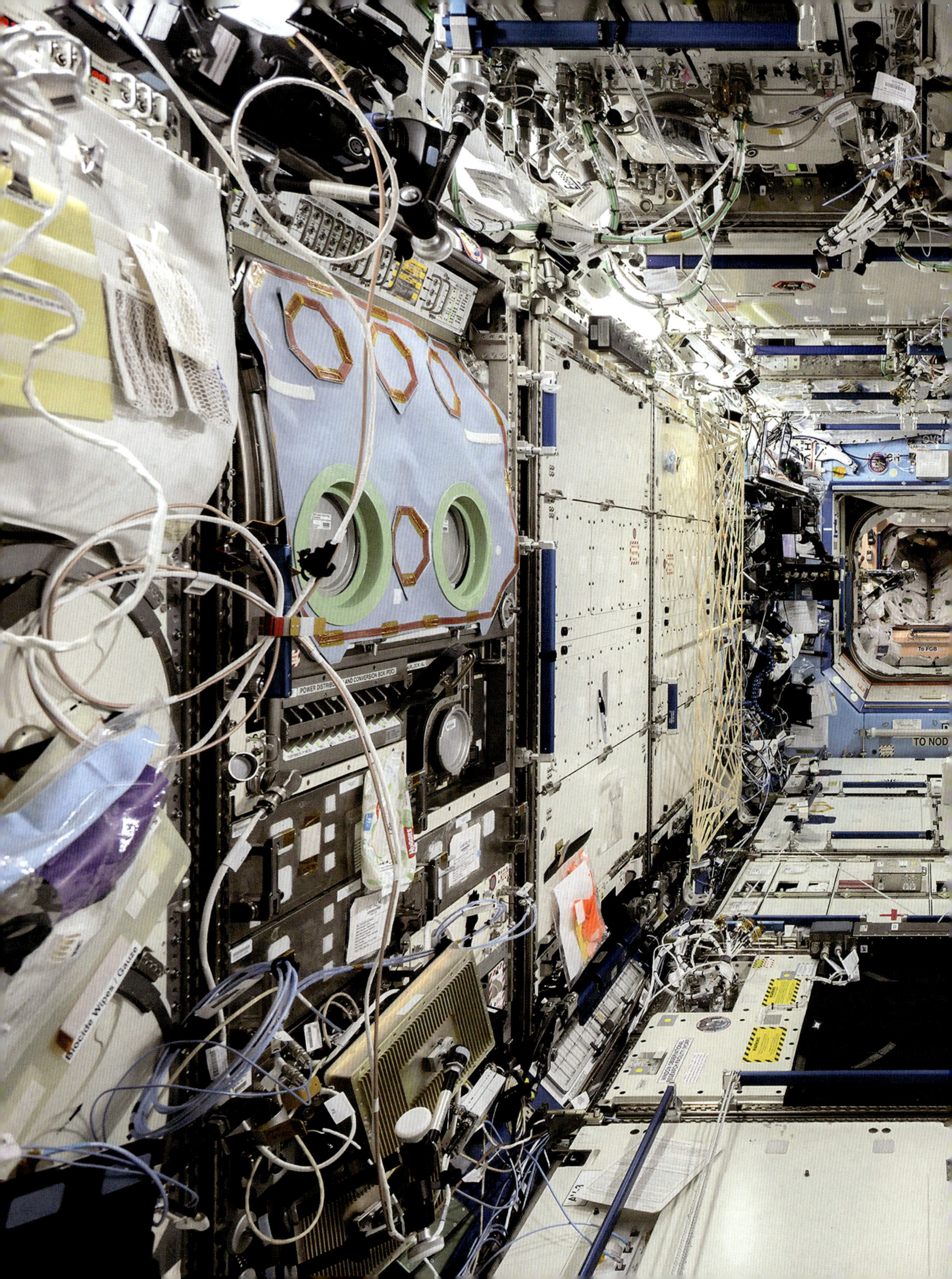
Biocide Wipes / Gauze
To FGB

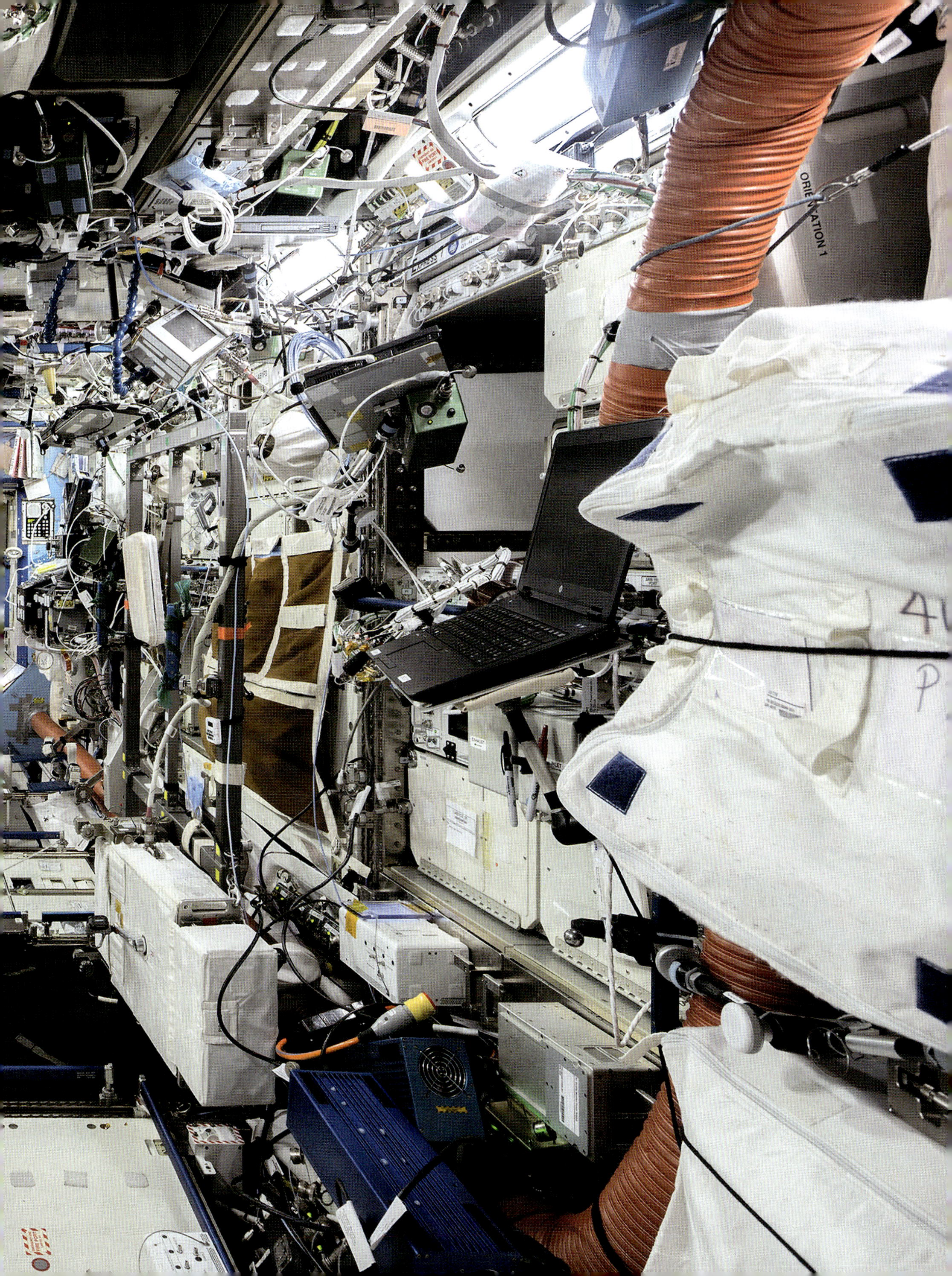

LAB
LAND OF MISFIT TOYS
EMER OBT
AUDIO TERMINAL UNIT
Sharpie
Tempo
RFID Logistics Antenna

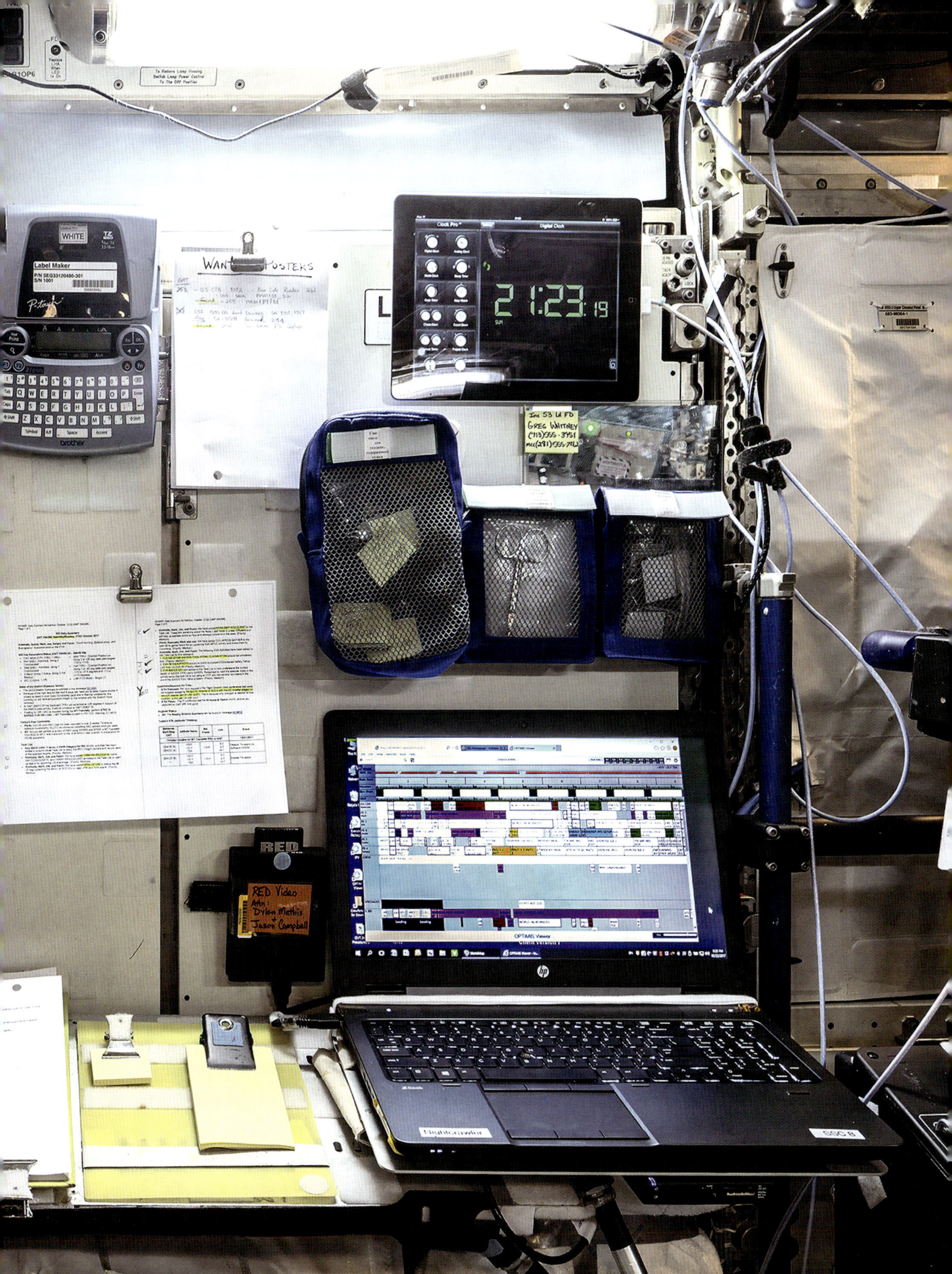

To Remove Lamp Housing
Switch Lamp Power Control
To The Off Position
WHITE
Label Maker
P/N SEG33120486-301
S/N 1001
brother
WANTED POSTERS
Clock Pro
Digital Clock
21:23 19
GREG WHITNEY
(713)555-3951
RED
RED Video
Attn:
Dylan Mathis
Jason Campbell
hp
Nightcrawler
SSC 8

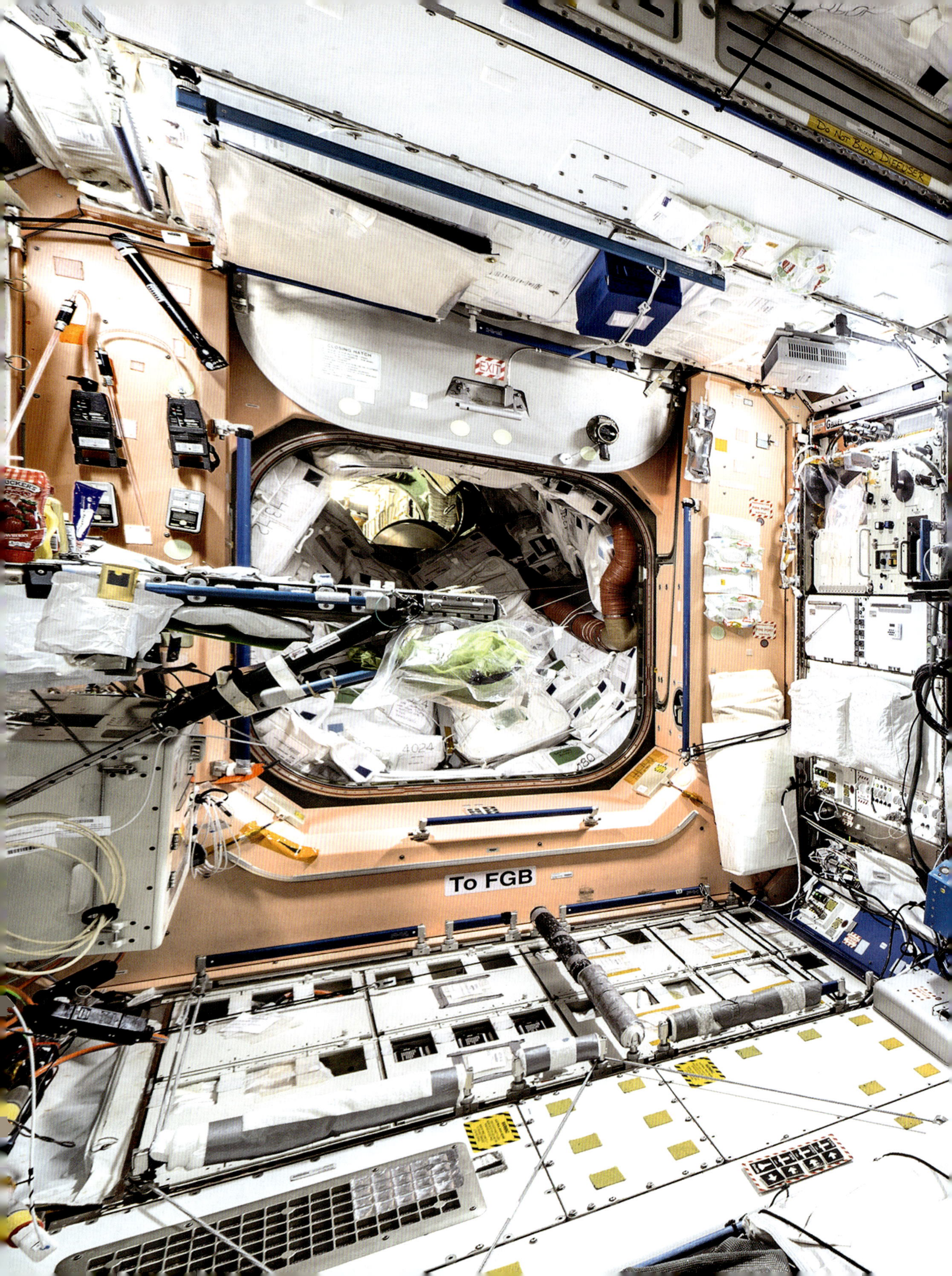
Do Not Block Diffuser
EXIT
To FGB

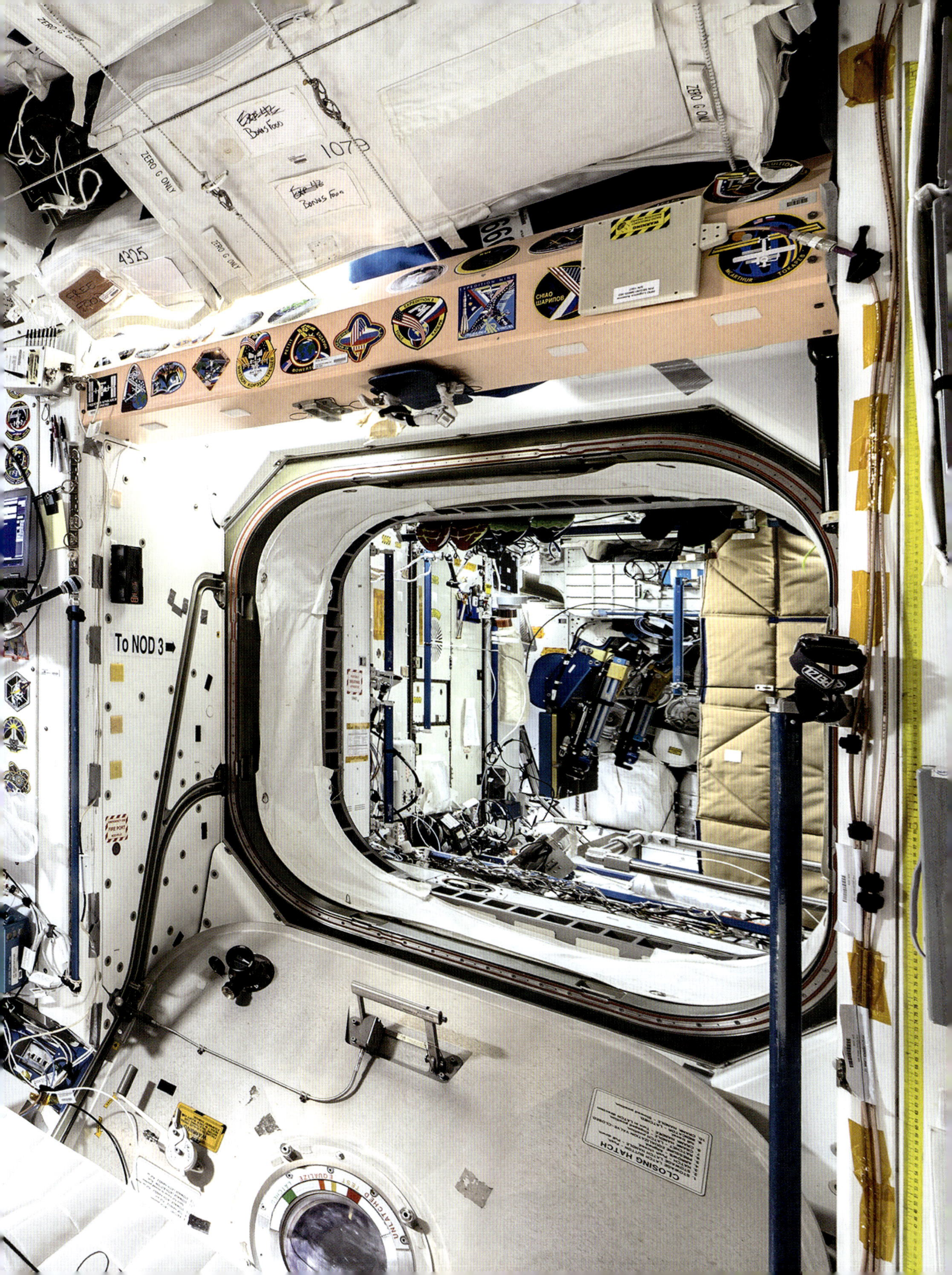
ZERO G ONLY
ZERO G ONLY
ZERO G ONLY
4325
To NOD 3

H
CUP1-W1

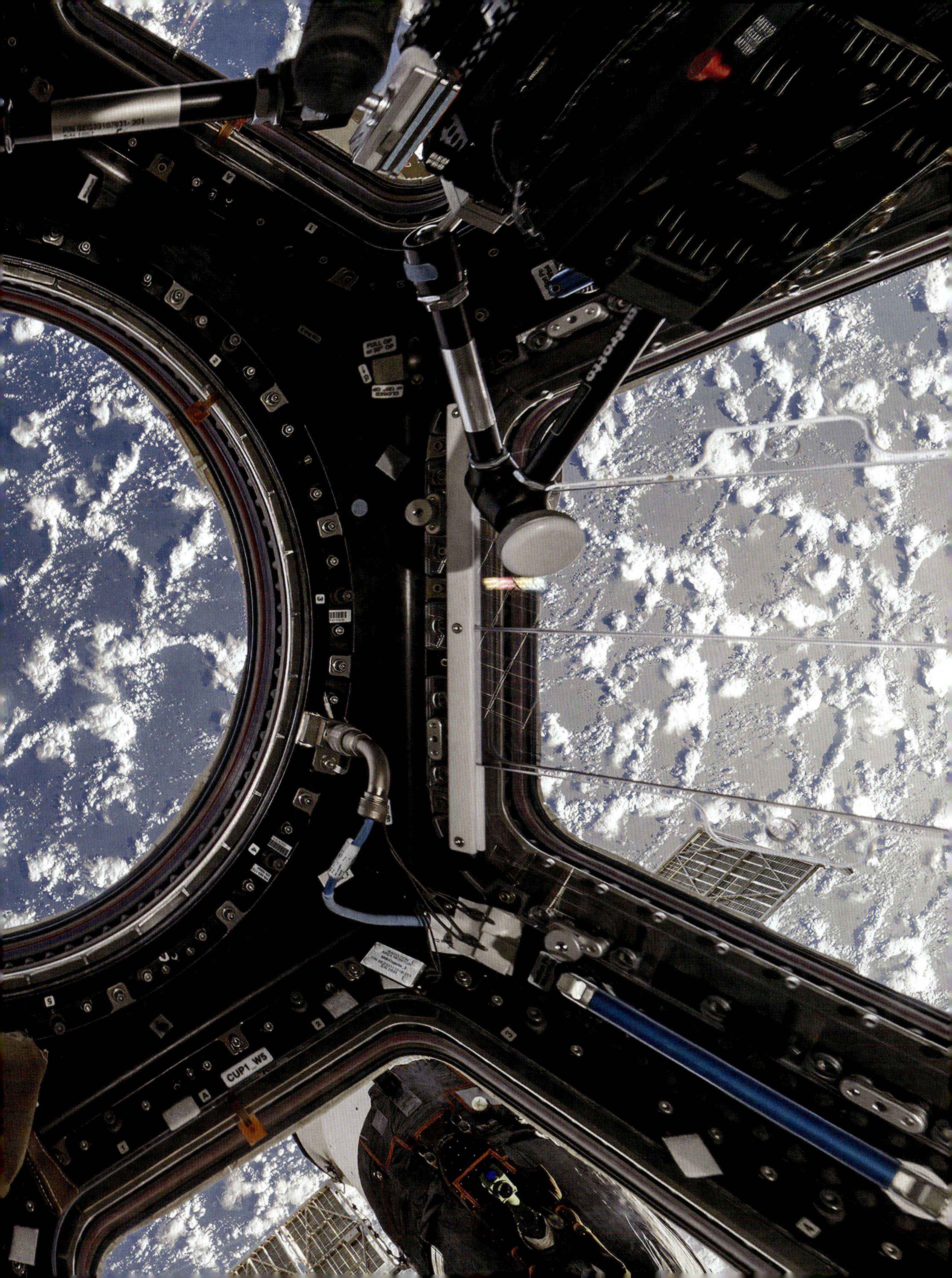
CUP1_W5

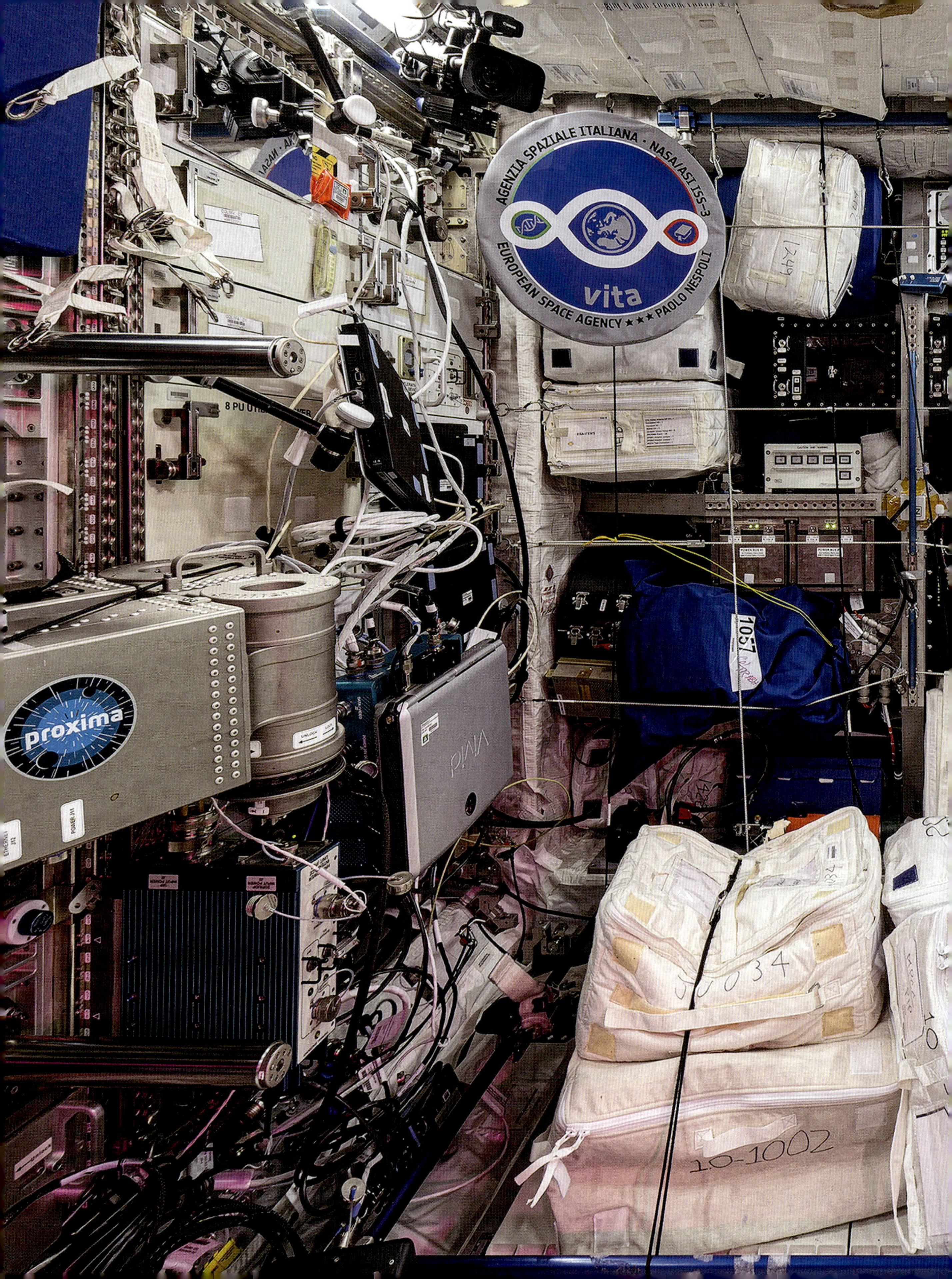
AGENZIA SPAZIALE ITALIANA • NASA/ASI ISS-3
vita
EUROPEAN SPACE AGENCY ★★★ PAOLO NESPOLI
proxima
8 PU
1057
10-1002

HRF COOLING STOWAGE DRAWER
WARNING
PAYLOAD
POWER SERVICE PANEL
MPCC PIP

Node 1 (Harmony) looking into Node 3 (Tranquility)
International Space Station
10.22.2017
Photograph by Paolo Nespoli and Roland Miller
Image courtesy of NASA and the Italian Space Agency (ASI)

View from Columbus Module (European Lab) to Node 2 (Tranquility) and the Japanese Experiment Module (Kibo)
International Space Station
10.22.2017
Photograph by Paolo Nespoli and Roland Miller
Image courtesy of NASA and the Italian Space Agency (ASI)

View Through Destiny Module (US Lab) to Node 1 (Unity) and Pressurized Mating Adaptor 1
International Space Station
8.13.2017
Photograph by Paolo Nespoli and Roland Miller
Image courtesy of NASA and the Italian Space Agency (ASI)

Work Desk, Destiny Module (US LAB)
International Space Station
10.22.2017
Photograph by Paolo Nespoli and Roland Miller
Image courtesy of NASA and the Italian Space Agency (ASI)

Node 1 (Unity) looking left into Pressurized Mating Adaptor 1 and right into Node 3 (Tranquility)
International Space Station
10.22.2017
Photograph by Paolo Nespoli and Roland Miller
Image courtesy of NASA and the Italian Space Agency (ASI))

Cupola with Clouds and Ocean
International Space Station
10.23.2017
Photograph by Paolo Nespoli and Roland Miller
Image courtesy of NASA and the Italian Space Agency (ASI)

Looking Starboard into the Columbus Module (European Lab)
International Space Station
10.22.2017
Photograph by Paolo Nespoli and Roland Miller
Image courtesy of NASA and the Italian Space Agency (ASI)

BIOGRAPHIES

Rachel Armstrong is professor of experimental architecture at the School of Architecture, Planning and Landscape, Newcastle University, United Kingdom. Her work explores how our buildings can incorporate some of the properties of living systems to become "living architectures." She was coordinator for the Future and Emerging Technologies Open *Living Architecture* project (April 2016–June 2019) and coordinates the EU Innovation Fund *Alliance for Logistics Innovation through Collaboration* project. She is a Rising Waters II Fellow with the Robert Rauschenberg Foundation (April–May 2016) and a 2010 Senior TED Fellow. She is also a member of the Hub for Biotechnology in the Built Environment at Newcastle University and director and founder of the Experimental Architecture Group (EAG) whose work has been published and exhibited internationally.

Katarzyna Balug is an instructor and PhD candidate in architecture history and theory at the Harvard University Graduate School of Design. Her research explores feedback loops between techno-political change and subjectivity as mediated by artistic practice. Her dissertation studies late 1960s inflatable structures in art and architecture and the postlunar imaginaries that they articulated in response to a confluence of 1960s scientific and social transformations. She is particularly interested in how the elemental aesthetics of the inflatable anticipated theorizations sensitive to non-human forces and entities increasingly prevalent across scholarly disciplines in subsequent decades. Kate's academic work is complemented by curatorial and artistic practice. Past research has been supported by the Sinclair Kennedy Fellowship.

Nicholas de Monchaux is the Craigslist Distinguished Chair of New Media and professor of architecture and urban design at UC Berkeley, as well as a partner in the Oakland-based architecture practice *modem*. He is the author of *Spacesuit: Fashioning Apollo* (MIT Press, 2011) and *Local Code: 3,659 Proposals about Data, Design, and the Nature of Cities* (Princeton Architectural Press, 2016). His work has been exhibited at the Venice Architecture Biennale, the Lisbon Architecture Triennial, The Storefront for Art and Architecture, SFMOMA, and the Museum of Contemporary Art Chicago. He is a Fellow of the American Academy in Rome.

Rajji Sanjay Desai is an architect and research associate at Harvard University Graduate School of Design's Critical Landscapes Design Lab and member of the Urban Theory Lab. Operating at the intersection of critical geography and visual studies, her research examines the hidden externalities of technological systems in the 21st century. Previously, Rajji worked as an urban researcher at Columbia University's GSAPP Studio X Mumbai where she was involved in projects spanning urban planning, art, and architecture. She holds a master in design studies in Urbanism, Landscape, and Ecology from the Harvard GSD (2019) and a bachelor of architecture from Mumbai University's Kamla Raheja Vidyanidhi Institute for Architecture and Environmental Studies (2015).

Daniel Daou is a doctor of design candidate at the Harvard University Graduate School of Design and an associate professor in the urban-environmental area of the architecture department at the National Autonomous University in Mexico. His research explores the relationship between the design disciplines and the ecological imagination from 1972 onward and the ways in which the ecological metaphor can help reconsider an emancipatory project for architecture today. His forthcoming *Planetary Design Reader* (forthcoming) traces the lineages of the planetary across literatures making the case for a more ambitious role for design vis-a-vis the planetary crisis.

Edward Eigen teaches the history of architecture and landscape at the Harvard University Graduate School of Design. His scholarly work focuses on intersections of the human and natural sciences with the built environment in the long 19th century. His book, *On Accident: Episodes in Architecture and Landscape* (2018), was just recently published by the MIT Press. His current research examines the landscapes of the modern American presidency, including studies of the "grassy knoll" and Watergate.

Rania Ghosn is partner of Design Earth and associate professor at Massachusetts Institute of Technology. Her research deploys architectural representation to make visible the geographic techno-political systems. The work of Design Earth was collected by MoMA and exhibited at Venice Biennale and other leading international events and museums. Her honors include Architectural League Prize for Young Architects, Boghossian Foundation Prize, and Association of Collegiate Schools of Architecture Faculty Design award. Rania holds a doctor of design degree from the Harvard University Graduate School of Design, where she was founding editor of *New Geographies* and editor-in-chief of *Landscapes* of *Energy*. She is co-author of *Geographies of Trash* (Actar, 2015) and *Geostories: Another Architecture for the Environment* (Actar, 2018).

Mariano Gomez-Luque is an architect from Argentina, a post-doctoral fellow at the Harvard University Graduate School of Design's Urban Theory Lab and the Office for Urbanization, and editor of *New Geographies*. Mariano's design research and teaching address the intersections between architecture and planetary urbanization through the lens of science fiction studies, with a particular emphasis on the status of architectural form within the cultural imaginaries and extended landscapes of the contemporary urban world. He holds a doctor of design and a master in architecture from the Harvard Graduate School of Design.

Gretchen Heefner is an associate professor of history at Northeastern University. She teaches and researches the history of the US in the world, with a focus on the Cold War, militarization, and the surprisingly intimate relations between national security regimes and the everyday. Her current research, *From the Red Desert to the Red Planet*, examines military engineering in extreme environments on earth and beyond. Articles based on this research have appeared in *Diplomatic History*, *Environmental History*, and *Endeavour*. Gretchen's first book, *The Missile Next Door: The Minuteman in the American Heartland*, was published by Harvard University Press in 2012.

El Hadi Jazairy is partner of Design Earth and Associate Professor at University of Michigan. The work of Design Earth has been exhibited internationally, including Venice Biennale (2018, 2016), Oslo Triennale (2017), Seoul Biennale (2017), 2018), Sursock Museum (Beirut, 2016), Times Museum (Guangzhou, 2018), and collected by MoMA. His honors include Architectural League Prize for Young Architects, Prix Europan, and Rougerie Foundation first prize. El Hadi holds a doctor of design degree from the Harvard University Graduate School of Design, where he was founding editor of *New Geographies* and editor-in-chief of *Scales of the Earth*. He is co-author of *Geographies of Trash* (Actar, 2015) and *Geostories: Another Architecture for the Environment* (Actar, 2018).

Elizabeth A. Kessler's research focuses on 20th and 21st century American visual culture, in particular the place of aesthetics, images, and media in astronomy. She earned a PhD from the University of Chicago, and she has been awarded the Society for the History of Technology-NASA History of Space Technology Fellowship, as well as fellowships from Stanford University and the Smithsonian Institution National Air and Space Museum. Her book, *Picturing the Cosmos: Hubble Space Telescope Images and the Astronomical Sublime*, on the aesthetics of deep space images, was published in 2012 by University of Minnesota Press. Currently, she is lecturer in American studies at Stanford University.

Scott Kirsch is professor in the Department of Geography, University of North Carolina at Chapel Hill. His research interests include nuclear landscapes; history of scientific exploration and cartography; US geopolitics, especially in the Philippines and Asia/Pacific; and geographies of war and peace. He is author of *Proving Grounds: Project Plowshare and the Unrealized Dream of Nuclear Earthmoving* (Rutgers University Press, 2005) and editor (with Colin Flint) of *Reconstructing Conflict: Integrating War and Post-War Geographies* (Routledge, 2011). He is writing a book about America's insular empire in the Philippines.

Dr. Julie Klinger (PhD Geography) is an Assistant Professor in the Department of Geography at the University of Delaware, where she is core faculty of the Minerals, Materials, and Society Program. Her recent book, *Rare Earth Frontiers: From Terrestrial Subsoils to Lunar Landscapes* (Cornell University Press, 2018) won the 2018 Meridian Award for its "unusually important contribution to the art and science of geography."

Neil Leach teaches at Florida International University, Tongji University and the European Graduate School and is an academician within the Academia Europaea. He has worked on two NASA-funded research projects to develop robotic fabrication technologies to print structures on the Moon and Mars. He has published over 40 books on architectural theory and digital practice. His books include *Rethinking Architecture* (Routledge, 1997), *Designing for a Digital World* (Wiley, 2002), *Digital Tectonics* (Wiley, 2004), *Camouflage* (MIT Press, 2006), *Digital Cities* (Wiley, 2009), *Machinic Processes* (CABP, 2010), *Scripting the Future*, (Tongji University Press, 2012), *Space Architecture* (Wiley, 2014), *Robotic Futures* (Tongji University Press, 2015), *Swarm Intelligence* (Tongji University Press, 2017) and *Interactive Futures* (Tongji University Press, 2017).

Michael Light is a photographer focused aerially over settled and unsettled areas of American space, pursuing themes of mapping, vertigo, human impact on the land, geologic time, and the sublime. A private pilot, he is currently working on a survey of the arid western states, publishing volumes *Bingham Mine/Garfield Stack* (Radius Books, 2014), *LA Day/LA Night* (Radius Books, 2011), *Lake Las Vegas/Black Mountain* (Radius Books, 2015), and *Lake Lahontan/Lake Bonneville* (Radius Books, 2019, forthcoming). Light is also known for his archival interventions. *Full Moon* (Knoff, 1999) used Apollo lunar survey imagery to show the moon both as a sublime desert and an embattled point of first human contact. *100 Suns* (Knoff, 2003) focused on the politics and landscape meanings of military photographs of US atmospheric nuclear detonations.

Lisa Messeri is an assistant professor of sociocultural anthropology at Yale University. Her research concerns how science and technology stretch our imagination of what place is and what it means to be in place and in the world. Messeri's book, *Placing Outer Space* (Duke University Press, 2016), examines how scientists transform planets into worlds. Her current research, supported by a National Science Foundation Scholars Award, focuses on the virtual reality community in Los Angeles. In addition to academic writing, Messeri has had essays published in the *New York Times*, *Slate*, and *Motherboard*. Her research has been featured in *Wired*, PBS's *NOVA ScienceNOW*, and on CNN.

Roland Miller is an aerospace photographer and former dean of the College of Lake County's Communication Arts, Humanities, and Fine Arts Division. His photography research focuses on documenting and interpreting the United States' space program. Recently, his images were included in the books *Sun and Moon* (Phaidon Press, 2019) and *Go Down Moses* (Candor Arts and the Museum of Contemporary Photography, 2019). His book, *Abandoned in Place: Preserving America's Space History* (University of New Mexico, 2016) is a collection of photographs on abandoned, deactivated, and repurposed space launch and test facilities.

Jeffrey S. Nesbit is an architect, urbanist, and doctoral candidate at the Harvard University Graduate School of Design. His research focuses on processes of urbanization and the urban landscape. Currently, his dissertation explores the 20th-century spaceport complex through the lens of architecture, technology, and aerospace history. Nesbit has written a number of journal articles and book chapters on infrastructural urbanization and is editor of *Chasing the City: Models for Extra-Urban Investigations* (Routledge, 2018) and editor of *New Geographies 11: Extraterrestrial*.

Alessandra Ponte is full professor at the École d'architecture, Université de Montreal. Since 2008, Alessandra has been responsible for the Phyllis Lambert International Seminar, a series of colloquia held at the Université de Montréal. She was curator of the exhibition *Total Environment: Montreal 1965-1975* (Canadian Center for Architecture, Montreal, 2009). She also collaborated on the exhibition and catalogue *God & Co: François Dallegret Beyond the Bubble* (with Laurent Stalder and Thomas Weaver, Architectural Association Publications, 2011), and contributed to the Canadian Pavilion at the Venice Biennale of Architecture in 2014 (*Arctic Adaptations*) and 2016 (*Extraction*). Recent publications include: *The House of Light and Entropy* (Architectural Association Publications, 2014) and *Architecture et Information 2.0//2017*, *Architecture et Information 2.0//2018* (École d'architecture, Université de Montréal, 2017, 2018).

David Salomon is an assistant professor of Art History at Ithaca College, where he is the coordinator of the architectural studies program. He is a co-curator of the traveling exhibition *Ambiguous Territory: Architecture, Landscape, and the Postnatural* (2019). He co-authored the book *The Architecture of Patterns* (Norton, 2010) and is the author of *Symmetry: The One and the Many* (DiTella, 2018). His work has appeared in *Grey Room*, *Log*, *Harvard Design Magazine*, *Places*, *The Journal of Landscape Architecture*, and the *Journal of Architectural Education*, on topics that include the relationship between minimal art and suburbia, the aesthetic function of infrastructure, and the history of the design thesis.

Fred Scharmen teaches architecture and urban design at Morgan State University. He is the co-founder of the Working Group on Adaptive Systems, an art and design consultancy based in Baltimore. His first book, *Space Settlements*—on NASA's 1970s proposal to construct large cities in space for millions of people—is out in 2019 from Columbia Books on Architecture and the City.

Felicity D. Scott is professor of architecture, director of the PhD program in architecture (history and theory) and co-director of the program in Critical, Curatorial and Conceptual Practices in Architecture (CCCP) at the Graduate School of Architecture, Planning and Preservation, Columbia University. Her books include *Architecture or Techno-Utopia: Politics After Modernism* (MIT Press, 2007), *Ant Farm* (Actar, 2008), *Outlaw Territories: Environments of Insecurity/Architectures of Counter-Insurgency* (Zone Books, 2016), and *Disorientations: Bernard Rudofsky in the Empire of Signs* (Sternberg Press, 2016).

Guy Trangoš is a doctor of design candidate at the Harvard University Graduate School of Design. He is a founding partner in Meshworks Architecture and Urbanism and the co-editor of *New Geographies 11: Extraterrestrial*. His doctoral research investigates the infrastructural, spatial, and political implications of large science projects on landscapes and society. Guy has written widely for various publications and journals and co-edited the book *Movement Johannesburg* (The City, 2015) with Zahira Asmal. Guy holds a MSc in city design and social science from the London School of Economics and Political Science and a master of architecture (professional) from the University of the Witwatersrand.

Neyran Turan is an assistant professor at the University of California-Berkeley and a partner at NEMESTUDIO, an architectural office that has been recognized with several awards, most recently the 2016 Architectural League New York Prize for Young Architects. Turan is the founding chief-editor of *New Geographies* and was the editor-in-chief of the first two volumes of the journal *New Geographies 0* and *New Geographies: After Zero*. Turan's book, *Architecture as Measure*, which has been awarded with a Graham Foundation grant, was released by ACTAR Publishers in Fall 2019. Turan was recently selected to curate the Turkish Pavilion in the 2020 Venice Architecture Biennale.

New Geographies 12:
Commons

Commons, as a contested and political idea, has been continually articulated and reproduced in relation to its historically and geographically specific context. NG 12 brings forward commons as a mode of thinking that goes beyond the fragmented discussions about material and immaterial resources, individual and collective life, local and regional geographies, and public and private interventions. It seeks to accentuate the relationship between the idea of commons and the production of space at a planetary scale. In doing so, it projects into an expanded territory of space and encompasses a global network of built and unbuilt environments, and human and non- human communities. This issue aspires to break through the disengaged agenda to restore the wholesomeness of the commons as a space of inclusion that fosters heterogenous existences all the way from the intimate and subjective scale of the body to the planetary material and immaterial spaces.

Editors
Mojdeh Mahdavi and Liang Wang